INFIGHTING ADMIRALS

INFIGHTING ADMIRALS

Fisher's Feud with Beresford and the Reactionaries

by

GEOFFREY PENN

LEO COOPER

DEDICATION

To Barbara
And to my brother, Tony,
Killed in the rearguard, 28 May 1940,
So that others could escape from
Dunkirk.

First Published in Great Britain 2000 by
Leo Cooper
an imprint of Pen & Sword Books
47 Church Street
Barnsley, S. Yorkshire, S70 2AS

ISBN 0 85052 756 2

A CIP record for this book is available from The British Library

Typeset in 10/12.5 Plantin by
Phoenix Typesetting, Ilkley, West Yorkshire.

Printed in England by Redwood Books, Trowbridge, Wiltshire.

CONTENTS

ACKNOWLEDGEMENTS

Again I have to thank the third Lord Fisher of Kilverstone for his unfailing courtesy and kindness in allowing me access to family records and to use photographs as illustrations. He must be weary of authors approaching him for information. Vice-Admiral Sir Louis Le Bailly and Professor Ian Beckett have also been of great assistance and given me sound advice. The staff of the Public Record Office and the Imperial War Museum have been as helpful as ever, as have the Warminster Public Library, who seem always to be able to obtain rare books and material for me, saving hours of travelling and much expense.

My gratitude goes to the authors and publishers of the many books I have studied and from which I have quoted for permission to do so. The extracts from the works of Winston Churchill are reproduced with permission from Curtis Brown Limited, London, on behalf of the estate of Sir Winston Churchill, copyright Winston S. Churchill. The extracts from the works of Randolph Churchill and Martin Gilbert are reproduced with permission of Curtis Brown Limited of London on behalf of C & T Publications Limited, copyright C & T Publications Limited.

Professor Marder's books on the Fisher era and the Nineteenth Century Royal Navy are indispensable. I also have to thank the Navy Records Society for permission to quote from their invaluable and accurate volumes.

If I have missed any authors or publishers I hope they will forgive me. There are some I failed to trace and to them too I offer my sincere apologies.

Geoffrey Penn

PREFACE

At the end of all wars British politicians think there will be everlasting peace and start to dismantle the fighting Services. It has happened after every war including the Napoleonic wars. In the Navy List of 1834 under the list of Lieutenants is a pathetic note which reads: '*The undermentioned officers, not having been heard of for several years, have been removed from the list*'. There follow eight names. But even so, there were 3,139 lieutenants listed, the senior of whom gained that rank in the year 1778.

It may therefore be recognized that in the nineteenth century competition for promotion was fierce, and progress could seldom be obtained without influence. But the century was one of extraordinary change. Not only was wood replaced by steel, sail by steam, bringing changes in strategy, tactics and the lives of officers and men, but weaponry changed from that of Trafalgar in the first years of the twentieth century to that of the First World War. Young men of higher social position were attracted as officers by vastly improved standards of comfort and many saw change as both unnecessary and inconvenient.

Lord Fisher of Kilverstone was an exception to almost every rule. With astounding foresight, years before the event, he predicted the date of the Great War to within two months. He fought the reactionaries all the way and introduced the submarine, the torpedo, the mine and the big gun, and insisted on keeping Britain ahead of Germany's growing navy. There can be little doubt that, had it not been for him, Britain would have lost the Great War. It is interesting to speculate how the world would have turned out without him. He had to fight all his life against resistance to change, conceit, self-aggrandisement and faulty doctrine. He has at last been recognized by one journal as one of this country's great men; but even so there is no statue of him in London, and historians have almost ignored him. He deserves better.

I hope this book will help to remedy the omission.

1

LONELY YOUTH AND WILD IRISHMAN.

Lord Fisher of Kilverstone was one of the most remarkable officers ever to serve in the Royal Navy. His immense achievements were accomplished against fierce opposition, arising from inter-related sources. He entered the Navy just at the time when sailing ships were disappearing. The result was a reluctance to accept steam, with its coal, oil, ashes and dirt, and an understandable belief that it could never replace sail, since the endurance of ships under steam was limited and, without sail, coaling stations were needed at intervals along the ship's passage, whereas the wind was free. Once steam was accepted and endurance increased by improved machinery, the life of the deck or 'military' officer changed totally. No longer did he have the worries and difficulties of handling sail; ships increased in size and comfort, yet occupation had to be found for the large ships' companies required to man the guns. So in the long peace of the nineteenth century cleanliness took a new meaning and ships became more like the private yachts of their admirals and captains, whose life was transformed into one of comparative ease, attracting into the Service many more men with society and titled backgrounds and the accompanying snobbery led them to look down on men of Fisher's kind. They looked back with nostalgia to the beauty of sail, perhaps forgetting the comforts that steam had brought them, seeing only its handicaps and objecting to almost any progress in ship design, weapons or machinery, except where it amplified their own basic magnificence.

Entry of officers in the nineteenth century depended upon gaining a 'nomination' from an admiral, enabling him to select his relations or friends, or those from whom he wished to obtain favour, especially with a voice to the rich and powerful. The rudimentary entrance examination was often waived. Consequently many Victorian officers belonged to titled families, often the younger sons, and though many were sound, lack of intelligence was not a handicap. Because there were too many officers and too few ships,

1

much time was spent idling on half-pay. Promotion after service in the Royal yacht was automatic, and an admiral, on hauling down his flag at the end of every appointment, was entitled to nominate an officer for promotion. The Admiralty had no say in the matter and haul-down nominations were accepted without demur. Once an officer achieved the rank of captain, he only had to serve in command of a seagoing ship for three years and for a further three years at sea (not necessarily in command) to gain promotion to rear-admiral. From then on promotion up the ranks of admirals was automatic on reaching the top of each list. So the Navy was overburdened with not very intelligent, inexperienced admirals whose desire was not to change anything, to oppose every new development and enhance their own grandeur.

But there were some men like Fisher, wholly devoted to the modernization and war efficiency of the Navy, who were not welcome in a reactionary profession and there were many who, under the tacit leadership of Lord Charles Beresford, opposed almost everything he did and tried to bring about his downfall. Fisher is remembered primarily for his brainchild, HMS *Dreadnought*, which changed the face of the British Navy (and all other navies). Yet this was only one part of his contribution to naval development. The submarine, the destroyer, the big gun, the mine, the torpedo, the steam turbine, oil fuel were all his. Churchill recognized his genius and brought him back from retirement in 1914.

John Arbuthnot Fisher was born in 1841 in Ceylon, son of William Fisher, ADC to Sir Robert Wilmot-Horton, the Governor. William married Sophie Lambe, daughter of a London wine merchant, and that year the Governor died; Captain Fisher left the Army and purchased a coffee plantation. With no school, Fisher had a splendidly wild and free early childhood. At the age of six he travelled home alone for his education, a two-day journey by bullock cart and a sea passage of about a hundred days. He never again saw his father, whose plantation failed leaving him almost penniless and who was killed riding. Fisher's Godmother, Lady Wilmot-Horton, the Governor's widow, had moved to her estate at Catton Hall, Burton on Trent, where he spent most of his school holidays and had happy days.

Fisher was nominated by Admiral Sir William Parker, the last of Nelson's captains, a neighbour of Lady Wilmot-Horton and entered in HMS *Victory* on 12 July 1854. On 29 July, at Plymouth, he joined HMS *Calcutta* an 84-gun two-decker, similar in size to HMS *Victory*, proceeding there by sea. 'I entered the Navy penniless, friendless and forlorn,' he wrote.

He had joined a composite navy; though steam had been introduced some thirty years earlier, it was the heyday of the sailing line-of-battleship. When Queen Victoria reviewed the Western Squadron the year before, it consisted of seven screw line-of-battleships, three sailing line-of-battleships, four screw frigates, four screw corvettes and sloops and one paddle corvette. But to the contemporary officer this seemed the most natural thing. That sailing ships were to go, paddles almost gone, did not occur to him and he assured himself that they would never pass away. Little attempt was made to prepare for war; manoeuvres and fighting exercises were hardly ever held, the guns seldom fired and, through neglect, were often in no condition to be fired with safety. Seamanship and cleanliness were the twin gods of the naval officer. The chief object was not fighting efficiency, but to keep the decks as white as snow, the ropes taut, the sails sparkling clean.

Apart from a short run to Falmouth, *Calcutta* remained in Plymouth until February the next year before recruiting an adequate crew. After briefly working up in the Channel she sailed to the Baltic Fleet with supernumeraries and shell. Fisher was violently seasick, and it exemplifies the difficulties of sailing ships than seven days after leaving Plymouth, *Calcutta* was off the Scilly Isles. Though present at the Bombardment of Helsingfors, she took no part, returning to Plymouth to pay off on 1 March 1856.

Calcutta's captain, James Stopford, was appointed to *Agamemnon* in the Mediterranean and asked for Fisher, who joined her on 19 May, and for the first time went up the Dardanelles. But almost immediately she too returned to Portsmouth to pay off. It was with joy, therefore, that the day after *Agamemnon* paid off Fisher, now a midshipman, joined *Highflyer*, a steam corvette bound for China, under Captain Charles Shadwell.

The midshipman's life was unpleasant, often deliberately made more so; the older generation having suffered thus, saw no reason why the new generation should not. An admiral of the day said that he never washed when he first went to sea and he saw no reason why midshipmen should want to wash now. Conditions at sea were quite appalling. 'Late as I came to sea,' wrote Fisher, 'I had to keep either the First or Middle Watch every night and was always hungry!' The water, in casks, was turgid, smelly and inhabited by living creatures.

Shadwell was a man whom he 'loved like a father' and remembered all his life, an eccentric, as were many naval officers of those days. He went into battle with a tall white hat with a gold stripe on the side, a captain's uniform tail coat, a yellow waistcoat, white trousers, and a white umbrella.[1] He soon recognized Fisher's promise and gave him lessons in nautical astronomy.

In Shanghai the boy was adopted by a Mrs. Warden, wife of the manager of the P & O Company who provided a temporary home for the lonely midshipmen away from England for three or four years, and whose letters might take many months to reach them. Fisher's mother was an infrequent correspondent and he had never met his youngest two brothers or his sister. When he was nineteen he received a picture of his mother, whose beauty astonished him, so long was it since he had seen her. Mrs. Warden was undoubtedly a substitute mother, writing regularly to him and to whom he wrote every mail.

In the Second China War Fisher took part, in charge of a boat, in a minor skirmish at Fatshan Creek in the mouth of the Canton River, clearing the way up to Canton which was captured at the end of the year. The war ended in 1858 and in June 1859 the 8th Earl of Elgin, Special High Commissioner and Envoy, was to go to Peking to sign the Treaty of Tientsin. Unknown to the British, the forts guarding the entrance to the Peiho had, with Russian assistance, been considerably strengthened, iron piles and ropes placed across the entrance, effectively barring the passage. Rear Admiral James Hope, the C-in-C, decided to clear away the obstacles by force. The entrance was narrow, with mudbanks on either side, the men getting stuck in the mud under a murderous fire from the forts. The attack failed, casualties were high and four small vessels sunk. Shadwell and the Admiral were wounded, the captain of marines drowned in the mud. The captain he adored was invalided home, and asked Fisher, for whom he had a great liking, what he could do for him.

'I said, "Give me a set of studs with your motto on them 'loyal au mort'".
He did, and I've worn them for sixty years.'[2]

Before he left, the Admiral came to say goodbye and asked Shadwell what favour he could do him. 'Look after that boy,' Shadwell said, and the Admiral adopted him as a personal assistant.

Soon Fisher passed 'first class' for lieutenant, an examination that had to be confirmed on arrival home, but gave him promotion to acting mate (later sub-lieutenant). He then had to wait for a vacancy for acting lieutenant and soon was offered an appointment to HMS *Esk*, which he refused because he did not want to miss the second attack on Peiho. Five days later he was appointed to fill a vacancy in HMS *Furious*. He was nineteen and bursting with pride, for in those days of nepotism most vacancies were given to young men with influence, aristocratic connections or to a relation of the admiral; the young man without 'interest' was sympathetically regarded as labouring under an unhappy disadvantage. Hope was convinced of Fisher's exceptional efficiency and probity, and appointed him to command HMS *Coromandel*, a little paddle vessel of 303 tons. His command lasted only four days, but in after years he was proud to have achieved it.

After a short spell in *Pearl*, a wooden steam corvette, which he liked, (though he found the messing expensive, 'Champagne and all the rest of it'), he joined *Furious*, a paddle frigate of 1,287 tons. Despite his description of the captain as a 'scoundrel' he admired him as an accomplished sailor, linguist, a master of hounds, skilled in the arts of navigation and surveying. *Furious* took part in the successful second attack on the Peiho Forts, but in March 1861 sailed for Portsmouth where she arrived on 20 August and paid off, Fisher receiving a certificate of praise.

He had been away from England for five years; he was twenty, had gained high commendation from all his senior officers and had served eighteen months as acting lieutenant. He now had to pass his 'official' examinations in gunnery at HMS *Excellent*, the gunnery schoolship, in navigation and 'steam' at the Royal Naval College, Portsmouth (the old Naval Academy). He obtained first class certificates in each, won the Beaufort Testimonial, (the top prize in navigation), was confirmed as lieutenant, backdated to 4 November 1860, and appointed to the staff of *Excellent* as a gunnery officer.

While Midshipman Fisher was attacking the Peiho Forts another cadet joined the Navy. These two men were to have an immense influence upon each other and end in bitter enmity. There could hardly have been a greater difference between their upbringing. Lord Charles William de la Poer Beresford was the second of five sons of the fourth Marquis of Waterford. Of his four brothers three joined fashionable regiments. The family home was Curraghmore, a beautiful Irish estate standing in 10,000 acres. He was brought up as a great horseman, a hard rider; out hunting he broke his chestbone, leaving a cavity, his pelvis, his right leg, his right hand, foot, five ribs, one collarbone three times, the other once, his nose three times.

Born in 1846, five years younger than Fisher, after school in England among a galaxy of titles, he joined HMS *Britannia* in Haslar Creek in December 1859 and then *Marlborough*, flagship of the Mediterranean Fleet. A ship of the old style, a three-decker, she was fitted with engines, but seldom used them.

Like all midshipmen Beresford learned in a tough school, aloft day and night, in freezing gales, rain and hail descending in icy sheets, underfed, overworked and suffering a discipline unrecognisable today, nearly killed when a footrope was accidentally kicked away from under him. But he brimmed over with enthusiasm and fun, sometimes leading him into trouble, as when he was discovered trying to gain an advantage in drill by unbending the foretopgallant sheet; he was reprimanded, taken out of his 'top', deprived of his boat and disrated to cadet. But though restored to his previous honours, for other pranks he was mastheaded, beaten, kept on board in harbour and given extra duties. An irrepressible sense of humour got him into repeated troubles. Posted home, awaiting passage, he heard his old ship was assisting a liner on the Filfola rocks, so he hired a shore boat and pulled himself the twelve miles from Grand Harbour and back alone at night to witness the spectacle.

Marlborough was Beresford's 'ship of happiest memory', but on returning home he joined *Defence*, his 'ship of unhappy memory', one of an inferior class which he thought a 'dreadful ship'. But his objections were based on the fact that she belonged to the new steam Navy; his joy stemmed from the white decks, the perfection and pride of the *Marlborough*. *Defence* was a 'slovenly, unhandy tin kettle, which could not sail without steam.' She was in the Channel Squadron; the blue waters and sunlit skies of the Mediterranean replaced by the cold grey seas of the Channel. He asked his father to remove him from the Navy.

Beresford's youthful views reflect those of the contemporary naval officer. The sailing line-of-battleship had reached her apogee just when she was becoming obsolete, to be replaced by the iron-built steamship, a clumsy, experimental hybrid, lacking identity, the hull shape based on the need to provide for the broadside, but modified to house machinery. Her coal capacity gave her insufficient endurance to proceed under steam alone, so she carried sail as well, and all the stores for both sail and steam. Space was taken up by boilers, engines, coal and accommodation for engineers and stokers. Beresford's description was justified, but it contrasted with Fisher's pleasure at his appointment to *Furious*.

While in *Defence* Beresford demonstrated his personal courage. He was awarded two medals by humane societies; later he was awarded the Bronze medal of the Royal Humane Society for saving a passenger when a shore boat was sunk in Plymouth. Later still, in Panama, he rescued a mess-mate from shark-infested waters.

Hopelessly in debt and unhappy, he stayed in *Defence* for less than a year, when his father used influence for his transfer to HMS *Clio*, a corvette of 2,106 tons whose engines were rarely used. He was happy among his glorious sails again. The ship sailed from Portsmouth in August 1864, via Ascension, the Falklands and the Magellan Straits to Mercy Bay, where, caught in a hurricane, she put to sea to clear the treacherous coast. But the ship was blown onto her beam ends and the captain decided to return to Mercy. The master having set a wrong course, Beresford, by wideawake seamanship, saw the coast ahead, just in time to avoid rocks in a smother of snow and spray.

But *Clio* was an easy-going ship and to tame the wild Irishman he was transferred to HMS *Tribune*, a frigate with 300 horsepower engines, a smart ship under Captain Lord Gilford (later Lord Clanwilliam), a fine seamen and strict disciplinarian, who never allowed sail to be shortened without his permission and could never be induced to use steam except in dire emergency.

While Beresford was in *Defence*, on 28 March 1863, in spite of his lack of 'interest', Fisher gained the appointment of gunnery officer of HMS *Warrior*, the most advanced ship of her day. The French had built *La Gloire*, an immense frigate, with 4¾-inch armour, a sensation comparable in public opinion with nuclear submarines a hundred years later. The Admiralty realized armour was now essential and would increase in thickness. Such weight could not be borne by wood; the days of sail and wood were gone, and in 1859 *Warrior* was laid down. Though the iron hull was unprotected fore and aft, the vital parts of the ship were armoured with 4½-inch plate, backed with 18 inches of teak. She was built essentially as a steamship, but full-rigged, with her guns in 'broadside'. With fine lines fore and aft, her performance under both sail and steam was good. No new major warship was ever again built of wood.

So Fisher, still only 22, after only fourteen months in *Excellent*, had been appointed gunnery officer of the latest British warship. She was sent round the British ports to be shown to eager taxpayers who visited her in droves. Fisher's sense of humour was developing; one day a group of young women stared through the wardroom skylight at the officers having lunch and made witty comments, until Fisher loudly remarked, 'If those young women only remembered the state of their lingerie, they would not stand right over our heads'. The visitors disappeared.

Fisher's high spirits were proverbial. The first sight one of his messmates gained of the gunnery officer was on the wardroom table, dancing grotesquely and singing a song he claimed to have picked up in China with the refrain 'Ching-a-ling Chow Chow'. Full of fun in the wardroom, he was different on duty. His carefully developed voice snapped men into action when the battery of 26-pounders and four 70-pounders was drilled. A gun weighing 4¾ tons would be moved the length of the ship and fired in just over three minutes. In his service in *Warrior* he trained more seaman-gunners than the rest of the Channel Squadron put together. It is possible that Fisher and Beresford met during this period, though neither mentions the other. Fisher's time in *Warrior* ended in March 1864, after just a year, when he returned to *Excellent* in command of her tender, the 60 horsepower screw gunboat *Stork*, remaining until 3 November 1866. when, as a senior staff officer, he lectured the qualifying gunnery lieutenants. But in April and May 1865 he attended the Hythe School of Musketry, where he gained a disdain for army officers that was to last many years, for the course was absurd. For example, the correct answer to the question 'What do you pour the water into the barrel of the rifle with when you are cleaning it?' was 'with care'! The army officers on the course were no less contemptuous.

In his lectures in *Excellent* he summarized the philosophy that was to guide him all his life:

> If you are a gunnery man you must believe and teach that the world must be saved by gunnery, and will only be saved by gunnery. If you are a torpedo man you must lecture and teach the same thing about torpedoes. But be in earnest, terribly in earnest. The man who doubts or is half-hearted never does anything for himself or for his country. You are missionaries; show the earnestness – if need be the fanaticism of missionaries.[3]

This illustrates Fisher's determination, his contempt for the man who did not devote himself completely to the Navy and his country, which was to earn him so many enemies in the future, foremost among them Beresford, who, on 2 January, 1866, was promoted to acting sub-lieutenant, Gilford endorsing his certificate that he had conducted himself 'with sobriety, diligence, attention and always obedient to command; I have been much pleased with the zealous manner in which he has performed his duties'. He was transferred to HMS *Sutlej*, a screw frigate of 3,066 tons, flagship of Rear Admiral the Hon. Joseph Denman. Again he experienced a hurricane, the ship putting in to San Francisco for repairs, before returning home round Cape Horn to Spithead.

Beresford now had to take his examinations in gunnery, navigation and 'steam' for which he was allowed three months' study. In contrast to Fisher's earnest approach, like many another officer of his generation, he treated the period with studied casualness, dividing his time between Portsmouth and Curraghmore, enjoying hunting, shooting and steeplechasing. Again it is likely that in *Excellent* the two young men met.

Soon afterwards a new regulation required gunnery officers to undergo a six-month course, when they would be divided into three classes, those already employed on gunnery duties being placed in the third class. Fisher – never third class in anything – studied in his own time, applied for a special examination and in March 1866 qualified first class. Uninterested in sport, his main recreation was to walk on Portsdown Hill where, in isolation, he practised his voice to stir men to activity. Many officers later commented on this ability. 'His orders were like peals of thunder.'

He was a terrifying examiner, staring vacantly at his victim as he noted down the accuracy of the answers, the stare remaining with him in later life, when digesting the arguments of colleagues or antagonists, lips slightly parted and his face assuming an expression of vacuity. His reputation already spreading, when the Board of the Admiralty paid a visit, one of them asked, 'Is this Lieutenant Fisher as good a seaman as a gunnery man?' He overheard the question and, stepping forward, said: 'My Lords, I am Lieutenant Fisher, just as good a seaman as a gunnery man'. The shyness of the boy who wrote to Mams for consolation was replaced by the brashness of the man.

In 1866 Fisher married Miss Frances Delves-Broughton, daughter of the Rector of Bletchley, whose two brothers were naval officers, and the marriage was a very happy one. The marriages of naval officers, interrupted by long absences from home, were not always successful, and a man of Fisher's commitment to the Service must have been a difficult husband, but his wife devoted herself to helping him in his career, unaffected by his restless vagaries, providing a domestic base, a serene refuge from his stormy life, her balance always preserved and confirming his profound religious convictions, which show in all their correspondence. He too was deeply fond of her, regretting in a letter that he had not married her a year earlier. His love never left him.

The next year Beresford was appointed to HMS *Research*, a small screw sloop stationed at Holyhead looking out for Fenians. This was convenient, enabling him to join a local hunt and often to cross to Ireland one night, hunting through the next day, returning the following night. But he did not stay long in *Research*. In the summer months of 1868 he joined the Royal yacht *Victoria and Albert*, where he first met the Prince of Wales, later Edward VII, with whom he struck up a close friendship. He met, too, the Prince's 22-year-old younger brother, Alfred, Duke of Edinburgh, who was appointed in command of *Galatea*, a screw frigate of 3,227 tons, in which an extensive tour was planned.

Service in the Royal Yacht gave Beresford promotion on 21 September 1868, when he was nowhere near the top of the seniority list (there were 140 officers above him) and appointment to *Galatea* for the Duke's tour. Calling at Madeira, St. Vincent and Cape Town, the ship voyaged to Perth and Sydney before visiting New Zealand, Tahiti and Yokohama, where the Duke paid a State Visit to the Mikado. While in Japan, Beresford had the Waterford Hounds in full cry tattooed on his back with the brush of the fox disappearing 'where it ought to disappear'. Leaving Yokohama the ship visited Peiho, where, ten years earlier, Fisher had seen so much bloodshed in the mud. Beresford accompanied the Duke to Peking before *Galatea* continued her journey to Chefoo, Shanghai and Hong Kong, Manila, Calcutta, Ceylon and Mauritius, returning to Cape Town, thence to the Falklands and home via Montevideo, almost exactly two years after leaving.

Such an extensive tour perhaps involved Beresford in some naval experience, but it was also the life of a courtier. It introduced him to Royalty and the great – Sir Harry Parke, British Minister in Japan, Admiral Sir Henry Keppel, Commander-in-Chief, China, A.B.F.Mitford (later Lord Redesdale). Beresford was happy with two years of splendour, pleasure and pageantry. He was 24 and on return placed on half-pay, enjoying the pleasures of the Irish country life for the next two years.

Fisher, meanwhile, in 1869 took over instruction in torpedo work in HMS *Excellent*. The term embraced all existing underwater weapons; guncotton charges were attached to the end of forty-foot spars stuck out from the sides of eight-knot steam gunboats which were sent on suicidal attempts to brush against enemy ships, the charges detonated by batteries. One-pound guncotton charges with detonators were connected to one end of an instantaneous fuse, with a pistol at the other, the charge thrown into enemy ships or boats and the moment it landed the pistol fired. To make it watertight, charge, detonator and all were dropped into boiling pitch and withdrawn before getting hot enough to explode, the operator ducking behind an iron plate for protection. The mobile torpedo, such as the Whitehead, had not been introduced and must be distinguished from these faltering experiments, which soon faded out, (though the US Bureau of Ordnance

9

issued Spar Torpedo Instructions for the US Navy as late as 1890) and from the mine, of which there were many types, surrounded by much confusion. Rudimentary mines were then regarded as largely defensive weapons for the protection of harbours, the responsibility of the Royal Engineers, who ran courses at Woolwich. The Admiralty was invited to send an officer and in March 1867 Lieutenant H.C.Kane (later Admiral Sir Henry) underwent the course. The War Office wanted to confine all mining instruction to Woolwich, but Rear-Admiral Astley Cooper-Key, formerly captain of *Excellent* and now Director General of Naval Ordnance, established a course there and selected Fisher to run it.

All who came in contact with Fisher were inspired with his enthusiasm; one officer remarked that he persuaded groups of captains, who tended to be dignified and pompous, to pull oars and handle wet cable 'as if once again they were midshipmen'. He wrote a manual of mines detonated from shore and electrical work *(A Short Treatise on Electricity and the Management of Electric Torpedoes)*, but he was dissatisfied with it and typically, while later serving at sea, rewrote it. In an appendix he wrote proposals for 'electric firing of guns', the forerunner of director firing, but the Ordnance Select Committee rejected it. The Foreign Office drew the attention of the the Admiralty to experiments being carried out at Fiume (now Rijeka, Croatia, but then in the Austrian Empire) by a Scotsman, Robert Whitehead, and the next year the Commander-in-Chief, Mediterranean, Vice-Admiral Lord Clarence Paget, reported on the weapon's potentialities and a committee of three officers of the Mediterranean Fleet, including Kane, went to Fiume. They reported favourably on their visit, though the Director of Naval Ordnance, Captain Arthur Hood, had reservations on accuracy.

In the meantime Fisher was selected by the Admiralty to join a distinguished party to attend the opening in June of Prussia's new naval port, Wilhelmshaven, at the fishing village of Heppens where Wilhelm I in his speech foreshadowed the future ambitions of Germany: 'I look forward with cheerful confidence to the further development and to the future of our young German Navy.'[4]

But Fisher was there to report on German development of mines and torpedoes, a fact that was evident to the King who asked him if he was the only one in Britain who knew about torpedoes. Fisher sent in a massive report recommending the horn of the 'mechanical' mines which, when struck, 'breaks a small glass tube containing sulphuric acid which thus escaping mixes with a powder [chlorate of potash] surrounding it, thereby causing a flame which ignites the charge'. The Hertz horn was identical, though the acid spilled onto plates which formed a battery, the current from which ignited the charge, and Fisher wrote in 1919, 'That same Hertz mine, in all its essentials, remains still "The King of Mines"',[5] and in 1917 the Navy was obliged to copy the German model. Fisher recommended that a

Torpedo Committee should be formed of two officers of the Navy, one of the Royal Engineers and a chemist from Woolwich, nominating Kane as one of the Admiralty representatives.

Promoted commander in August 1869, at the early age of 28, (not spectacular; Key was promoted at 24, Hornby at 25, Richards at 26) in November he left *Excellent* and joined *Donegal*, taking out a relief crew for *Ocean* on the China Station. In those days ships recommissioned on the station, relief crews taking a ship out, transferring to their new ship, while the old crew sailed the relief ship home. Such ships were grossly overcrowded and *Donegal*, a wooden screw ship of 5,481 tons, carried 1,300 men and fifty officers. But Fisher had worked everything out in advance and she was organized as if in commission for years.

His thoroughness, enthusiasm and fairness stirred the men to adore him. The passage to China was accompanied by continual drills and on arrival at Hong Kong the crews were efficient in gunnery, rifle and sail drill. He was said to know the name of every man on board, where he was born and his religion. He picked the best men for *Ocean*, a wooden 'iron-cased' ship of 6,832 tons. The drill of the main deck battery was impressive, Fisher standing aft, his powerful voice moving the whole battery as one, the perfection of contemporary gunnery. Sail drill was similar, Fisher giving the order, 'Make plain sail in two minutes!' followed by 'Way aloft!' He enjoyed landing a platoon for field days at Kowloon and invented the white gaiters still worn by sailors drilling ashore.

A strict disciplinarian, he tempered punishments with humour, adopting many unofficial ones if they fitted the crime, but when necessary dealt out severe punishments, many recorded in pencil, so that if a man showed improvement they could be rubbed out so as not to affect his future or pension. *Ocean* was a happy and efficient ship, drills worked out in minute detail, the officers and petty officers often consulted. Suggestions were welcomed and if adopted the details were left to the man making them. When coaling ship, he always went down into the lighters and worked with the men, a practice which later became standard, every officer except the captain being expected to join in. He was not interested in making his ship 'pretty', putting efficiency first, something not calculated to bring him favour, but on arrival at Cape Town on the way home to pay off, the ship was battered after her passage from China, and the men longed to get ashore. Fisher, using meat tins as extra paint 'kettles', got nearly all the ship's company over the side and the whole ship was painted in half an hour.

Though always a convinced Christian, in *Ocean* Fisher read and studied theology. He read the Bible every day and his beliefs remained with him all his life. Yet his was a private Christianity; he never inflicted his views on others, though his letters to his wife devoted much space to long quotations from the Bible.

11

In the contemporary Navy the study of past operations, the principles of war and gunnery efficiency were all ignored, giving way to the technology of the day, the intricacies of masts, yards and sails and cleanliness. Fisher recognized the significance of the changes taking place: steam, armour, electricity, breech-loaders and quick-firing guns, torpedoes and mines. In December 1870 he wrote to the Admiralty a letter 'which will puzzle Captain Hood. It's pointing out an awful lot of humbug in the way our guns are arranged on board ship. I have been having a very great success with electric firing and introduced a lot of new dodges, all of which I have sent to the Admiralty.'[6] He had hoped to be appointed Assistant Director of Naval Ordnance and was disappointed when the existing incumbent remained after promotion. But he was being consulted by many of his superiors on gunnery matters, and in reply to Captain Henry Boys, captain of *Excellent*, he wrote: 'The great failing of *Excellent* is aversion to change' and complained of the permanent committees sitting at Woolwich, Shoeburyness and Chatham. 'It makes my blood boil when I remember the studied and deliberate manner in which the Navy is ignored in all these places.' The War Office controlled all ordnance stores and ammunition, 'from a 35-ton gun down to a boarding pike and a common shovel'.[7] The needs of the Navy were not understood by the soldiers.

In a postscript he drew attention to *The Soldier's Pocket Book for Field Service* published in 1869 by Colonel Garnet Wolseley, then Deputy Quartermaster General in Canada, who had said: 'The system of placing ships employed by the commissariat for stores and provisions under naval control is most injurious to the public interest.' and recommended that a harbourmaster should be under Army control. 'No naval officer, no matter what may be his rank, should in any way interfere,' and, further, that 'The transport of troops by sea is, unfortunately for the Army, entirely subject to the Admiralty control,' which Fisher described as 'cool impertinence', and added, 'The next time the Navy and the Army are associated with one another, they will be fighting one another instead of the enemy'.[8]

He wrote (30 March 1871) an eight-page pamphlet, intended as a preface to a book by Captain James Goodenough, who had the preface printed separately for private circulation. Though Fisher was surprised, it demonstrates his original thinking. At that time he supported Captain Philip H. Colomb, though later he became impatient with the historian, who was falling behind the times: 'He is not a naval authority, and he never comes to the point'.[9] In a letter to his wife in January 1872 he referred to 'my new book about which you must not be too sanguine' (he was right for it seems never to have appeared) and 'what I think is a very good pamphlet about things in general in the Navy'. There is no trace of that either.

His views were revolutionary. There were only two tactical formations needed, line abreast and line ahead, from which the former

12

could easily be attained in any direction. Ships should be constructed to protect their vital parts by compartmentation and armour. Masts and sails should be done away with; the weight and space they occupied should be taken by coal; extreme rates of speed should not be aimed at; the space occupied by engines and boilers was out of proportion to the coal that could be carried.[10]

But Professor Marder's remark[11] that Fisher's ideas on protection and speed were to change overlooks the fact that conditions changed too. Improvements in steam engines were so great that the relationship between coal carried and size of boilers and machinery altered dramatically. Increases in gunnery ranges were also dramatic. When someone accused him of inconsistency, Fisher said, 'Inconsistency is the bugbear of fools. I wouldn't give a damn for a fellow who couldn't change his mind with a change of conditions! Ain't I to wear a waterproof because I didn't when the sun was shining?'[12]

Ocean was ordered home in the middle of 1872 and on passage demonstrated the weakness of wooden-built ironclads. At every roll the weight of the plates opened the seams, water squirted in and as the ship rolled the other way the seams closed again. 'At one time the sea washed up to my waist in my cabin.'

About the time Fisher returned home Beresford was recalled from half-pay. Sir Henry Keppel had returned from China and hoisted his flag as Commander-in-Chief, Plymouth, and, at the suggestion of the Prince of Wales, invited Beresford to become his Flag Lieutenant.

Keppel, born in 1809, entered the Navy only seven years after Waterloo. Uninterested in the professional aspects of the Service, he was a classic example of the nineteenth century naval officer. With ample courage, he enjoyed a good fight in which he displayed great leadership. The Navy was a convenient vehicle for the rumbustious life he liked to lead. He pursued sport and amusing company; Beresford and he soon becoming fast friends. The duties of a flag lieutenant included control of the C-in-C's signal organization, 'a science which, as it was understood in those days, I mastered completely'. But his duties were largely social and by now he had acquired all the graces and supreme self-confidence. A polished, good-looking, titled young man, active, exuberant, with a sense of humour (though sometimes malicious), immense charm and a smooth tongue, he could hardly fail in such duties. The titled families of the west country rallied to him and he had as much pleasure as he could desire; steeplechasing, riding point-to-point with the Dartmoor Hounds, travelling with the C-in-C, sharing house parties with the Prince of Wales.

Even allowing for the overweening pride of the Victorian landed aristocracy, Beresford's insolence exceeded all bounds. Driving home in the early hours he reached a turnpike gate then outside Plymouth. The keeper was asleep and, despite knocking and shouting, would not be disturbed. Beresford heaved a stone through his window which brought him out, when Beresford gave him half a sovereign. But he retreated inside leaving Beresford and his friends on the wrong side of the gate whereupon they broke all the remaining windows, removed the gate from its hinges, tied it to the back of their 'cart' and reduced it to firewood. He ran a string of horses which he lent to senior officers and titled people; he ran a coach and four in which he took the whole Board of Admiralty to some manoeuvres. Rear Admiral Beauchamp, with unconscious prescience, called out: 'Get down! Gentlemen, you must get down. He'll upset you on purpose, just to say he's upset the whole Board of the Admiralty!' Though claiming to be short of money, he also ran a small yacht in which he and Keppel sailed in the Sound and he lived in lavish extravagance.

While on half-pay Beresford had campaigned for the anti-home-rule candidate for Kerry, which gave him an appetite for politics and he stood for County Waterford, for which he was obliged to give up his appointment as flag lieutenant. He fought a hard campaign and won with a substantial majority. It was not unusual for active naval officers also to be Members of Parliament. Though he stood on anti-home-rule and denominational education (the right of every parent to have his child educated in his own religion), Keppel encouraged him, believing the Navy might gain through such an individualistic and dedicated a character to promote the interests of the Service. But a lieutenant of 28 with limited experience could hardly represent the Navy in Parliament and since the early 1900s, largely as a result of his activities, officers have been prohibited from membership of the House of Commons while still on the active list (though at first it was permitted when on half-pay). The objections were obvious, for a junior officer who disagreed with his superior was free to catch the next train to London and with the protection of Parliamentary privilege criticize the decisions of his superior. It gave him direct access to ministers, including the First Lord and Prime Minister; it gave him an almost automatic route to promotion, for he could speak in Parliament with impunity in terms that would destroy the careers of his seniors. As time went on, it became an intolerable burden on authority.

Beresford made his maiden speech on 8 May 1874, but as a man-about-town he spent little time in the House. His position and charm gave him access to the company he enjoyed, which the Queen so pungently described as 'that independent, haughty, fault-finding, fashionable set, repulsive, vulgar, bad and frivolous in every way'.[13] He spent much of his time enjoying the pleasures of London society, country house parties and out hunting. He soon became a member of the 'Marlborough House set' and his friendship with the Prince of Wales grew, even to attending as the Prince's guest the state banquet for the Czar Alexander II in May 1874. He was established as a Victorian 'buck' among the high-living. He once rode down Park Lane on a pig for a bet.

He spoke in the House in April 1875, his speech having been prepared by Commander Gerard Noel (later Admiral of the Fleet), advocating improvements in naval training. He advocated that Britain should withdraw from the Declaration of Paris of 1856, which attempted to define the rules of blockade stating that blockade must not merely be declared, but must be enforced. The motion was lost, to the inconvenience of the Allies in the First World War. He spoke on the retirement of officers. The Navy List was so swollen that about half the officers were on half-pay. In 1873 Gladstone had retired some 2,000 officers but there were still as many as 640 unemployed. Promotion came from the top of the list, or to men with 'interest'. Beresford wanted to see promotion by selection, a system thought likely to encourage nepotism. He spoke again demanding increased numbers of fast cruisers for trade protection 'to be rigged as frigates'. But a visit to India by the Prince of Wales was planned and the Queen was reluctantly persuaded to allow the Prince to take many of his Marlborough House friends with him, including Beresford, who was appointed an ADC. Before his thirtieth birthday, two months after the cruise started, Beresford was promoted commander, though he had no war service and had only served 7½ years as a lieutenant (there was no rank of lieutenant commander then), of which only two years and four months had been spent at sea, all in Royal cruises. He had spent more than four years on half-pay, yet was promoted over the heads of some 170 officers, some of whom were to earn high rank and fame. He was nominated for promotion by Sir Henry Keppel on a 'haul-down' vacancy. As already discussed, haul-down nominations were accepted without demur. On promotion, an officer was often left unemployed, and Beresford returned to the House of Commons, speaking in support of the retention of flogging, which he afterwards regretted.

At the end of the Parliamentary session in the autumn of 1876 he joined HMS *Vernon* to qualify in torpedoes and then applied for an appointment as second in command of a big ship, joining HMS *Thunderer* as commander, remaining a Member of Parliament. His name was suggested for *Victoria and Albert*, but the Queen refused him: 'I don't think any of the officers of my yacht ought to be Members of Parliament. It might be very inconvenient in various ways.'[14]

When Beresford joined her, *Thunderer* was undergoing a refit after one of her box boilers had exploded with sixty-five casualties. She recommissioned in May 1877, but cruised only as far as Queenstown, giving her commander ample opportunities to visit Curraghmore and London, speaking in the House on the Whitehead torpedo. An anonymous account had recently been published of a fictitious action in which the British fleet had been disabled by torpedoes. Beresford confirmed to the House that such an event was quite possible and inaccurately claimed that a Whitehead torpedo could achieve a range of 1,000 yards at 20 knots. At that time its speed was little more than seven knots and its range about 300 yards. To a non-technical House of Commons he spoke imaginatively and with self-confidence on a technical subject, giving exact details of the damage likely to be sustained by British ships.

What Beresford had said had some truth in it; the torpedo indeed had a profound effect on naval warfare. But when an inexperienced officer pontificated on naval tactics, especially as a report was awaited from the Admiralty Torpedo Committee, the Admiralty were both embarrassed and angry. The First Lord, George Ward Hunt, pointing out the impropriety of his action, told Beresford he should make up his mind whether he wished to follow a career in politics or the Navy. With hauteur he responded that as there was no regulation that forbade a naval officer to sit in Parliament; what he said was his own business. Ward Hunt was not satisfied, but Beresford went to Disraeli. 'Mr Ward Hunt soon found, like many another statesman imbued with good intentions, that patriotism weighed but lightly in the balance compared with party and political convenience.'[15] Beresford heard no more about it, but the Prince of Wales wrote to him: 'You will I think have to make up your mind to give up your seat and stick to your profession, or else it will damage your professional interests. I have real reasons for saying this.'[16] But the Prince's advice was ignored. Beresford made the concession that he did not stand for Parliament when on full pay, and on receiving a new appointment, applied for the Chiltern Hundreds. But the Admiralty either had to keep him fully employed or suffer the embarrassment of having their policies pulled to pieces with impunity by a serving officer, whose incursions into Parliament gave him power to make demands denied to others, ensuring his progress in the Service.

When not in the Commons he returned to his ship, where he entertained the Queen, who went into a turret and saw a torpedo. That evening he attended a dinner at Osborne, where the Queen found him 'very funny' though 'a trifle cracky'. The boiler accident had given *Thunderer* a reputation among the sailors as an unlucky ship, so to dispel this Beresford invited the Prince of Wales on board. He fired one of the 38-ton guns, which did little to change the ship's reputation, for after Beresford left her, one of them exploded with the loss of twelve killed and thirty-five injured. Beresford was at Curraghmore. Basing his views on what he could read in the newspapers and with only his sub-lieutenant's training in gunnery, he wrote to *The Times* offering an explanation. The muzzle-loading guns had to be depressed below the horizontal for loading and when withdrawing the rammer the papier-mache wad could come out a little way. While true, this was irrelevant; but having been raised by a man gaining in the lay mind a reputation as an expert in everything naval, *Excellent*, the Gunnery School, and Woolwich were

16

obliged to experiment to establish the facts and concluded the explosion was due to a misfire. Beresford was reprimanded for publishing a letter while on full pay, but he was quite unconcerned and continued to attend Parliament whenever naval matters were discussed.

The Admiralty then refused him employment as long as he remained in Parliament and he appealed to the Prince of Wales, who, in sharp contrast to the views of the Queen, asked for him to command his yacht *Osborne*, a small paddle vessel of 1,860 tons. Normally a commander's command, she was a sinecure; she seldom went to sea. Beresford did not live on board, but in London during the social season, touring the great houses of his friends and relations. In March 1878 he had married Ellen Jeromina Gardner, known as 'Mina' to her friends. The granddaughter of a minor German count, a beautiful heiress with a taste for expensive antiques, who used make-up lavishly in an age when it was ill-favoured, she was known as 'the Painted Lady' and had great social ambitions. The yacht took Prince and Princess Arthur of Connaught for a honeymoon cruise in the Mediterranean in the autumn of 1879, but otherwise was only called upon to attend Cowes Week, where Beresford sailed his own yacht.

Beresford's reputation as a naval expert was now established. In 1877 Russia went to war with Turkey and in the spring of 1879 defeated the Turks and was on the point of taking Constantinople. The situation was critical and when a Particular Service Squadron (today a Task Force) was formed for the Baltic under Admiral Sir Astley Cooper Key few ships were available, but three were being built in British shipyards for Turkey and one for Brazil. Instead of leaving the matter to the Admiralty, Disraeli asked Beresford's opinion and the ships were commandeered. Beresford explained that Disraeli asked him because 'I could, if necessary, speak on the matter in Parliament'. But clearly the First Lord would speak, and the affair remains a mystery.

Less surprising, the Prince of Wales consulted Beresford on the selection of officers to serve in HMS *Bacchante* which was carrying his sons, the Duke of Clarence and Prince George (later King George V), to Australia. He could hardly refuse, but a word with the Second Sea Lord might have saved the Board irritation at being by-passed again.

With advancing technology, amateurs happily splashed about in the depth of technicalities and in March 1878 the House debated the design of battleships, a matter of great complexity. HMS *Inflexible* had been protected with the heaviest armour ever fitted (24") over her vitals, but fore and aft the armour did not extend below the waterline and it was argued that she could be made unstable. To extend it the whole length would have been impractical. In a speech the obscurity of which surely justified Churchill's description of Beresford, 'When he gets up, he does not know what he is going to say; when he is speaking he does not know what he is saying; and when he sits down he does not know what he has said', on this occasion he gave welcome support to the First Lord who convinced the House of *Inflexible*'s stability. A week later he spoke on pensions for naval widows and dependents and the following year claimed that one-third of the ratings were 'non-combatants' – a statement with which, even then, few would agree. He continued to ask questions – about a smallpox epidemic in HMS *Boadicea*, the use of seamen and marines in the Zulu War, the provision of sports grounds at Portsmouth.

But the Tory government fell on 24 March 1880, Beresford losing his seat and leaving him with only his sinecure appointment in *Osborne* counting only as harbour service. For promotion to Captain two more years' service in a seagoing ship were required. His service in *Thunderer* had only been a year, so he asked the Prince to release him and applied for an appointment at sea. It is difficult to understand why the Admiralty did not take the opportunity to rid themselves of this truculent officer. There were many others on half-pay and if they had left him unemployed for five years he would no longer have been eligible for promotion and could have been retired. But the new Liberal Board failed to grasp the nettle and he was given command of HMS *Condor*, a composite single-screw gun-vessel of only 780 tons, stationed in the Mediterranean.

2

WELL DONE *CONDOR*

On 19 September 1872 Fisher, having paid off *Ocean*, returned to *Excellent* as 'commander for torpedo service'; he was little concerned with gunnery. HMS *Vernon*, an old fourth rate was attached to *Excellent* as a torpedo school including every sort of underwater weapon. Many of his friends, with little faith in them, advised against the appointment, but with greater foresight, he accepted. Effectively he was head of the torpedo department of the Navy, for there was no higher authority and he demanded personal control, writing to his wife that he would resign 'if I find I am not independent'.

He ran courses ranging from captains to seamen, to which he applied his usual vigour and in October 1873, after visiting *Vernon*, Rear-Admiral J.W.Tarleton, Second Naval Lord, concluded that the torpedo had a great future before it and that in future mechanical training would be essential for officers. 'Made a note to speak to Goschen [First Lord] about young Fisher.'[1]

In April 1874 the good relationship between Germany and Britain permitted a visit to Vernon by Dr Albert Hertz, whose electromechanical 'horn' had now been accepted by the German Navy. Fisher reported that Hertz had gone closely into the British mining and torpedo organization and had given him details of the Hertz horn. The visit was conditional on a return visit by Fisher to Wilhelmshaven and Kiel which took place in July. He reported in detail on both the Hertz mine and those detonated from shore and took the opportunity of reporting on the defences of Kiel and Wilhelmshaven and on harbour defence by mines, fast developing. Germany had already obtained a Whitehead torpedo for trial.

In the same month the final report was issued by the Torpedo Committee, suggested earlier by Fisher who had been associated with it throughout. The original terms of reference he drafted included determining 'the most efficient manner of protecting vessels, both at sea and at anchor, from the attacks of offensive torpedoes of the various natures known; viz. the Whitehead, the locomotive torpedo invented by Lay, and Von Scheliha, the Harvey torpedo and the outrigger [spar] torpedo'.[2] The committee report emphasized the need to protect ships against offensive torpedoes, particularly the Whitehead, and said 'none of our large vessels could remain for any length of time during war off an enemy's port without the imminent risk of destruction by offensive torpedoes'.

In the meantime Fisher again revised the *Treatise* which included an *Addendum*, with a preface dated January 1873, in which he discussed the Whitehead torpedo, though he was much irritated by delays in printing and publishing. The next week he went with Captain Morgan Singer, President of the Torpedo Committee, to Fiume, where they bought a Whitehead torpedo and brought it home for examination and trials at Sheerness. It was a primitive weapon armed with only 100 pounds of gunpowder with three speeds 10, 8 or 6 knots, tottering for two or three hundred yards. Fisher wrote to Boys, the Captain of *Excellent*, 'I have sent you the official letter with respect to the Whitehead torpedo. It is certainly a wonderful invention. . . . I shall be about a fortnight over it. On Tuesday week we go down to Sheerness to have some sea trials with it.' After these trials he wrote: 'I shall try to get back on Wednesday if I can, but I want if possible to take the Whitehead to pieces and put it all together by myself (if I can) before leaving.'[3] The equipment needed for experiment and instruction in *Vernon* was increasing at an alarming rate, unwelcome in *Excellent*, and gunnery officers unfamiliar with torpedoes despised them. Accordingly Fisher proposed the segregation of *Vernon* from *Excellent*. But he also saw the even greater need for experiment and development and demanded more staff for this work, since his existing staff, even with his extraordinary energy, was almost wholly occupied in teaching and examining officers and men. He listed numerous items requiring attention – electric steering of torpedoes, countermining (the use of electrically detonated mines to destroy enemy minefields), extemporized mining, experiments with foreign electric fuses, and so on. He demonstrated a circuit closer designed by the Army at Woolwich which cost £7 10s, (about £420 in 1990) whereas *Vernon* made one from an old meat tin for 1s. But though Boys supported him in an increase in staff for instructional duties, he believed experimental work should be carried out at Woolwich – a short-sighted view, since the Army was interested only in defence work – and having stifled the vital research he then tried to get Fisher to revise the *Treatise* yet again, which Fisher firmly said should be done by the Torpedo Committee.

The suggestion that it was the Admiralty rather than Fisher who initiated the segregation from *Excellent* cannot be sustained, for he had written in the covering letter to his report on the visit to Fiume in February 1873, 'I mentioned casually to Captain Hood yesterday that I thought I should receive some sort of definite instructions or some definite position, in turning over to the *Vernon*; but I will reserve my ideas on this subject till I see you, as I couldn't explain in a letter as clearly as I should wish what my views are.'[4]

On 26 April 1876 *Vernon* was commissioned under Captain William Arthur, with Commander A.K.Wilson as principal instructor. Though promoted to captain in October 1874 at the age of 33, Fisher stayed in *Vernon* until August 1876 to inculcate the new captain, commander and officers. He wrote then, 38 years before the First World War, 'The issue of the next naval war will chiefly depend upon the use that is made of the torpedo and mines, not only in ocean warfare, but for purposes of blockade.'[5] He invited politicians and journalists to displays and demonstrations, which did not endear him to the reactionaries.

His interest in gunnery remained, however, and his opinion was sought by Boys on a proposal to introduce a 75-ton gun: 'I am most decidedly of opinion that the projectile of every rifled gun in the Service might be very greatly increased in weight with very great advantages *for naval purposes* PROVIDED that every gun can be warranted to withstand an internal pressure of 30 tons upon the square inch. . . . Putting it broadly, we are now using guns . . . capable of hitting a barn door at 3,000 yards under conditions which frequently render it doubtful whether we shall ever hit a haystack at 1,500 yards.'[6] He argued that until new and better gunnery control was developed the hard punch, which would inflict more damage on the enemy when hits were scored, should be substituted for accurate guns, whose qualities could not be utilized, refuting some historians' claims that Fisher paid little attention to fire control until the advent of the journalist, Pollen, in the early twentieth century, discussed later. A Board minute of 4 September 1876 praising his work said, 'He should be thanked and placed on half pay at the end of the month and he should shortly be considered for employment next year.'[7] It was the first time he had been placed on half pay – a remarkable distinction in those days. Even then he was called upon to serve on a committee preparing a torpedo manual and for 2½ months was placed in command of HMS *Pallas* in the Mediterranean to witness Whitehead's experiments and then to HMS *Hercules*, the flagship, to continue the work.

While there, he wrote again to Boys, now Director of Naval Ordnance, concerning discussions he had had with a Colonel Wray of the Royal Engineers about torpedo defences of Malta which he described as 'quite inadequate' suggesting the introduction of large Whiteheads as the telegraph companies objected to moored mines. He had heard from some engineers working in Constantinople claiming to have invented a method of detecting torpedoes at a distance. He was cautious, and we hear no more about it.

In January, 1877 Sir Geoffrey Phipps Hornby, a fine tactician and

21

progressive admiral, became Commander-in-Chief Mediterranean and Fisher decided to remain on the station 'even if put on half pay, as I should like to see a little of Hornby's way of managing a fleet'. But in March he was appointed flag captain to Cooper Key, Commander-in-Chief, North West Coast of America, in HMS *Bellerophon*.

His reputation had preceded him. Joseph Honnor, a midshipman, wrote:

> When Captain Fisher was appointed to us there was something like consternation in the ship, for his reputation as a strict disciplinarian was known. The state of the ship was undoubtedly slack. . . . Captain Fisher . . . fell the officers and crew in on the quarterdeck; and having told them what he thought of the want of smartness and proficiency, said, 'Now I intend to give you Hell for three months, and if you have not come up to my standard in that time you'll have Hell for another three months.' He was as good as his word . . . and in three months the ship was as smart as any. . . . The Captain . . . threw himself heart and soul into the amusements of the officers and men.[8]

At Bermuda a humourless Captain Superintendent reported to the Admiral that two midshipmen had broken into the yard and Fisher wrote to the Admiral, 'regretting . . . a serious case of probable attempted burglary by two officers of his flagship whose heights were respectively 4 feet 4 inches and 5 feet and who had scaled a wall two inches higher than the shorter offender. A 90-cwt anchor was missing from the dockyard and a hole had been found in the pocket of the elder and most desperate criminal'.[9] Another midshipman, A.G.H.W.Moore (later Admiral Sir Gordon Moore) described Fisher as 'a very exacting master, the least inattention being punished, but who was kind to the younger midshipmen for whom he laid on lavish suppers in his cabin.'[10]

At Halifax Fisher developed a passion for ballroom dancing which lasted all his life and later he insisted on all midshipmen learning to dance as a social accomplishment. This, of course had nothing to do with the old order, 'Hands to dance and skylark', claimed elsewhere.

Cooper Key who had been in command of *Excellent* when Fisher was a lieutenant on the staff, admired Fisher's progressive views and his daughter recalled: 'He was so much a sailor in every meaning of the word – was so essentially part of the sea and the Navy. His genuine love for both shone through everything. . . . my father's opinion of him often repeated [was] that he was bound for the **TOP**. "One of the finest brains in the Navy . . . with an inexhaustible capacity for hard work," a born optimist.'[11]

When Cooper Key hauled down his flag, Fisher accompanied him as his flag captain in HMS *Hercules*. Russian ambitions in Turkey, with the connivance of Bismarck, had led to a European crisis, and in June 1878 Cooper Key commanded a Special Service Squadron. But Disraeli's diplomacy settled the problem in the Treaty of Berlin and after six months Cooper Key hauled down his flag.

In January 1879 Fisher returned to *Pallas*, then in the Sea of Marmora, after the Russian scare. At an hour's notice he travelled across Europe and arrived in Malta to see a tramp steamer weighing, destined for Constantinople. He climbed a rope ladder and hauled his luggage aboard. The master, seeing the figure in plain clothes, said,

'Hullo!'

'Hullo!'

'What is it you want?'

'I'm going with you to Constantinople to join my ship.'

'There ain't room: there's only one bunk, and when I ain't in it the mate is.'

'All right, I don't want a bunk.'

'We ain't got no cook.'

'That don't matter either.'

In due course Fisher arrived at his ship, part of a squadron under Phipps Hornby, whose presence was instrumental in persuading Russia to make peace with Turkey. There followed a visit to Constantinople, when Fisher took the opportunity to study the topography and defences of the Dardanelles of which he took careful note and which was to be of importance to him in 1915.

Six months later he returned home and was appointed flag captain to Vice Admiral Sir Leopold M'Clintock in HMS *Northampton*, one of the most modern ships, fitted with every sort of novelty. As usual, he spared no one. Admiral Sir George Egerton, then a Lieutenant, described it:

> The amount of work put into [the first] week was prodigious. Steam trials under steam alone, trials under steam and sail, trials under sail alone, tacking, wearing, making and shortening sail, gun trials, general quarters, searchlight tests and frequent coaling ship. . . . When a Sunday came everyone hoped we were going to have a day's rest. Not a bit of it. . . . Captain's inspection and short prayers . . . were followed by reading the Articles of War, finishing up with a reading of forty punishment warrants . . . but it had its effect throughout the commission, which was a very happy one.[12]

Fisher was irregular both in meals and sleep, dining any time between 6 and 10 pm and often not at all, working late, at any hour of the night sending for specialist officers to discuss his latest ideas, demanding a report the following day. His second in command, Commander Wilmot Fawkes, never understood and complained 'he will not stick enough to routine. . . . I have had such a time of it. . . . Anyone serving with Captain Fisher ought to have the temper of an angel and the hide of a rhinoceros. . . . We had 150 runs with

Whitehead torpedoes in the last ten days and the whole Navy had only 200 last year.'[13]

But Fisher liked Fawkes and they got on well. On 14 January 1881 Fawkes wrote: 'Very sad news for the ship, but very good news for Captain Fisher . . . He is appointed to the *Inflexible*, the new large ironclad. It is a **VERY** great compliment to him, as those ships are generally given to men very much senior to him. . . . but he is very sorry to leave the ship . . . there are nothing but long faces in her.'[14]

Fawkes arranged an elaborate farewell, but the emotion of leaving this happy ship was too much for Fisher, who 'crept unseen into a shore boat' to take him to the mail steamer, *Northampton*'s band playing his favourite waltz, *La Berceuse*, and *Old Lang Syne* as the steamer passed.

His appointment to *Inflexible* when only half way up the captains' list was a great distinction. If the demise of the sailing warship can be dated, it is the commissioning in 1881 of *Inflexible*, the biggest ship of her day, 11,880 tons, 320 feet long, 75 feet beam, armed with four 80-ton, 16-inch muzzle-loading guns, far the largest to date, in two 750-ton turrets abreast her funnels, with 24-inch armour. Two three-cylinder compound engines drove two shafts, 8,407 horsepower giving her 14 knots. Electric light was provided by AC generators at 600 volts, which was not thought to be dangerous until a stoker was electrocuted. Fitted with submerged torpedo tubes, she was subdivided into many compartments, the first realistic attempt at watertight sub-division. She carried two 60-foot torpedo-boats. Yet she was fitted with sails, which Fisher said 'had as much effect upon her in a gale of wind as a fly would have on a hippopotamus'.[15] They were removed, cut down to pole masts with fighting tops.

The Admiralty's confidence in Fisher was demonstrated when he asked for a forebridge to be fitted. The Admiral Superintendent opposed him, but was told 'all Captain Fisher's requests are to be complied with'. Trials and work-up followed Fisher's strenuous pattern and the ship sailed for the Mediterranean, where Vice-Admiral Sir Frederick Beauchamp Seymour was now Commander-in-Chief, stopping at Villefranche as Guardship while Queen Victoria was at Mentone. The Queen had little regard for the Navy since the Admiralty had refused to make the Prince Consort an admiral of the fleet, but Fisher's frankness and humour won her favour, his first intro-duction to Court circles.

Egypt, under Turkish suzerainty, was in chaos. Khedive Ismail in a 'carnival of extravagance and oppression' had run up huge debts and to miti-gate his position, in 1875, had sold his 176,000 shares in the Suez Canal Co. to Great Britain. The next year his debts rose to £94m and the Sultan was induced to procure his abdication.

His son, Khedive Tewfik, was weak, the country seething with discontent. An obscure colonel, Arabi Bey (also known as Ahmed Arabi or Arabi

Pasha), led a revolt and Bismarck, seeking to discredit Britain and France, encouraged Turkey to claim exclusive rights to restore order. Neither Britain nor France took decisive action until both their consuls general warned that the lives of foreigners were in danger, when Seymour and the French Admiral Conrad were ordered to Alexandria with one ironclad and two gun-vessels each.

Beresford, serving under Seymour, wrote a long letter to T.G.Bowles, editor of *Vanity Fair*, opposing Gladstone's policy, ending: 'If I have told you anything you did not know, I am so glad, but do not let my name appear; you know how particular I am to do everything strictly according to the Service, and our orders are that we are not to appear as having written to any paper'. Bowles was discreet, but Beresford was writing letters to the Prince of Wales, who showed some to Lord Granville, the Foreign Secretary, from which it was evident that Beresford had disclosed confidential information to Bowles. At last the Board decided that he must be court-martialled. But before the Warrant could be issued, the Prince heard of the matter and rescued his friend by indicating that he considered the action a breach of Royal trust, though he agreed to advise him to refrain from further indiscretions.

Egypt deteriorated; France apostatized. On 11 June 1882 150 Europeans were slaughtered, men women and children. Alexandria was looted, Europeans and natives were murdered and 14,000 Christians fled the country. Refugees of all nations were evacuated by Britain in any available vessels, including the holds of colliers.

With German assistance Arabi fortified the city and nine miles of coast, twelve forts or batteries mounting 261 guns, and Seymour was ordered to demand its cessation, which was ignored. The French refused to take part in operations so the British fleet stood in to Alexandria and began a bombardment lasting all day. Seymour divided his heavy ships into two groups; *Inflexible*, with her massive guns, placed between the two, one turret firing ahead and the other aft, supporting each group.

The gunboats had been ordered to take such opportunities as presented themselves. *Condor*, under Beresford, was repeating ship, passing signals from one section to the other. He had as his guest an 'artist war-correspondent', Frederic Villiers, and at the last moment embarked Moberley Bell, the *Times* war correspondent, according to Beresford on the instructions of the admiral.

Beresford noticing two 10-inch guns firing accurately on some ships unable to reply, went in close to the shore where the fort's guns could not bear and attacked them at close range, dispersing the big guns' crews. The Admiral made a signal, 'Well done, *Condor*' and afterwards sent for Beresford to congratulate him. With two war correspondents aboard, Beresford's gallant action was given much publicity and at home he was regarded as the hero of the hour. Seymour had also signalled 'Well done *Inflexible*', but there was no reporter aboard her.

By morning all Arabi's fortifications had been abandoned and he turned his soldiers loose, opening the gaols. There followed a carnage of loot, pillage, arson, rape and murder, unreasoned and ferocious. The Khedive was surrounded in his palace and *Condor* was ordered to lie off the shore, her guns covering the approaches. The next day the palace was relieved by 400 sailors and marines, the Khedive making his way to Ras-el-Tin, where he was met by Seymour.

Seymour placed Fisher in command of forces ashore to secure the outer defences of Alexandria, but behind him was a zone of anarchy, incendiarism and chaos and he asked the Admiral for an officer as Provost Marshal. Beresford claimed Fisher asked for him, but whether or not, he was appointed 'Chief of Police and Provost Marshal' with orders to 'restore order . . . put out fires, bury the dead and clear the streets'. He wrote home: 'I never saw anything so awful . . . Streets, squares, and blocks of buildings all on fire, roaring and crackling and tumbling about like a hell let loose, Arabs murdering each other for loot under my nose . . . streets with many corpses in them.'[16]

Beresford, with 140 men, announced that arsonists, murderers and looters would be publicly shot at once; arson stopped and looting was much reduced. Fire brigades were formed of sailors and Arabs, at first recruited at the point of the bayonet, but after being well rewarded, as willing volunteers. Europeans began to return to the city, most armed, and behaving as victors over the Arabs. They were disarmed and sentenced in the same way as the Arabs. Tactfully, he set up Egyptian courts to try serious offences and insisted that death sentences were carried out by Egyptian soldiers. On 1 August the Army arrived and took over Beresford's task.

Meantime, Fisher held the perimeter, and with ships' artificers constructed an 'armoured train' – a locomotive and a few trucks protected by boiler plate, carrying a gun, an idea subsequently repeated many times. Beresford, engaged in destroying stocks of Arabi's guncotton, became surrounded and signalled for help. Fisher manned and armed boats, came ashore and drove off the enemy, rescuing Beresford.

In recognition of Beresford's work in the bombardment he was promoted captain and was relieved of his commander's command. Beresford and Fisher received cordial letters from the Queen and the Khedive, the latter offering Beresford an appointment on his staff, which he wished to accept, as his only alternative was another period on half pay. But he discussed the matter with Wolseley, now in command of land operations, who refused to allow him to accept it. He was immediately offered the position of war correspondent for the *New York Herald* but was again refused permission. Beresford gives no reason for these refusals, but his Parliamentary influence and correspondence with politicians may have been seen as a danger by Wolseley, himself a political intriguer.

By the end of August Fisher was seriously ill with dysentery, to which he refused to give in, taking eight pills of ipecacuanha and opium, the proper dose of which was one a day. Lord Northbrook, now First Lord, wrote telling him to come home: 'We can get many *Inflexibles*, but only one Jack Fisher'. But passage home would not then have been paid from public funds and cost £50, which was all he had in his bank account. He wrote to his wife that he dared not risk losing his command; he was a poor man with a family and was paying his mother an allowance. So he rejoined *Inflexible*, but at Malta was obliged to give in and come home.

The regard with which he was held by his ship's company is testified by the following perhaps unique letter:

HMS *Inflexible*.
27th August 1882

Sir,

    We, the ship's company of HMS *Inflexible*, take the earliest opportunity of expressing to you our deep sorrow and sympathy on this sad occasion of your sickness, and it is our whole wish that you may speedily recover and be amongst us again, who are so proud to be serving under you. Sir, we are all aware of the responsible duties you had to perform, and the great number of men you had to see to during your long stay ashore at Alexandria, which must have brought the strongest to a bed of sickness; but we trust shortly to see you again amongst us and on the field of active service, where you are as much at home as you are on your own grand ship, and at the end may receive your share of rewards and laurels, and your ship's company will feel as proud and prouder than if it was bestowed on themselves.

    Sir, trusting that you will overlook the liberty we have taken in sending this to you,

We beg to remain,
Your faithful and sympathising ship's company
INFLEXIBLES [17]

On return home Fisher was entertained by Northbrook, who introduced him to Gladstone, the latter pompously remarking of *Inflexible*,

'Portentous weapons! I really wonder the human mind can bear such a responsibility!'

'Oh, Sir,' replied Fisher waggishly, 'the common vulgar mind doesn't feel that sort of thing.' [18]

After his recovery, the Queen invited him to dinner at Osborne and to stay the night, an invitation repeated every year thereafter. For their services at

Alexandria Fisher was made CB and Beresford was mentioned in dispatches. This may have been the first time the two had met, and was certainly the first time they served afloat together. Each had earned the respect of the other.

Beresford arrived home a hero. Newspaper reports suggested he had played the major part in the bombardment and his role as Provost Marshal caught public imagination. His reception was typified at Highcliffe, the home of his Aunt Louisa, dowager Marchioness of Waterford, where the streets were lined with sailors, flag signals draped along the route, while he was drawn in a carriage by fourteen men on drag ropes to her house, where he made 'a nice little speech'.

Wrote Beresford: 'Mr. Gladstone sent for me; and after most courteously expressing his appreciation of my services, he discussed the question of compensation to the inhabitants of Alexandria who had suffered loss and damage. The information he required I had carefully collected in Alexandria.'[19]

The publicity given to Beresford and his own letters made him unpopular in the Admiralty and he was indignant at receiving no decoration other than the Khedive's medal. Seymour had been created Baron Alcester and was now Second Naval Lord. Fisher wrote to him: 'I have been a good deal worried by receiving letters from and about fellows landed at Alexandria after the bombardment, implying that I have not sufficiently represented what they did. . . . I think Beresford might have received a CMG if nothing else. . . . It's a mercy they gave me nothing!'[20]

Fisher's support for Beresford was reciprocated by the latter's friendly telegram: 'Old fellow, so concerned to hear you are ill. For sake of Service [come home] and recruit.'[21]

3

THE TRUTH ABOUT THE NAVY

Believing himself recovered, short of money and anxious for a new appointment, in April 1883 Fisher was given command of *Excellent* which met his enthusiastic approval and needed his energy, for what was called the 'forty year routine' was well established. It was said that nothing had changed for forty years. On the staff he had been powerless to change its torpid state, but now he could.

Founded in the early 1830s, *Excellent*'s first captain was Sir Thomas Hastings. In 1834 the First Naval Lord of the time, Sir John Poo Beresford, an antecedent of Lord Charles, described gunnery as 'Tom Hastings' scientific bosh', and proposed to close the establishment down. Practices were performed with outdated smooth-bore guns. The same old routine, the same old drills were carried out from year to year. 'The whole place was in a state of Rip-van-Winkleism.'[1] Fisher replaced the smooth-bore guns with modern quick-firing ones and exercises took on a more realistic form. His house was in the dockyard, but he was in the establishment daily at 8 am, disturbing the peace of the staff, who were unaccustomed to being in attendance when the day's work began.

On the staff were two young lieutenants, John Jellicoe, a highly competent gunnery officer, and Percy Scott, whose name became a byword in gunnery. The establishment consisted of two old hulks, *Excellent* and *Calcutta*. Whale Island was then the dumping ground for the excavations for Portsmouth Dockyard. Scott sketched a new and elaborate establishment for gunnery training, which Fisher seized on and pressed on the Admiralty. By 1890 barracks, batteries, drill and recreation grounds were being built. Fisher's period in command initiated the transition from the 'broadside' of hand-operated, muzzle-loaded guns to the breech-loaded, mechanically operated weapons of 1914. But his illness recurred and in the summer of 1885, to his bitter disappointment, he was placed on half pay while attempts were made to cure him.

Also on half pay and unable to obtain a seat in Parliament, Beresford went with his wife to visit his brother in India, taking passage in a P & O liner, which was rammed in the Suez Canal, whereupon Beresford 'at once made for the bridge' and offered the master advice.

In Cairo he dined Hicks Pasha on the night before his departure on his fatal mission in which all his force was slaughtered by the Mahdi. Beresford wished to join him, but permission was refused. During his journey he wrote a long politically motivated letter to *The Times*, criticizing the Egyptian War and concluding: 'Where is England's justification for the late "military operations" in Egypt? . . . it must surely be thought that, without sufficient cause England drifted into a war as arbitrary as it was unnecessary.'[2]

Again the Prince of Wales warned him: 'Take my advice, my dear Charlie, and leave Egyptian affairs alone,' and later, 'having been promoted for the bombardment of Alexandria, it would be perhaps better if you were not to criticise the action of the Government concerning Egypt.'[3] Since the only opponent in Parliament to the action was Randolph Churchill, the Prince was well justified.

On his return Beresford gave a lecture on machine guns to the Royal United Service Institution, attended by the Prince and many Army officers, who seem to have made little study of the subject. But during questions he claimed that British warships were inferior to French. Several admirals disagreed, both with his comparisons and his conclusions, challenging his right, as a serving officer, to make criticisms. Then it was stated that no British machine gun design existed, the War Office, who controlled the Ordnance Department, being blamed. The meeting broke up in acrimonious disorder. There was much truth in what Beresford said, but it was hardly tactful, especially since he repeated his criticisms in a letter to the *Standard*. He again lectured on 'Machine Guns in the Field' in July 1884. His popularity in the Admiralty was indeed at a low ebb, exacerbated when he was adopted as Tory candidate for Pembroke.

Much soured at not receiving a sea-going appointment, when captains junior to him were, he threatened resignation. But the Prince dissuaded him: 'Depend upon it, you will be employed, and there would be no greater pity than for you to leave the Navy in a huff.'[4] But the Admiralty refused him an appointment.

When Mahomet Ahmed, claiming to be the Holy Mahdi, began his insurrection and Hicks Pasha's force was annihilated, General Gordon was sent to Cairo in January 1884 to arrange the evacuation of Europeans. Astonishingly, Gladstone withdrew the force protecting the short route from the Red Sea port of Suakin, isolating Gordon. In August agitation led by W.T.Stead persuaded him to send Wolseley to the Sudan with 7,000 troops to relieve Gordon and the Prince advised Beresford to join it, sending him a letter addressed to Buller, Wolseley's Chief of Staff, which he could forward if the idea appealed to him. Wolseley, with little option, agreed, whereupon the Prince wrote, 'Let me know if "My Lords" make any objection,' to which Beresford replied, 'Northbrook has been very kind and told me that the Admiralty were very glad to send me out'.[5] Perhaps with relief in the Admiralty, Beresford was appointed Naval ADC to Wolseley. He was in the company he enjoyed, the whole expedition littered with titles and famous names. The stores included 1,000 pints of champagne and Gladstone's radicals described it as a 'social stunt'. Against the advice of Admiral Lord John Hay, Commander-in-Chief, Mediterranean, Wolseley decided to attempt the 1,650-mile journey up the Nile, hazardous most of the way, and impeded by six rocky cataracts. A number of Nile steamers were requisitioned and Hay allocated 220 naval personnel under Captain F.R.Boardman, a few months junior to Beresford. As an ADC Beresford had no authority; he therefore got his appointment changed to that of Staff Officer, which enabled him to use Wolseley's name to give orders to Boardman, who, he claimed, was slow and incapable. But for Boardman, he said, three extra steamers would have been over the first cataract when he arrived with Wolseley in September. 'All the naval officers and men are delighted I have come,' he wrote, 'as organization makes things go so much easier and better.'[6]

Gordon's situation was becoming desperate. It took Beresford eight weeks to get through the second cataract, with four more and 850 miles to go. Wolseley decided that Beresford, with a naval brigade, should accompany a column commanded by Major General Sir Herbert Stewart and travel overland from Korti to Shendi, about 170 miles, avoiding the huge arc in the Nile of 450 miles, there to take over Gordon's steamers and attack from the river while Stewart attacked from land. But Stewart was mortally wounded and turned over the command to Colonel Sir Charles Wilson of the Royal Engineers. 'At my request,' wrote Beresford, 'Sir Charles Wilson conferred upon Mr Ingram, of the *Illustrated London News*, the rank of acting lieutenant in the Royal Navy.'[7] The authority for this was dubious, but Beresford had ensured adequate Press coverage.

Wilson launched an attack on Khartoum unaccompanied by the naval brigade. He 'had had enough of the constant prodding to which Beresford had subjected him,'[8] and the colonels of the regiments insisted that he be left behind at Gubat. News came of the fall of Khartoum and death of Gordon. Wilson became isolated just above the fort of Wad Habeshi and Beresford set off in the old river steamer *Safieh* with all available officers including Ingram. The channel lay within eighty yards of the fort and the strong current was such that the ship could only crawl past it, keeping up an overwhelming fire. But when about 200 yards above the fort *Safieh*'s guns no

31

longer bore. Suddenly a great cloud of smoke and steam rose from the after hatchway. Chief Engineer Henry Benbow (later Chief Inspector of Machinery Sir Henry), who was with Beresford on the quarterdeck, ran to the engine room, while Beresford headed towards the opposite bank and anchored. A shot had penetrated the boiler and two engine room artificers were brought up terribly scalded. Benbow decided he could repair the boiler, which took about ten hours. Wilson brought his force to a point opposite the steamer. At 5 am the next morning the vessel had a full head of steam; Beresford proceeded upstream for a quarter of a mile and came down at speed, passing the fort without casualties, and picked up Wilson's force a mile further down.

On 14 February, short of camels, stores and provisions, the column retired, most of the sailors marching in bare feet on the scorching sand, arriving at Korti on 8 March. Beresford rejoined Wolseley at Cairo and the naval brigade was broken up. At the end of June Beresford was again welcomed home as a hero. He was made a CB and basked in the adulation of the public. The Prince of Wales wrote to him: 'The conduct of officers and men . . . has been the universal theme of admiration of everyone . . . Your gallantry in the steamer when your boiler came to grief and your saving of Wilson's party has filled everyone with admiration. . . . it is just what one would have expected from Old Charlie.'[9] Clearly Walter Ingram had done his work and Beresford wrote to the Queen describing his experiences. When he arrived home the Liberals had been defeated. Salisbury formed a caretaker Government with every intention of going to the country.

On 30 March 1885 Russian troops attacked the Afghans at Penjdeh. Public opinion was much excited at the apparently unprovoked attack and the reserves were called out. Phipps Hornby was appointed to command a fleet in the Baltic. But, as always happens in periods of peace, for many years the Navy had been neglected by both political parties, neither understanding the time required to design and build ships and the even greater time needed to train the officers and men to man them. So, in addition to a supplementary estimate of £5½m, a vote of credit of £11m passed through Parliament without a dissenting voice, and was spent in a hopelessly profligate attempt to rectify neglect.

Beresford appears to have believed war unlikely. He thought Gladstone's belligerence was intended to divert attention from the mishandled, messy and expensive Nile expedition. His lack of seagoing command, limited to about nine months in *Condor*, rendered it unlikely that he would be given a seagoing appointment, especially as his continued self-advertisement had further lowered his popularity in the Admiralty. At the suggestion of the Prince of Wales he applied for command of one of Hornby's ships, but was refused, and with a Tory victory in sight he turned his attention to his political career. He wrote repeatedly to the Press and to W.H.Smith, the First

Lord, rightly urging changes in naval policy and the building programme: 'Nearly all, if not all, of the officers of HM Navy view with grave concern the misplaced confidence the British public have in the power of the Navy.'[10] At length he was adopted for East Marylebone and elected with a majority of 944. But Gladstone was returned, with the Irish Nationalists holding the balance. Beresford spoke on strategy and tactics, basing his views on the Nile campaign and making the curious proposal that Britain should block the Suez canal and revert to the Cape route. Even his adulatory biographer calls this an 'irresponsible comment' and the Prince of Wales wrote, emphatically disagreeing. But he spoke authoritatively on naval development, then moving at a confusing rate, aggravated by each Government's false economies. Successive Boards of Admiralty had drawn attention to well-founded apprehension that the Navy had fallen far below a standard of safety. France, Italy, Germany, Russia and the United States had greatly increased their naval estimates, while Britain's remained unchanged when increased expenditure was essential to maintain equality of development. The somewhat unexpected defeat of France in 1870, the rise of Germany to ascendancy in Europe, the protective rapprochement between Russia and France, French loans to Russia and the projected building of the Trans-Siberian Railway, together with the emergence of the Triple Alliance, led inexorably toward a Russo-French Alliance. Even if Britain could contend with the French Navy alone, the two together represented too great a threat. But both political parties ignored warnings from their naval advisers, even though expansion of the Empire, foreign trade, increasing population and the need to import food amply justified expenditure the country was quite able to afford. But Northbrook (First Lord from May 1880) was a politician, and a strong party man adopting the strong views advocated by his party in regard to economy and retrenchment and was consequently more solicitous to keep down the estimates than to add to the efficiency of the Navy.[11]

In 1884 Lord Salisbury visited Plymouth and was shaken by the unpreparedness of the Navy, provoking Northbrook to make a long speech in the House of Lords, exaggerating the efficiency of the Service and saying that if £3m were 'thrust into his hand' he would be at a loss to know how to spend it. But his contentions were based on the false argument of tonnage, including old sailing line-of-battleships, paddle sloops and other outdated vessels.

Northbrook's speech angered all thinking officers and an anonymous Press agitation began attacking it. The climax came in a series of articles by W.T.Stead in the *Pall Mall Gazette* entitled *What is the Truth about the Navy?* under the pseudonym of *One Who Knows the Facts* disguising the identity of Fisher, who supplied Stead with almost all the information. His action might be criticized as much as Beresford's, but the difference was one of motive; Fisher was concerned about the Navy, Beresford about self-advancement.

Lord Esher, a remarkable son of an outstanding Master of the Rolls, who had unfettered access to Buckingham Palace and No 10 Downing Street, wrote:

> Fortunately in the eighties, when the isolation of England was more splendid than usual, when our relations with Germany were frigid, when our confused policy in Egypt had led to strained relations with France, when Russia was particularly active on the Afghan frontier, W.T.Stead, a publicist of courage and virtue, equipped with curious antennae without which genius in journalism is ineffective, came into touch with one John Fisher. . . . The minds of these two men flashed at each other across Europe, the outcome being a new naval policy for England – a policy . . . to which we owe in large measure the victory of 1918.[12]

The articles drew dramatic attention to changes in naval warfare and shocked the country out of complacency, though with little effect on the politicians. Beresford believed they 'did more than any Press representations, before or since, to awaken public opinion to the true condition of our defences'.[13] He took up Fisher's arguments; Northbrook's building programme was 'hopelessly inadequate'. Though Britain had more ships than France, they were inferior. More cruisers and torpedo boats should be built. Only eight of the latter could have accompanied Hornby's squadron, whereas the Russians had ninety-eight. He was supported by Admiral Sir John Commerell, former C-in-C North America, and by Lord George Hamilton, his former schoolfellow, First Lord in Salisbury's short administration the year before. But Sir William Harcourt, Chancellor of the Exchequer, said there was no possibility of finding more money for the Navy. Beresford persevered, speaking of improving the Royal Dockyards. His arguments were reinforced in May 1886 by a gun bursting in *Collingwood* due to faulty design, and asked if *Colossus*, with the same guns, was to join the Channel Squadron. Foolishly, A.B.Forwood, Parliamentary Secretary, replied that this was so, but she had been instructed not to fire her guns for practice. Her usefulness was therefore a mystery. In May Beresford drew attention to seventy-four outdated smaller ships, whose retention was a waste of money.

Though elected because of his interest in Irish affairs, he failed to speak when Gladstone's Home Rule Bill was debated. It was lost, and in the following election Gladstone was defeated with only 191 seats. and Lord George Hamilton returned to the Admiralty.

Encouraged by his socialite wife, Beresford had eagerly entered London Society. From his house in Eaton Square, he was sought by hostesses anxious to take advantage of his friendship with the Prince of Wales, and enjoyed a constant round of country house parties, his skill in the hunting field much admired. A frequent guest at Marlborough House and Sandringham, he kept up a correspondence with the Prince, who encouraged him to 'go at the Admiralty'. But to gain office he approached the Prince, whose suggestion that he might be head of the Irish Police Force did not appeal to him, nor the Home Secretary's of Commissioner of Police of the Metropolis. But in August 1886 Salisbury, influenced by Beresford's schoolfriend, Hamilton, agreed to his appointment as Junior Naval Lord.

That year Fisher was advised to take the waters at Marienbad, a popular Victorian health spa, which cured his dysentery and became his favourite resort which he frequently visited in future years. To his joy, in November he was appointed Director of Naval Ordnance, an important position, with access to the Board and politicians, just when his drive was needed. The supply of ordnance and ordnance stores were then in a state that now seems incomprehensible, but it had evolved over the centuries. Until the Crimean War guns for the two Services differed little, the carriages varying only slightly. Responsibility for the supply of guns, ammunition and stores was given to the Army just when naval guns were increasing in size far beyond those of the Army which had to remain small enough to be moved across country by men and horses. Money for Ordnance and stores was included in the Army Estimates, the hands of the Admiralty completely tied. Their worst fears were realized in 1868, when the commissioning of *Hercules*, the most powerful ironclad afloat, was seriously delayed because the War Office had not asked for the money for the guns. Many ships could not sail because their guns or carriages had not been delivered, or ammunition delayed. In July 1872 a trial was carried out between *Glatton* and *Hotspur*, the latter armed with a smooth-bore muzzle-loader, designed to penetrate 13-inch wrought iron armour at 1,000 yards. At 200 yards, with selected gunnery ratings from *Excellent*, *Glatton*'s armour and turret were undamaged. But Woolwich still refused to accept that the day of the muzzle-loader was finished and they were fitted to Fisher's *Inflexible*, though *Orion* completed a year later was the last so equipped, and the French method of breech-loading employing an interrupted thread was adopted with rifling and the copper driving-bands still used today. Between 1881 and 1887 the average sum submitted by the War Office for the Navy was only one third of that the Admiralty had requested. Home reserves of ammunition were pooled and the Admiralty was in total ignorance of quantities available for naval guns or the sums being spent. In war the Army would get the bulk of supplies and the Navy what was left over. The design and manufacture of guns was concentrated at Woolwich, under Army control and the Navy was not empowered to buy guns elsewhere.

Woolwich was a monopoly and the civilian officials ensured that private enterprise was driven out of the trade.[14] It was 'a huge job worked by a ring of interested officials, who by means of a great expenditure of national money, crush competition, suppress inventors, keep the country years behind Continental nations in guns, powder, and projectiles and saddle it with abortions.'[15] In 1886 *Conquest* was commissioned with old muzzle-loaded 64-pounders, because no others were available; *Pylades* on gun trials reported three guns defective in different parts of the breech pieces, and the others of weak action in the tube plates. The gun explosions in *Thunderer* and *Collingwood* gave concern; other incidents due to designs developed when fine grain gunpowder was used and retained after the introduction of increased charges and slower burning powder which gave higher muzzle velocities, greater range and accuracy but demanded increased strength and length of barrel.

These were the problems facing Fisher, yet he still found no officer responsible for mines and torpedoes. Almost alone in recognizing their tactical and strategic impact, he gained approval for his office to be changed to Director of Naval Ordnance *and Torpedoes*, the wider title demonstrating that no weapon could be considered in isolation. When only a young lieutenant, he had foretold to the amused contempt of the then First Naval Lord that the mine he had seen in Kiel would revolutionize sea warfare.

There were many versions of torpedoes and mines, but few made an impact on future war. Whitehead's short range created a need for a vessel from which to launch it. The 'torpedo boat' resulted, a fast vessel designed to dash in to range of the enemy, discharge its torpedoes and dash out of range. This was highly effective, for both muzzle- and breech-loading guns were slow in operation. By the time a ranging shot had been fired and the gun reloaded, the torpedo was on its way. Thornycroft and Yarrow in Britain and Normand in France developed them. The first was *Lightning* of 1877, 28.7 tons, a single-screw vessel 81 feet long, with a speed of 18.55 knots. The Admiralty ordered twelve more, one achieving 21.9 knots. Initially, they were operated from harbours or carried in big ships like *Inflexible*, but larger boats were built that could cross the Channel, and by 1885 the largest was 127½ feet. *Ariete*, built by Yarrows for Spain, achieved 26 knots in short bursts. When Fisher joined the Admiralty France had 210, Britain 206, Germany 180, Italy 152 and Russia 143. Fisher's problem was to provide defence for big ships against torpedo boats. Secondary armament consisted of cumbersome 6-inch guns and he introduced quick-firing guns, *Nile* of 1890 being fitted with six 4.7-inch QF guns, *Royal Sovereign* of 1892 with ten 6-inch QF and from about 1895 to 1900 most were fitted with twelve 6-inch QF.

But there were other problems. After the sinking of the *Re D'Italia* by the Austrian flagship by ramming in the battle of Lissa in 1866 Philip Colomb lectured at the RUSI on 'The Lessons of Lissa'. Many naval officers, including Fisher, believed, in those days of short range and inaccurate gunnery, that the ram was an effective weapon, visualizing mêlées in which ships would manoeuvre and sink each other by ramming. *Bellerophon* in 1866 was completed with the first realistic ram and two years later *Hercules* was fitted with a massive stem protruding under water. The accidental sinking of *Vanguard* by *Iron Duke* in fog in 1875, that of the German *Grosser Kurfürst*, the Chilean *Esmeralda* by the Peruvian *Huascar* convinced navies that the ram was a weapon to be taken seriously. Technological developments created turmoil in naval warfare, with little agreement on tactics, and Fisher was presented with new concepts, of increasing the power, range and effectiveness of gunfire, of combating the ram, the mine, torpedo and torpedo boat, which he tackled with his usual energy. 'I came to the definite conclusion that the fleet was in a very bad way and the only remedy was to take the whole business [of gunnery] from the War Office.'[16]

On 4 August 1888, probably inspired by Fisher, Beresford spoke in Parliament on the failure of the War Office to serve the Navy, quoting nine new ships lacking guns. The Admiralty, he said, should be allowed to obtain its guns from Armstrong's and Whitworth's, exactly what Fisher was pressing for.

The situation was serious: 'The cartridges supplied for revolvers often would not go off, and if they did they burnt like squibs . . . and owing to the pig-headed obstinacy of the Artillery General, the Navy at that time was armed with inefficient, inaccurate and dangerous muzzle-loading guns, while every continental nation had breech-loaders.'[17]

Lord Salisbury's brother-in-law, General Alderson, was Director of Ordnance at the War Office. When the Army estimates were cut, Alderson reduced provision for naval ordnance. Fisher went to Hamilton, who backed him 'through thick and thin', and approached Salisbury, who formed a committee under his own chairmanship, consisting of W.H.Smith, former Minister for War, Hamilton, Alderson and Fisher. Acrimonious discussion followed, but Fisher had the facts and argued with tenacity; the committee recommended that the Navy should have custody of its own war stores and design its own ordnance. No longer tied to the restrictions of land warfare, naval gunnery made strides. Fisher, by his determination, obtained equal representation on the Ordnance Committee, created a Corps of Naval Inspection and obtained authority to place orders for ordnance details. But even in 1900 naval contracts were often set aside for Army orders and it was not until 1909 that segregation was complete.

While Fisher was pressing the adoption of QF guns he had many discussions with Josiah Vavasseur, a director of the merged Armstrong Whitworth, who contributed greatly to the transition, and they became fast friends. Childless, Vavasseur and his wife left their property, Kilverstone

37

Hall, to Fisher's only son, later the second Baron Fisher of Kilverstone, provided he added Vavasseur to his name.

Fisher reached the top of the captains' list and was promoted rear admiral on 2 August 1890, at the age of 49, but he remained in his post after promotion and vacated it in May 1891.

4

THE NAVAL DEFENCE ACT

Beresford's membership of the Board and simultaneously of Parliament was by no means a precedent; there were many previous examples. But he was a captain of only four years' seniority, had never held a captain's command at sea, and there were at least 170 active admirals and captains senior to him. His qualification for the office was therefore dubious and inevitably it caused embarrassment and difficulty. Now it was his duty to defend the Admiralty, and no doubt Salisbury felt he had silenced a critic.

'The weak spot in my team was Beresford,' wrote Hamilton, '[His] heavy dull work did not come before the public. He did not like his post of subordination. . . . Beresford was always overflowing with spirits and had an uncontrollable tongue. Reporters were to be found by shoals in the House of Commons lobby . . . there were constantly appearing little notices about naval affairs in which his name figured, and which, as a rule, related to contemplated changes and reforms.'[1] He constantly interfered with the duties of the other Naval Lords and almost daily one of the Board would bring in newspaper clippings complaining that the papers concerned had never left his office and Hamilton had to haul Beresford over the coals.[2]

> Superintendence of an Intelligence Department was under the First Naval Lord. Hood had undertaken to reorganize and expand this service. . . . One day there appeared in a newspaper [*The Pall Mall Gazette*] a long memorandum which almost from beginning to end was a violent diatribe against the Admiralty for its neglect in organizing this department. Schoolboy expletives of the most pronounced character ran throughout this document, and to it was attached the signature 'Charles Beresford'. The paper had been circulated in the Admiralty, but I do not think that any of my colleagues had read it.[3]

39

The memorandum included the establishment of 'Section 2' of an 'Intelligence Department', an organization to prepare plans for war – a naval staff. The originality and soundness of the paper is such that it seems doubtful if it came from Beresford's pen alone; he may have been assisted by the newly promoted Captain Reginald Custance, (later Admiral Sir Reginald) and possibly others, A Foreign Intelligence Committee had been founded by Captain George Tryon (later Vice-Admiral), when Junior Naval Lord, 1882–84, but its sole duty was to inform Admiralty of foreign activity. It was the association of Beresford's proposals with the Intelligence Department that created much opposition. It was unlikely that a staff would have much influence; there was no staff course, no staff college and therefore no trained staff officers. But the First Lord allowed him to show his memorandum to Salisbury, a liberty that would only be extended to a politician. The Prime Minister told Beresford he was asking him to set his opinion above that of his superiors and their predecessors, but agreed to consult three admirals nominated by Beresford.

The basis of the paper was that steam, modern weaponry and communication by telegraph made it impossible to leave all operational decisions to Commanders-in-Chief. Coal and stores had to be provided, and information came to the Admiralty from many sources, which for security reasons could not be relayed to local admirals, so decisions had to be made in London. In Nelson's day the Admiralty consisted of the Sea Lords and a small staff of clerks. This little band could no longer perform all the tasks and a staff was essential. 'The departmental duties entailed upon the First Sea Lord were so arduous and multifarious that it was with difficulty that he could get through the daily routine of office work, much less find time for the careful consideration of those grave and important questions of national defence and commercial protection which rightly devolve upon [him].'[4]

The Admiralty was put into commission in the reign of Charles I and duties clarified in an Order in Council dated 4 October 1710:

> AND KNOW YEE further that WE reposing especiall trust and confidence in the approved Wisdom, Fidelity and Experience of you . . . do nominate ordaine constitute and appoint you to be Our Commissioners for executing the said Office of Our High Admirall . . . GIVEING and by these presents granting unto you our said Commissioners or any three or more of you during our pleasure full power and authority to doe execute exercise and perform all and every Act matter and thing which to the office of Our Lord High Admirall . . . as well in and touching all those things which concern Our Navy and Shipping as those which concern the Rights and Jurisdictions of or appertaining to the office of Our Lord High Admirall . . . AND WE

do further by these presents give and grant unto you our said Commissioners or any three or more of you full power and authority to make such orders and issue such warrants . . . and We do hereby strictly charge and command all our Officers and Ministers of or belonging to our Navy or Shipps . . . do carefully and diligently observe execute and perform all such Order Warrants and Commandments as you Our said Commissioners or any three or more of you shall make give and direct.

The words *Our said Commissioners or any three or more of you* (repeated thirteen times in the full text) made it impossible for the political head of the Admiralty to act without the express sanction of a majority of the Board. But in 1832, on the abolition of the Navy and Victualling Boards, each of its members was given specific functions and the First Lord, Sir James Graham, appropriated power and responsibility. When he relinquished office for the second time in 1855 the new letters patent required only two Commissioners to make binding decisions. This was eroded by Childers in 1868 and by Goschen in 1872, who assumed the supremacy of the First Lord, 'responsible to Your Majesty and Parliament for all the business of the Admiralty', the naval members relegated to advisers only. Beresford rightly objected to this power of a politician, entirely ignorant of naval affairs: 'The country has no means of knowing whether the recommendations of the Sea Lords are being carried into execution. I said at the time that such means should be instituted; afterwards, perceiving that no such demand would be granted, I urged the Cabinet ought at least to be precisely informed what were the requirements stated by the Sea Lords to be necessary in order to carry into execution the policy of the Government.'[5]

The subsequent Hartington Commission of 1890, which inquired into the administration of both Services, considered that the original patent had been varied by usage: 'The responsibility and consequently the power of the First Lord has continually increased, and he is at present practically the Minister of Marine.'[6]

The naval profession is complex, demanding extensive sea experience, and wrong decisions are often made by politicians whose views are weighted by party allegiance and personal ambition. One historian has said this view 'seems to be striking at the fundamentals of democracy, namely the control of the Services by a civilian Minister.' But democracy is defined as 'government by the people, by a majority vote', which cannot be exercised with wisdom without full knowledge of the facts, to which, in a democracy the voter has a right, undistorted by politics. Hitler gained power democratically and acted autocratically.

The absurdity was demonstrated when a clerk entered Beresford's office, inviting him to sign the estimates, which he had not seen. The clerk said that

41

the other lords had signed them. Beresford refused and the clerk informed him that he would have to tell the First Lord. '"I don't care a fig whom [*sic*] you tell," said I, "I can't sign the estimates because I have not read them."'[7] But Hamilton said 'it did not really matter' and they were brought before Parliament without Beresford's signature.

Sir John Briggs supported Beresford's paper. 'It is only the naval lords who are able to make a just and accurate estimate of what is absolutely necessary to meet the duties the Navy will be called upon to discharge; and yet their voices are never heard, nor their representations laid before the Cabinet.'[8]

From 1815 to 1889 both parties encouraged retrenchment for political reasons and when the international situation deteriorated panics ensued. The Penjdeh incident of 1885, discussed above, was typical, and the hotch-potch mixture of experimental designs often obsolescent before completion, was totally inadequate. It has been said, 'The remarkable fact is that the Victorian Navy performed adequately the tasks demanded of it.' Fortunately very little was demanded of it.

The soundness of Beresford's ideas was obfuscated by his insistence on executive authority for the Intelligence Department, reducing the Board to a mere administrative organization, by-passed by direct communication between the political head and the staff, which brought disaster in 1914–15. 'I am firmly convinced that in all matters of purely naval operations, the First Sea Lord should be held solely responsible, the same as the Commander-in-Chief in the Army, and that the former should have the same rank and position as the latter . . . and deciding upon the naval defences of the Empire, the responsibility for the advice should rest upon the First Sea Lord, and not upon the Board as such.'[9] This was the accepted wisdom with which Beresford refused to agree. 'I had the rest of the Sea Lords against me,' he complained.

But the crux of the matter was Beresford's insistence on inflexible plans which ignored the thousand factors to be considered. Such inflexibility presumed that the enemy would make no plans of his own. Plans could be prepared in great detail provided they were adaptable to the prevailing circumstances. Enemies are not always so obliging as to comply with their opponent's purpose; surprise is the essence of war.

The two sides could not be reconciled. Had they accepted that flexible planning was essential, details of possible attacks, strategy, tactics, locations in which to seek action, logistics, numbers and types of ships needed, final responsibility lying with the Board and especially with the First Naval Lord, much blood would have been saved in 1914–15. But fixed plans such as Beresford wanted were as great a danger as no plans at all. Those of the War Office in 1911 led to the bloody stalemate of trench warfare.

The publication of Beresford's paper made it impossible for the Board to delay any further and a Naval Intelligence Department was established, divided into two sections, 'Intelligence' and 'Mobilization', whose functions were purely advisory, the decisions to be made by the Board.

But the following July an attack by Randolph Churchill on the cost of ship-building in the Royal dockyards provoked Beresford to sum up succinctly the change in attitude necessary if the Navy was to fulfil its tasks: 'You may undertake what plan of campaign you like; you may build what vessels you like; and all your work is useless unless officers and men are taught how to use the ships and vessels you put them in. The sooner we grasp the fact that the man or boy who has worked a torpedo for three months is more desirable to the admiral who is about to go into action than the man who has been in a brig for three years, the better for the British Navy.'[10]

Beresford's memorandum and its publication had made him thoroughly unpopular with his companions on the Board and he did little to repair the damage. In public speeches he claimed reforms were due solely to him and his interference with other members of the Board, including the First Lord, offended them greatly. He failed to recognize that he was the junior in rank and far behind his colleagues in experience. He told Parliament later: 'As long as I sat at the Board, where there were men of so much greater experience, far higher in seniority and far higher in rank than myself, I treated them outside the Board with the courtesy and respect which that higher rank called for, but at the Board I intended to have my say level with everybody else.'[11]

This was reasonable, but his methods were devious. Early in 1887 he again introduced a motion in the House to abolish obsolete vessels, of which he now specified fifty-nine, suggesting the use of the money saved for new construction. Obviously such a matter should be introduced by the First Lord. The scheme, Beresford claimed, 'was carried into execution by degrees', but in fact nothing of the sort took place. As ships became unserviceable due to age or obsolescence they were paid off in the ordinary course.

At that time officers employed in the Admiralty received a civil salary in addition to their pay and when the Intelligence Department was instituted a schedule of salaries was included. This became a matter of acrimonious contention between the Admiralty and Treasury. After some months, Hamilton capitulated. The Board consented and Beresford agreed that when the existing officers were replaced the lower salaries should come into force, but he understandably objected to the reduction of salaries of existing officers. On 9 January 1888 he sent in his resignation to the Prime Minister, itself a breach of procedure, for it should have been sent to the First Lord.

But Hamilton took the politician's view: 'Lord Charles Beresford has resigned because he objects to the First Lord having supreme power, and because he considers that in a particular instance, I made an improper use of it.'[12] Beresford confirmed Hamilton's statement: 'I was constantly urging that Parliament and the country had a right to know . . . that any given course of action was founded upon professional advice.'[13]

But Hamilton complained that Beresford's threat of resignation had often been made on matters of trivial importance. In resigning, Beresford was jeopardizing his whole career. He never again had a seat on the Board, and though he reached the rank of admiral and hoisted his flag afloat, his further career in the Navy was of little significance and he achieved no office in politics.

Acknowledging Salisbury's acceptance of his resignation, Beresford wrote: 'The First Lord has every right to carry on the whole administration of the Navy without consulting his Board at all, or to give decisions in direct opposition to it. . . . It was the continued and persistent use of that power which put the Navy into the disgraceful state of disorganization and un-preparedness which existed when you took office.'[14]

The point of principle on which Beresford had finally resigned was important – the power of a politician for political reasons to override the professional views of the naval officers on the Board. This power begat the horrors of Gallipoli.

Salisbury wrote of Beresford to the Queen: 'He is too greedy of popular applause to get on in a public department. He is constantly playing his own game at the expense of his colleagues.'[15] Hamilton described him as difficult as a colleague and almost impossible as a subordinate,[16] while the Prince of Wales wrote: 'Beresford has resigned his seat in the Admiralty for the hundredth time, and it has been accepted, as I fancy his colleagues could not get on any more with him, as *entre nous* he laid down the law too much.'[17]

Beresford now felt free to speak in Parliament. To do so immediately after leaving the Board and with so much official information in his possession may be questionable, but it was little different from the resignation of a minister to free himself to speak openly. His views were widely shared and he was supported by many distinguished officers, including Hornby and Colomb. He had seen many weaknesses in office and, after the Queen's Golden Jubilee Review in 1887, for the first time strategical exercises took place in the Channel, which revealed a Navy deficient in coal capacity and speed, weak in gunpower and alarmingly short in numbers. The Government paid no attention. Little more than a month after his resignation, on 15 February 1888, he gave notice of a motion for a committee to be appointed 'to enquire into the system of administration of both the War Office and the Admiralty', and early in March he correctly stated that both ministers frequently expressed views contrary to those of their professional advisers, sometimes without consulting them.

Beresford spoilt his case, as he so often did, by going too far and demanding that the Services should be freed from Parliamentary control.

But means by which the views of the professionals could be represented was urgently needed. He was well supported by Lord Randolph Churchill and it was agreed to set up a Royal Commission. Lord Hartington (later Duke of Devonshire), both a former First Lord and a former Secretary of State for War was appointed chairman with Churchill, W.H.Smith, Campbell Bannerman, Rear Admiral Sir Frederick Richards and Lieutenant-General Brackenbury as members.

When the Navy Estimates for 1888–9 were debated Beresford challenged the votes for shipbuilding, the Secretary's department, the Intelligence Department, the reserve of merchant cruisers, the Royal Naval Reserve and naval armaments. 'It should be impossible,' he said, 'for the First Lord to rule the Navy without consulting the Board.'[18] Hamilton responded that 'at no time was the Navy more ready or better organized for any work which it might be called upon to do than today',[19] to which Beresford replied that these words had 'rung in our ears as often as the tune *Britannia rules the Waves* and have been invariably falsified when war appeared imminent'.[20]

The following May Beresford spoke at a meeting in the City, at which Hamilton admitted there might be 'room for improvement'. The admission was fatal, for it raised the question of how far the Navy fell short of needs. On 13 July 1888 Hood, First Naval Lord, told the Select Committee on Naval Estimates, 'I should have preferred, by the end of 1890, to have had six more fast cruisers. I do not consider it a point of vital importance.' But Beresford argued that without a naval staff no attempt had been made to determine requirements. He had made a 'careful calculation of the work the fleet might, under probable contingencies, be required to perform, and upon that calculation, based an estimate of the classes and numbers of ships that would be needed'.[21] In an attempt to rebut his claims the Admiralty collected as large a force as possible in the Channel under Tryon and Vice-Admiral John Baird, in command of the Channel Squadron, including all the Channel and Reserve Training Squadrons, the battleships, cruisers, and first-class gunboats in the Steam Reserve and twenty-four torpedo boats. After weeks of preparation the mobilization order was issued and in twelve days the fleet assembled at Spithead and Portland. Compared with the expensive panic of the Russian scare this was admirable, but a 'British' force blockaded an 'enemy' fleet in Bantry Bay and Lough Swilly. Thirteen British battleships and eleven cruisers failed to prevent nine battleships and eight cruisers from eluding the blockade, raiding British coasts and shipping. If anything, the exercise had supported Beresford. On 13 December 1888 he introduced his programme, claiming the shipbuilding vote was based on no policy, no theory, no businesslike or definite idea whatever to enable it to meet the requirements of the country. The Government should first lay down a definite standard for the fleet, which standard should be a force capable of defending Britain's shores and commerce, together with the

45

punctual and certain delivery of food supply against the fleets of two powers combined, one of which should be France; and that the experts should then be called together to say what was necessary to get that standard and give the reasons for their statement.[22]

Beresford's programme included four first-class and ten second-class ironclads, forty cruisers of various classes and sixteen torpedo craft – seventy ships costing £21.1m. Hamilton replied that, far from saying that the fleet was strong enough, next year he hoped to lay before the House a larger and more comprehensive programme than the current estimates. Twelve weeks later he introduced a programme of exactly seventy ships, costing £21½m. Beresford claimed the Board copied his programme; but it would be impossible to check his figures, formulate, design, estimate such a programme, and get Treasury approval, all in twelve weeks; further, he quoted the views of Hoskins, the Second Naval Lord, the Secretary of the Admiralty and the Civil Lord, 'to the effect that "the British Fleet should be more than a match for the combined fleets of any two European powers that were likely to be our foes, one of which must necessarily be France". Here, so far as I am aware was the first definite demand for the two-power standard.'[23] But the programme was under discussion while he was a member of the Board, and he was afterwards kept informed by officers in Admiralty, including Custance, whose opportunist support of Beresford was close and was to grow with the years. Hamilton was clear on the matter; when the proposals were introduced to the House, he said the one person who systematically opposed the propositions was Beresford, though he never took part in a hostile division; but he did his best, throughout, to discredit the scheme. So hostile was his attitude that a meeting of a number of distinguished admirals was held under the presidency of Admiral Lord Clanwilliam, who was authorized by this meeting to represent to him that if he continued his tactics he would be repudiated by the Service generally.[24]

The manoeuvres of 1888, intended by the politicians to demonstrate the Navy's adequacy, revealed a number of problems, especially that of close blockade in the age of steam. Nelson's ships had remained off enemy ports for months and even years, maintaining themselves. But steamships needed coal and stores. Coaling at sea was difficult, and impossible in bad weather. The Admiralty therefore appointed a committee of three experienced admirals, Sir William Dowell, Sir R. Vesey Hamilton and Sir Frederick Richards, to study the feasibility of maintaining blockade; whether this could be achieved by close blockade or 'keeping the main body of the blockading fleet at a base, with a squadron of fast cruisers and scouts [light cruisers] off the blockaded ports, having means of rapid communication with the fleet,' and the ships required, the value of torpedo gunboats, both with the blockading fleet and defenders, the feasibility and expediency of cruisers making raids on an enemy's coast and 'the behaviour and sea-going qualities of, or the defects in the new and most recently commissioned vessels, as obtained in the reports of the admirals in command of the respective squadrons' and finally 'the general conclusions to be drawn from the recent operations'.

They reported that steam and torpedoes made close blockade impractical and, 'provided that a suitable anchorage can be secured in the immediate neighbourhood of the enemy stronghold, the advantages would be in favour of the ironclad fleet occupying such a position, and maintaining a sufficient number of swift look-out vessels off the port in direct communication by signal, or cable from a telegraph look-out ship. . . . We do not consider that a distant base would answer in this case.'[25] The report said that coastal raids were both feasible and efficacious for an enemy possessed of sufficient power.

The prescience of the report was demonstrated in 1914–18. It was presented to both Houses of Parliament in February 1889 and stated that the Navy was 'altogether inadequate' to take the offensive in a war against only one great power. 'As there seems nothing to support the belief that [Britain] would have any option in the matter, when it suited another great power to challenge her maritime position, we are decidedly of opinion that no time should be lost in placing the Navy beyond comparison with that of any two Powers.'[26]

Whether or not Beresford could claim to have originated the Two-Power Standard, the naval members of the Board would never have persuaded the politicians without him; the Navy would have decayed beyond redemption. The proposals were adopted by the Government and Parliament as the Naval Defence Act, 1889, which authorized the construction of seventy ships, including ten battleships.

The Hartington Commission had no influence on these decisions; its report was not produced until 1890, when it stated there was little or no regular communication between the Admiralty and War Office; 'no combined plan . . . for the defence of the Empire has ever been worked out.' They considered a Ministry of Defence, but rejected it, recommending that each department should be placed under a professional head under one Minister. Means should be provided for regular and constant communication between the two departments, possibly by 'the formation of a Naval and Military Council' presided over by the Prime Minister, which five years later led to the joint Naval and Military Committee and a Defence Committee of the Cabinet, the forerunners of the Committee of Imperial Defence.

Criticizing the Admiralty organization, they advocated a return to the position before 1872. The Board should be regarded as 'a standing Council for Naval Affairs, but this should in no way diminish the responsibility of the First Lord to Parliament and the country for all matters connected with Her Majesty's Navy'. A contradiction in itself, this conflicted with the proposal for a single Minister for both services. The Naval Lords should be appointed for specific periods and their duties needed definition, especially that of the First Naval Lord, who should be chief adviser on all matters of naval policy. Richards disagreed with this, believing that the Board should be collectively responsible for advice. They proposed the appointment of more naval officers to the Admiralty, supporting the move Beresford had long pressed, for the Board was insufficiently sustained by officers with professional and technical knowledge.

The proposals for Army reform were more far-reaching, including re-organization on lines similar to those of the Admiralty, abolition of the post of Commander-in-Chief, held since 1856 by the Duke of Cambridge, a stubborn, unyielding man. Campbell-Bannerman disagreed, and as the Queen, on behalf of her first cousin, opposed them, no such reforms took place until after the disappointments of the South African War, when they were watered down.

The Hartington Report was issued almost simultaneously with Fisher's promotion to rear admiral. He could normally expect to be left on half-pay, but was immediately appointed Admiral Superintendent, Portsmouth Dockyard, a purely administrative post normally regarded as a backwater, which would have dissatisfied him had he not known he was to join the Board as Third Naval Lord and Controller in nine months' time. The dockyards were regarded by the Navy as torpid establishments governed by slothful routine, of which the Admiral Superintendent was a figurehead expected to take no part in management. This would not do for Fisher and soon everybody knew it. His unconventional methods followed his usual pattern. 'I felt positive of the fearful loss to the country in the slow construction of ships, and equally positive there was a remedy by ruthless dealing with contractors, with dockyard employees, and with the distribution of labour, and, backed up by each of the three First Lords I had the pleasure of serving with, and by "re-potting" the chief constructors and other obstructionists, the time of building a battleship of 15,000 tons was reduced by nearly half!'[27]

He concentrated labour on *Royal Sovereign*, a battleship of 15,585 tons, designed by Sir William White, the biggest ship so far built in Portsmouth, the first steel battleship, with 18-inch armour. She was a great advance and urgently needed in the fleet. 'If you build two ships in the same time as it formerly took to build one,' Fisher wrote, 'then you want half the number of slips and half the plant . . . and instead of a ship being almost obsolete by the time she is commissioned, she is in the prime of her power.'[28]

He greeted some workmen by their names, and soon he was said to know that of every man. One civil servant spent too much time in his office and Fisher sent him, without comment, a memorandum mentioning a vacancy in Trincomalee for which he was eminently suitable. Within minutes the miscreant was out supervising work he would otherwise have comfortably left to his subordinates. *Royal Sovereign* was completed in two years and seven months compared with an average for a comparable ship of three to four years. His detractors said that he had delayed the completion of other ships, but all were completed well within the average.

Dissatisfied with the time it took to change barbette guns, he had a chair and table placed on a barbette where he ate his lunch, indicating that he would stay there until the task was finished. The job was done in four hours instead of the usual two days, and later the time reduced to two hours. He left a reputation at Portsmouth that endures to this day and soured many civil servants who never even knew him.

The appointment was a useful apprenticeship; on 1 February 1892 he took up his post as Controller with an intimate knowledge of one of the most important aspects of his new task, which included supervising design departments, building, arming and repair of all ships. He had begun to walk the corridors of power as DNO, but now he was on the Board with a real influence on events, at a time when his energetic foresight was most needed. After six years in office Hamilton, unusually well acquainted with the problems of advancing technology, was enthusiastic about Fisher's appointment.

The difficulties were manifold. Torpedo boats demanded high speed which could not be provided by the cylindrical boilers then in use, unless pressure was increased, which could not be sustained in existing boiler designs. The boiler explosion in 1876 in *Thunderer*, fitted with 'box' boilers, in which forty-five men were killed, had drawn attention to the dangers. Sir John Durston, Engineer-in-Chief of the Fleet, pressed for the adoption of water-tube boilers, which could safely sustain higher pressures and whose content of water was much smaller than the cylindrical boiler, substantially reducing weight, enabling steam to be raised quickly from cold, and responding rapidly to sudden demands for increased speed. The same arguments applied to big ships, but the benefits were limited by the sheer hard work of stoking larger quantities of coal.

Fisher instituted a committee to determine the advantages of water-tube boilers and decide on the best type. A multitude of designs came on the market, inventors and patentees lobbying Parliament. Existing manufacturers, threatened with investing in designs unsuitable for the merchant navy, opposed them. 'Whenever a non-expert body like the House of Commons meddles with technical development,' wrote Admiral Sir Reginald Bacon, a close friend and supporter of Fisher, who later wrote his biography, 'its interference retards progress and does harm.'[29] Indeed, there was more nonsense talked in Parliament than usual.

Experiments with a boiler designed by the French engineer Julien Belleville were carried out in the gunboat *Sharpshooter* in 1894 and they were fitted in the cruisers *Powerful* and *Terrible* against intense opposition in

Parliament and Press. A few months later Salisbury's Government fell and Lord Spencer became First Lord, supporting Fisher fully, but in 1895 the Tories were restored and Goschen returned as First Lord. Sixty supporters of the Government in the House intended to vote against the Navy Estimates if water-tube boilers were adopted. Goschen appointed another committee under Rear Admiral Compton Domvile, and insisted that none of the Admiralty contractors should be represented. The one naval engineer officer, the only person with knowledge of the subject, had to instruct the members in the matter they had to decide.

The 'Battle of the Boilers' went on for ten years. By 1904 all major navies had adopted water-tube boilers, Bellevilles accounting for nearly 40 per cent. Troubles with Bellevilles were ascribed to water-tube boilers in general; *Powerful* developed numerous defects, most quite unrelated to her boilers, but attributed to them by the uninformed and by opportunists. Fisher was of course blamed; Lord George Hamilton wrote:

> The Belleville boiler was, I believe, tried in the *Sharpshooter*. Fisher then proceeded to put into the two largest cruisers ever built, viz., the *Terrible* and *Powerful* . . . this same boiler, and having adopted water-tube boilers of this system and on this scale, he persisted in so boilering all subsequent cruisers. . . . The pressure . . . of the water-tube boiler is very much heavier than that of a cylindrical boiler, and every portion of machinery or packing coming in contact with this increased pressure ought to have been previously strengthened. . . . This elementary precaution was ignored.[30]

Fisher was precipitate in agreeing to fit Belleville boilers before experience had exposed their defects and longer trials were desirable, but the blame should be placed on the engineer officers who advised him, especially the Engineer-in-Chief. But in any case Hamilton shows the ignorance of the politician; the pressure in a water-tube boiler is not *necessarily* greater than that of a cylindrical boiler; it is *capable* of withstanding higher pressures, one of the reasons for its adoption.

The only engineer in the House was W.H.Allen (later Sir William), himself a boiler manufacturer faced with a large capital outlay. In 1901 he said, 'I say briefly that the water-tube boiler for marine purposes cannot work. . . . If you experiment more with these water-tubes, you will come to grief again.'[31]

There was divided opinion in the Navy. Admiral Sir George King-Hall noted in his diary when the war in South Africa was going badly: 'I understand the men-of-war are ready to embark the ladies at the Cape if necessary – this with the knowledge that so many of our ships are hors-de-combat from Belleville boilers is very depressing.'[32]

But at least he identified the problem: the wrong boiler. Wrong decisions pressed on the Navy by amateurs retarded development. But in 1892 Alfred Yarrow obtained details of the latest French torpedo-boat and asked Fisher if he would like faster ones. Fisher jumped at the idea and became deeply involved in planning them, which soon changed them from faster versions of the French vessels to larger vessels to combat them. Fisher adopted a term used by *The Times* in 1884, 'Torpedo-boat-destroyers', the words 'torpedo-boat' being later dropped.

The first was *Havock*, launched in 1893, followed by *Daring*, *Hornet*, and *Decoy*, the last 275 tons, 185 feet long and 19 feet beam, achieving 28 knots. These were the first of forty-two known as '27-knotters'. But the 'Battle of the Boilers' continued, politicians insisting that every outlandish boiler should be tried. There were six with locomotive boilers, ten with Yarrows, eight with Thornycrofts, three Blechynden, four White, eight Normand, two Reeds and one Du Temple. When the French *Forban* achieved 31 knots it was evident that the destroyer was a new menace to big ships.

Larger destroyers followed, known as '30-knotters', up to 370 tons and 6,400 horsepower, with a design speed of 30 knots, of which Britain built nearly seventy. Development between *Warrior* and Fisher's destroyers is illustrated by the fact that *Warrior's* machinery of 5,400 horsepower weighed 898 tons, more than twice the total weight of *Quail*, which developed 6,000 horsepower.

As the century ended the reciprocating engine passed its zenith, *Express* having engines running at 400 revolutions per minute. Such speeds demanded maintenance of the highest order, and engine room staff were strained to the utmost, only the most skilled stokers able to maintain steam. Men worked in a smother of oil and water, heat, noise and vibration. Many accidents occurred ranging from bending of rods to the bursting of cylinders.

In 1897 Charles Parsons spectacularly demonstrated his steam turbine at Queen Victoria's jubilee review and the next year Fisher ordered a turbine-driven destroyer, V*iper*, developing 10,000 horsepower, achieving 36.5 knots in a one-hour trial. By 1914 all the more important ships were driven by turbines, changing the strategy and tactics of all navies.

Gladstone was not devoted to strengthening the armed Services. In 1893 the naval estimates met with the disapproval of the Chancellor of the Exchequer, Sir William Vernon Harcourt. Gladstone backed the Chancellor, who stated in the Commons that the Admiralty had agreed to a reduction, which was simply not true, though he may have been misled by Spencer. The Naval Lords refused to budge, threatening to resign in a body. A meeting was arranged in the First Lord's room at which Harcourt and Campbell-Bannerman attacked the Board. Neither Spencer nor the First Naval Lord, Richards, were conspicuously articulate, the latter becoming speechless with anger, and Fisher doing most of the talking. He wrote to Austen Chamberlain: 'Sir William Harcourt told an unmitigated lie when he said that the professional officers of the Admiralty were satisfied with the present condition of the Navy. We gave Lord Spencer to understand that unless Sir W. Harcourt explained, we would resign. . . . We don't intend to stand any repetition of such misrepresentation of our views, and further . . . we will not stand much further delay in dealing with pressing naval requirements.'[33]

'It was enough,' wrote Beresford, 'the Government yielded.'

The threatened resignation of the Board persuaded the Government to introduce a programme of £31m, spread over five years, to include seven battleships, thirty cruisers and 112 destroyers and gunboats. The stand taken by the Naval Lords induced Gladstone, in a bid to save his Government, to increase the programme to nine battleships, though the number of cruisers was reduced to twenty-one, all the smaller vessels remaining in the programme. The outcome was not the resignation of the Board but of the Prime Minister, a testimony to the determination of Fisher, who carried the rest of the Board with him. Beresford's public speeches added to the pressure on Gladstone, who had other problems. In February 1894 the House of Lords rejected his Home Rule Bill, the Employers' Liability Bill and his reforms of local Government, all the important bills of that Parliament. Gladstone resigned on 3 March 1894 and was succeeded by Lord Rosebery, who struggled on until the Tories gained a majority in the subsequent election, Salisbury again becoming Prime Minister and, as we have seen, Goschen returning as First Lord after 21 years. With a strong Board and a First Lord willing to listen to professional advice, and in view of the Franco-Russian alliance of January 1894, there was now little difficulty in upholding the programme. The 1896 estimates included six 12-inch battleships ('Canopus' class); 1897 a further three 'Formidables'. Five 'London' Class were included in 1898 and 1900, and six 'Duncan' Class in 1898–99. Between 1894 and 1900, Britain built the largest battle fleet in the world, of the most advanced design.

However, in a newspaper interview in September 1894 Beresford proposed that seventeen 'old but useful' ships should be rearmed with modern guns, in addition to those in the programme. Fisher wrote to the First Lord:

Macgregor [Permanent Secretary] and I discussed yesterday whether we had better draw your attention to Beresford's indirect criticism of the Admiralty in his interview as to rearming certain ships. . . . He really is very stupid, but he can't resist self-advertisement. What I fear is an explosion by Sir Frederick [Richards], who justly thinks that no officer on full pay should act in this way. However, Sir Frederick may not have seen it, as he is travelling in Belgium at the time and you may think the best course is to take no notice. Perhaps it is.[34]

Beresford had overlooked the obsolescence of the ships' machinery, their insufficient speed and protection, the time it would take to obtain new guns in addition to those for new ships and the extra personnel required.

In May 1894 Fisher was made KCB and in 1896 was promoted vice-admiral in his turn. At the end of the summer of 1897, after 5½ gruelling years, he left the Admiralty. His successor, Rear Admiral A.K.Wilson VC, inherited a programme of fourteen battleships, eight first-class cruisers, nine second-class, ten third-class, two sloops, four gunboats, fifty-two destroyers, eight light draught steamers for special service and one royal yacht.

5

SAILOR OR POLITICIAN?

Beresford's political activities led him to hope for office in Salisbury's government. He might even be appointed First Lord, for which as an MP he was eligible, despite his commission in the Navy, becoming head of the Service, with little sea experience. But Salisbury had no such intention and, disappointed, Beresford returned to his naval career. For promotion to rear-admiral he needed at least three years in command of a sea-going ship. He resigned from Parliament and in November 1889 obtained command of *Undaunted* a twin-screw, first-class armoured cruiser of 5,600 tons, which left for the Mediterranean in January. Despite scant knowledge of naval architecture, he immediately criticized the ship's design, especially her unprotected bow and stern, reiterating the contemporary view that damage there would cause her to sink through lost stability. With adequate water-tight subdivision, this was unlikely, though the current low freeboard and negative trim resulting from damage forward might cause flooding above the armoured deck with consequent loss of stability due to 'free surface', not appreciated at the time. Vice-Admiral Sir Anthony Hoskins, now Commander-in Chief, commented that this was a matter for the constructor. But Beresford inundated him with matters far outside his authority, to which the Admiralty responded that such matters were not the business of a captain.

While in *Undaunted* he read Mahan's *The Influence of Sea Power upon History*, which had caused a sensation in international naval circles and, in a letter, praised his work. Now he wrote on matters even further outside his province, sending copies to various MPs. Following a visit to Toulon in July, he wrote to Hoskins of the strength of the French fleet, but sent a copy to Salisbury, by-passing his C-in-C and the Admiralty, even including the First Lord. He had earlier advocated an alliance with the Italians, but, having seen them, now wrote of their unreliability. He wrote to the Queen complaining

54

of lack of naval funds, especially attacking Lord George Hamilton. Ponsonby minuted to the Queen: 'What Lord Charles wants to do is to agitate in the Navy to force the Admiralty – and no doubt also bring his own name forward, as he likes doing, before the public.'[1] He had written further newspaper articles which earned him a rebuke from the Admiralty, though Tryon, who succeeded Hoskins, tended to support him.

Undaunted took part in experimental high-speed mine-laying, during which his ship grounded slightly, though, in the absence of damage, no action was taken. But on leaving Alexandria, the ship struck a rock, holing her. Beresford claimed his navigator had ordered 'port' instead of 'starboard', but was reprimanded by the court-martial.

Undaunted was ordered to Jaffa to assist the French ship *Seignelay* which had gone aground. French, Russian and Austrian steamers with HMS *Melita* were trying to get her off, the last fouling her screw with a hawser. Beresford claimed to have warned her captain, George King-Hall, a man of considerable sea experience, of the danger. In his memoirs Beresford praises himself for not reprimanding King-Hall. 'He deeply appreciated my motives.'[2]

Beresford criticized everything on the Mediterranean station: The fleet would have 'a very poor chance' against the French; stocks of coal and ammunition were inadequate; there was no breakwater at Gibraltar; in war the fleet would be blockaded at Malta, or would have to evacuate the Mediterranean. Tryon forwarded his letter, but Beresford contrived to send a copy to the Queen. Ponsonby minuted that he was seeking her support and threatening to publish letters which he claimed represented the views of the whole Service. He had written to Salisbury and 'he appeals to Your Majesty to protect the Empire. Lord Charles's energy may do good in supporting the demands of sailors of the Admiralty, but a public attack from an officer in the Service on the Finance Minister, would place him in an awkward position.'[3]

Beresford's attempts to gain office were, however, frustrated. He and his wife had been close friends with Lord and Lady Brooke, later Earl and Countess of Warwick, his letters to his wife constantly inquiring after the 'Brookies'. Lady Brooke was a beautiful woman and Beresford fell for her, his indiscretions widely known in society. In 1886 she had announced to Lady Charles her intention of eloping with Beresford. Lady Charles prevented this and Beresford discovered that Lady Brooke was enjoying the attentions of others beside himself, so broke off the association. But while he was on a visit to the Kaiser, she sent a compromising letter to the Beresfords' house at Eaton Square. He had left instructions for his wife to open all letters and naturally this fell into her hands. It demanded that Beresford should leave his wife and join Lady Brooke on the Riviera, claiming that one of her children had been fathered by him. Lady Charles later wrote to Lord Salisbury that 'To satisfy her feelings of wounded vanity

[Lady Brooke] started the most disgraceful and disagreeable stories about Lord Charles, . . . that she went in fear of her life, was persecuted by his attention, and so forth.'[4]

Lady Charles consulted George Lewis, a society solicitor specializing in such matters, who wrote to Lady Brooke warning her of the consequences of her actions. Lady Brooke appealed for advice to the Prince of Wales, who promptly in turn fell for her and persuaded Lewis to show him Lady Brooke's letter, attempting to induce Lady Charles to return it to the writer, which she agreed to do, but only if the latter absented herself from London for the entire season. This was unacceptable and the Prince sided with Lady Brooke, removing Lady Charles's name from the Marlborough House invitation list, and having it deleted from a house party he was attending, substituting that of Lady Brooke. Beresford now knew of the matter and, just before leaving in *Undaunted*, called on the Prince, protesting heatedly at his reading a private letter and calling his conduct 'dishonourable and blackguardly'. Beresford was said to have struck the Prince, though his biographer quotes Sir Shane Leslie, 'The truth was that he pushed the Prince, who dropped into a sofa, murmuring: "Really, Lord Charles, you forget yourself!"'[5] – which certainly seems uncharacteristically mild!

For eighteen months the matter simmered while Beresford was in *Undaunted*, until in June 1891 he wrote accusing the Prince of ranging himself 'on the side of the other person against my wife, many people thinking she must be in the wrong. The days of duelling are past, but there is a more just way of getting right done . . . and that is – publicity,' and threatened to state his opinion of the Prince that he was a 'blackguard and a coward'. But, realizing the dangers, he asked his wife to discuss the letter with Salisbury first, and this gave rise to her lengthy letter already mentioned, in which she assured him that, failing a public apology, her husband would 'bring the matter to public notice' and was able to precipitate a scandal which would be 'damning to the Prince of Wales'.

But on Salisbury's advice Lady Charles withheld the letter, whereupon Beresford assured him of his determination to exact retribution, to which Salisbury wrote a reasoned reply: 'Ill considered publicity would be of no possible service to Lady Charles; it would do you most serious harm. . . . I strongly advise you . . . to do nothing.'[6] But Lady Charles had a pamphlet printed describing the events and thinly disguising Lady Brooke, which she then circulated through society.

Beresford's brother, Marcus, who managed the Prince of Wales' stud at Sandringham, stepped in and advised Lady Charles that she was damaging herself more than her antagonist. She telegraphed Beresford to come home, where he arrived just before Christmas, 1891, only to inform Salisbury that he again intended to demand an apology. The Queen had been informed and Salisbury attempted conciliation, but Beresford had already sent another offensive letter to the Prince demanding an apology, 'failing which . . . I shall no longer intervene to prevent these matters becoming public'. The Prince sent a somewhat conciliatory reply, but Beresford responded in uncompromising fashion. Salisbury obtained this last letter from the Prince and persuaded Beresford to substitute one less offensive, to which the Prince sent a stiff reply which Beresford unwillingly accepted.

His breach with the Prince was total. In April 1892 the Prince wrote to Waterford: 'I can never forget, and shall never forgive the conduct of your brother and his wife . . . his base ingratitude, after a friendship of about twenty years, has hurt me more than words can say.'[7]

Beresford's surrender of the friendship of the Prince and his display to Salisbury of bullheaded arrogance dispelled any last chance of political office. His naval career too was suffering. That he was given leave to deal with the matter and not required to relinquish his command can only be attributed to official cowardice. But he returned to the Mediterranean and during exercises narrowly avoided ramming *Dreadnought*, for which Tryon mildly rebuked him, commenting that Beresford had only escaped catastrophe 'by a fluke'.

In Egypt Khediv Tewfik died in 1892 and his son, Abbas, wishing to free himself from British influence, dismissed his pro-British Prime Minister. Anti-British riots were expected and Beresford was ordered to Alexandria to reinforce the guardship. He immediately wrote a lengthy report direct to Salisbury, giving his assessment of the situation, even criticizing Lord Cromer (formerly Evelyn Baring) as British representative. The troubles faded and *Undaunted* returned to UK to pay off.

In May 1892 Beresford attempted to circumvent the regulations for promotion by applying to count his 315 days in the Sudan as war service and, because he was nominally borne on the books of *Alexandra*, as sea service. He tried again when *Undaunted* paid off in April 1893. He was refused. On return home he again went on half-pay and the day he arrived attended the debate on the Navy Estimates. A general election had been held only the year before, with the return of Gladstone, still in precarious office. Without a seat in Parliament and no employment in the Navy, Beresford devoted himself to journalism and speaking engagements, advocating the abrogation of the Treaty of Paris and urging that the two-power standard had not yet been achieved.

He would reach the top of the captains' list in 1897, so the need to qualify for promotion was becoming urgent. But, determined to qualify with the least disturbance and remain in touch with the seat of power, he applied for an appointment to the Steam Reserve at Chatham, equivalent to the modern Reserve Fleet, which he took up in July 1893 and which, oddly enough, counted as sea service. That month he was due to give an address to the London Chamber of Commerce in which he was to propose another great

57

building programme costing £25m, but he said, 'It would have been improper for me to have published a paper while on active service'.[8] He passed it on to a member of the Chamber who 'caused it to be published on his own responsibility'.[9]

Beresford described his post as a 'dockyard appointment. . . . All vessels under construction and repair were under the Admiral Superintendent; I was his executive officer.'[10] This is untrue. The Admiral Superintendent was in charge of the dockyard and all its managers, civilian and naval; Beresford had no part in its management. He was responsible to the Admiral for the naval personnel in ships in reserve and refitting, an undemanding task, his main function being to take ships to sea on trials, so his attendance was intermittent. On average he went to sea once a month, leaving him ample opportunity to live at Park Gate House, Ham Common, within easy reach of London society and politics.

When *Magnificent* was completed he invited Lord Wolseley to accompany him on trials. On returning to Chatham in a torpedo boat, determined Wolseley should not miss his train, he ordered the lieutenant in command to proceed at full speed in the dark up the Medway. It was hardly surprising that the young officer lost the channel and ran across a mud spit, provoking Wolseley to ask if the Navy 'always took short cuts across the land?'[11] Returning guests from a ball at Sheerness in a tug in thick fog, the master refused to start, so Beresford took over and 'found the channel by the simple method of hitting its banks, and, cannoning off and on all the way, we made the passage'.[12] Any other officer would probably have been court-martialled.

With increasing gun ranges, the flirtation of navies with the ram was rapidly disappearing, yet Beresford, in an interview with the *Standard*, stated, 'In my opinion the ram is the most fatal weapon in naval warfare – more fatal even than the torpedo.'

In May 1894 Mahan, the American naval historian, visited Gravesend in the cruiser USS *Chicago*. Beresford took the opportunity to meet him and subsequently wrote contributions to the *North American Review*, suggesting an alliance between Britain and the United States, which was supported neither by Mahan nor Britain, since the US Navy then included only five battleships and twenty-one cruisers.

In 1895 the Kiel Canal was opened amid great celebrations and the Kaiser invited the navies of the world to send representative ships and the Royal Navy sent four 'Royal Sovereign' class battleships under Lord Walter Kerr. At Kiel were the world's most modern battleships: the French *Hoche*, which Chatfield described as a monstrosity, the Italian *Re Umberto* and *Sardegna*, the German Navy's small ugly 'Worth' class and the impressive Russian cruiser *Rurik*, in reply to which Fisher built *Terrible* and *Powerful*. Beresford managed to get himself invited and afterwards claimed that the Admiralty had greatly over-estimated *Rurik* and suggested the 'Grafton' class of protected cruisers with two 9.2-inch, and ten 6-inch guns were a 'fair match for her'. Later, while on leave in France, he attempted to visit the French submarine *Gustav Zédé*, the first in any navy, but the French gave nothing away and he made the extraordinary statement that the officers 'appeared to think that when it fired its own torpedo the concussion could smash the boat',

When, in March 1896, Beresford had just completed the minimum 'sea' time for promotion, including minor periods earlier, he was returned to half-pay, embarking on a campaign writing to the newspapers, speaking at various societies, on how the Navy should be reorganized. He claimed the Service was 27,562 men short of requirements. But the Admiralty had already laid plans to increase its strength by about 6,000 men for each of the next four years. Beresford criticized this figure, claiming that deaths and retirements had not been taken into account, reducing the four-year increase to 17,262. Such precise figures could not have been stated, whether correct or not, without access to official information, and obviously it was being leaked to him. In 1896 he announced that the Navy required a total of 105,000 men and it cannot be coincidence that the following year the Navy estimates provided for 106,390. He suggested that the Admiralty and Treasury had tamely accepted his figures. In the *Nineteenth Century* he proposed reorganizing the Royal Naval Reserve, again suggesting the re-arming of old ships with quick-firing guns and the scrapping of obsolete vessels. He proposed annual joint operations between the Navy and the Army, (though he well knew this was being pressed by Fisher), and new strategically placed overseas coaling bases, the promotion of admirals at an earlier age, improvements in pay for officers and men, the abolition of half-pay, all of which commanded much support. Visiting Cairo, he expressed himself pleased with developments in defences since his day. He witnessed Marconi's experiments in wireless telegraphy.

Beresford never understood how his tactlessness and self-advertisement were damaging him and the Navy. He could have expected appointment as ADC to the Queen on 1 January 1895, but he was not honoured until two years later, perhaps due to the embarrassment he had caused the Admiralty or opposition from the Prince of Wales.

Promotion to rear-admiral was a matter of dead men's shoes. Once a Post-Captain there was no incentive. There was a fixed number, and as vacancies arose due to retirement or death, the next captain on the list, no matter how incompetent, was promoted, subject to sea service, (though he could be left on half-pay until he reached retiring age). Beresford was promoted on 16 September 1897, aged 51. On promotion, rear-admirals remained on half-pay for three or four years, so he applied to join Kitchener's expedition to reconquer the Sudan, but was refused and reverted to politics. He was returned as member for York in December 1897, with a majority of eleven.

Again criticizing his superiors with impunity, in a civilian Parliament many untutored members were convinced. In February 1898 he forced from Austen Chamberlain, Civil Lord, the admission that the new Gibraltar dockyard was behind schedule, noted no doubt, in the European chancelleries. Despite having three times hazarded his ship, he asked why *Victorious* had grounded at the entrance to the Suez canal; he forced Goschen to admit defects had developed in *Powerful* and asked, justifiably, 'Does the Council of Defence ever meet; and if so, what was the date of the last meeting?' Then Goschen had to admit that fourteen battleships and thirteen smaller ships were being built in Britain for her potential enemies, such as Russia.

Much of what Beresford said deserved raising. The 1872 reform of the Board of Admiralty[13] left Parliament and public ignorant of the views of the naval Lords, which could be disregarded by the political head. Their only recourse was resignation, a serious step unless with private means, and he provided an avenue by which such matters were brought to public attention.

Meanwhile, with virtually no interval, on 24 August 1897 Fisher handed over the task of Controller to A.K.Wilson and hoisted his flag in *Renown*, a new battleship of 12,350 tons with four 10-inch and ten 6-inch guns, the only big ship on the North American Station, which limited fleet exercises. But Fisher as usual ensured his flagship was highly efficient. One of his lieutenants later said she was 'one of the smartest ships in the Navy, but also one of the happiest. There were no half-measures with Jacky; it was first in everything, or – look out. . . . He always had at heart the comfort of officers and men . . . and there were few among those who served under him who had not some good reason to be grateful to him.'[14] He seldom played games but encouraged ship's teams. When one was beaten, he said, 'We'll win next time, even if I have to play myself.'[15] Immaculately dressed, he had some idiosyncrasies, a roll-neck tunic covering a linen collar and black bow tie. He wore blue spats.

Convinced that war would come soon, a view not widely shared, he repeated his habit of *Bellerophon* days, sending at all hours for the brains of the ship to discuss some idea for the future. He liked a man to stand up for himself and despised yes-men. Then in the early hours of the morning he would evaluate and note down the discussions to fit the great Navy he planned. His restless spirit would never allow sloth or slackness. At Antigua he met the newly-commissioned *Talbot* and four ships of the training squadron and he gave orders that he would review their ship's companies on shore, specifying that hats were to be worn, at that time interchangeable with caps, and the commander of *Talbot* Lewis Bayly, (afterwards Admiral Sir Lewis), overlooked the order, his men the only ones wearing caps. Fisher believed the most insignificant detail should never be missed, which in more important matters, might have serious consequences. He displayed theatrical fury, making a signal demanding to know who was at fault. *Talbot*'s captain, E.H.Gamble, loyally took the blame. But Fisher was not deceived, called the Captain to his flagship and signalled again. Bayly was obliged to answer and admitted the fault was his, whereupon Fisher made a long flag signal placing Bayly under arrest, ordering all ships to repeat it. 'The display of flags of all colours,' wrote Bayly, 'was beautiful.' Fisher then demanded Bayly's 'reasons in writing', a common disciplinary custom and the latter replied that it was due to carelessness and stupidity. Fisher respected the honest reply and, having taught the lesson, released him from arrest and there the matter ended. Most admirals would merely have sent a private reprimand to Gamble, but Fisher was determined to exaggerate the incident to show that inefficiency would not be tolerated. But there was no malice in it; Bayly bore none and the matter was treated as a joke.

The station was something of a backwater, but Fisher paid ceremonial and courtesy visits to ports in Canada, the United States and French and Spanish possessions, making many friends, his bluff and informal manner appealing especially to the Americans. Many of these contacts proved of value in later years. The visits were planned and adhered to meticulously. He liked to drop anchor at the precise moment he had arranged. In summer it was customary to spend most of the time in North American latitudes and in winter in the West Indies. There was an Admiralty House at Halifax and another at Bermuda, so when in the ports Fisher enjoyed the company of Lady Fisher, for once in luxury. He invited the midshipmen in turn to spend weekends at Admiralty House, where they were lavishly entertained, much port consumed and repartee exchanged, Fisher going into 'convulsions of merriment and laughter'.

Admirals then had to provide domestic staff at their own expense. Despite his relative poverty Fisher believed entertainment was important and employed a French chef. When Admiral Sampson brought his US Navy squadron to Bermuda Fisher gave a magnificent dinner in his honour. Sampson's speech was brief: 'It was a damn fine old hen that hatched the American eagle!' On another occasion a delegation of forty distinguished Americans arrived at an hour's notice. He sent for his chef and announced 'Lunch for forty in one hour's time.' The Chef replied calmly, '*Oui, Monsieur,*' and produced a splendid meal. Both events paid dividends in 1914–18 and helped cement Anglo-American relations.

On 21 April 1898 war broke out between the United States and Spain. Some years of insurrection in Cuba culminated in a rebellion in 1895, which Spain believed was aided by agitators in the United States, whose Government offered mediation, which was refused, creating indignation. In an attempt at reconciliation USS *Maine* was sent to Havana on a courtesy call, but confusion resulted in her arriving somewhat unexpectedly on 24 January 1898. During that night she blew up and sank in the harbour. A US Board of enquiry concluded that she had been mined and war was declared. A subsequent investigation by Lieutenant-Colonel J.T.Bucknill, Royal Engineers, established that the explosion was due to spontaneous combustion in a bunker directly adjacent to a magazine.[16]

The Spanish Army and Navy were blockaded by American forces and Fisher ordered *Talbot* to rescue British nationals. She made three visits to Havana, on the last finding the Cuban people starving. Fisher's friendly relations with Sampson persuaded the latter to lift the blockade to evacuate British subjects.

Shortly afterwards, relations between Britain and France deteriorated. Britain had accepted a protectorate over the Upper Nile Basin from the Khedive and in March 1895 Sir Edward Grey had declared that French penetration of the area would be regarded as an unfriendly act, but in June 1896 a French officer, Major Marchand, took an expeditionary force to the Congo, from where, against incredible difficulties, he pushed across central Africa, arriving at Fashoda two years later, to plant the French flag. Kitchener steamed up from Khartoum and denied Marchand's right to be at Fashoda and war threatened. The zealous Fisher immediately planned to sail direct to Gibraltar, sending for Gamble in *Talbot*, whom he ordered to Halifax to coal and go to the West Indies as senior officer. He then asked Gamble for a copy of his plans. Gamble had made none, but he and Bayly set to work overnight and sent one to Fisher, which, after modification, he issued to the rest of the squadron. Fisher's orders were worked out in detail in conjunction with the general at Halifax, Lord William Seymour, including attacks against Miquelon, Iles des Saintes and all French West Indian islands. A few years earlier a French Officer, Major Dreyfus had been convicted of treason and imprisoned in Devil's Island, creating bitter feelings in France. Fisher drew up an outlandish plan to kidnap Dreyfus, land him in France and revive the dissension. But the French Navy had been neglected in favour of her Army; she was helpless and the confrontation subsided.

Fisher's thoroughness was again demonstrated when trouble flared between Britain and the United States over Venezuela; despite the improbability, refusing to be caught unprepared for a conflict, Fisher planned it in detail.

In March 1899, to wide astonishment, he was called home by Salisbury to serve as naval representative at the Hague Conference. Salisbury had been impressed by his tenacity in winning the transfer of naval ordnance from the Army and remarked that, having fought so well against his brother-in-law, he would fight as well at the Conference. He submitted Fisher's name to the Queen without discussing it with the First Lord, causing some antagonism.

Resulting from an idealistic six-volume book *The Future of War*, written in Russia by Ivan Bloch, Russia proposed the conference with unrealistic terms of reference which included the limitation of armaments, alleviation of the terrors of war and settlement of international disputes by arbitration, all by mutual agreement.

Britain insisted on her right to stop and search neutral ships on the high seas. 'Suppose that war breaks out and I am expecting to fight a new Trafalgar on the morrow,' said Fisher, 'Some neutral colliers try to steam past us into enemy's waters. If the enemy gets their coal into his bunker, it will make all the difference in the coming fight. You tell me I must not seize those colliers. I tell you that nothing that you, or any power on earth, can say will stop me seizing them or sending them to the bottom, if I can in no other way keep that coal out of the enemy's hands.'[17]

Admiral Sir Cyprian Bridge put the same thing more succinctly: 'To expect nations so engaged to regulate their action by rules drawn up in circumstances as different as can be would be as futile as trying to stop a dog fight by singing a hymn.'[18]

Though it did result in the Hague Convention, the Conference was not a success; Germany refused to consider arms limitations and Russia herself displayed little enthusiasm. But Fisher's stature was hugely enhanced; it was now internationally recognized that Britain had an admiral who would confront anyone. His views, expressed forcefully by a man with his religious outlook, were obviously not intended to be taken literally. But later in life his enemies used his exaggeration to portray him as a cruel and merciless man who could not be trusted with power. Even today writers have taken his words literally.

Fisher's position was far stronger than any admiral at the second conference in 1907. Britain's naval power was then universally recognized. Germany was a fourth-rate naval power; Japan had not proved herself. The Americans worked closely with Britain, and Stead said Fisher was

> like a little god. As he was personally modest, gracious, put on no airs and danced like a middy till all the hours of the morning, no man at The Hague was more popular than he. He was a bit of a barbarian who talked like a savage at times to the no small scandal of his colleagues at The Hague. 'The humanizing of war!' he declared, 'You might as well talk of humanizing Hell! . . . As if war could be civilized! If I'm in command when war breaks out I shall issue my orders [quoting Macaulay]

> > The essence of war is violence.
> > Moderation in war is imbecility
> > Hit first, hit hard and hit anywhere.

He had the not uncommon notion – which the uniform experience of mankind has shown to be false – that nations are deterred from going to war for fear of the atrocities that accompany conflict. 'If you rub it

63

in both at home and abroad, that you are ready for instant war with every unit of your strength in the first line and intend to be first in and hit your enemy in the belly, and kick him when he is down and boil your prisoners in oil (if you take any!) and torture his women and children, then people will keep clear of you!'[19]

It was a cogent view. War is by its very nature inhuman. In later life Fisher admitted that it was a mistake to speak so, but there was then, especially in Britain, a belief that war could be conducted according to gentlemanly rules of behaviour. It was this doctrine that later brought Britain close to defeat; Churchill believed no civilized nation would sink merchant ships without warning. The suggestion that poison gas would be used in war would have been treated as insanity, like the Holocaust, Hiroshima, Nagasaki and the failure of the League of Nations. And in AD 2000 the futility of declaring 'nuclear-free zones' is surely evident.

Fisher was a realist. He knew the totality of war. He knew that as countries approach defeat they will use any means at their disposal, however unspeakable, and he knew that the best safeguard is strength. No man attacks the giant; even David had a special weapon. Stead was wrong. 'The uniform experience of mankind' demonstrates that no country will start a war unless it believes it has at least an even chance of success.

But he had a hard time at The Hague; he wrote to Wilmot Fawkes, his commander in *Northampton*, now captain and Naval Secretary to the First Lord, 'It's very hard work here. It's a case of *Britannia contra Mundum*'.[20] His realism did not cause the failure of the Hague Conference, but it expressed the facts: the insincerity of agreements based on chivalry. He starkly exposed that insincerity, and there was no answer. Salisbury's choice of Fisher was astute, for he awakened Britain's potential opponents to the existence of an admiral whose determination they would have to contest. 'He exclaimed impatiently, "I am not for War, I am for Peace. That is why I am for a supreme Navy. . . . The supremacy of the British Navy is the best security for the peace of the world".'[21]

In 1883, when Wilhelm II ascended the throne, Germany had only four battleships. The following year William reorganized the German Admiralty, giving himself personal control. In 1889 Beresford visited Bismarck and later wrote: 'Bismarck said that he could not understand why my own people did not listen to me (nor could I!); for (said he) the British Fleet was the greatest factor for peace in Europe.'[22]

In 1894, following an explosion in a German battleship, Beresford sent a message of sympathy to the Kaiser, a strange thing for a serving officer of captain's rank to do. A year later Tirpitz persuaded the Kaiser that the increase in Germany's population entitled her to the status of a world power, for which an overseas cruiser force was needed. This could only be for commerce raiding and colonial expansion, posing a threat to Britain.

After the foolish and abortive Jameson raid in 1896 the German Emperor telegraphed to President Kruger: 'I express my sincere congratulations that, supported by your people and without appealing for the help of friendly Powers, you have succeeded by your own energetic action against armed bands which invaded your country as disturbers of the peace and have thus been enabled to restore peace and safeguard the independence of the country against attacks from the outside.'[23]

The Kruger telegram was intended to encourage the Boers and facilitate German expansion in Africa, creating great indignation in Britain. The Boers' declaration of war tempted Germany to expand her Empire and render active assistance to them; invasion by the large and well-organized German Army was deterred by the power of the Royal Navy and the danger Germany saw in exposing her flank. Once again the importance of sea power to Britain was demonstrated. Russia, and France too, admired the tenacity and skill of the Boers against a professional army, every Boer victory received with delirium and every setback with disappointment. France, cheated of Napoleon's spoils in Egypt, had built the Suez Canal, yet Britain had gained dominance over the canal and Egypt. Lutz said in 1928 'It is . . . an open question whether popular feeling in Germany during the Boer War was actually more hostile to Britain than in France.'[24] Russia's historic desire for a warm-water port led her to cast covetous eyes on Constantinople; only Britain barred the way and Russia proposed an alliance of the three powers against her. But the Navy deterred them and German eyes were opened to the need for a Navy.

In 1897 Tirpitz, a skilful naval officer and natural politician, achieved control of German naval policy and with little difficulty persuaded the Kaiser to pass the first German Navy Law, the second following on a more ambitious scale in 1900. The opening of the Kiel Canal had effectively doubled the German Navy by obviating the need to keep half in the Baltic and half in the North Sea. 'I will never rest,' said the Kaiser, 'until I have raised my Navy to a position similar to that occupied by my Army. German colonial aims can only be gained when Germany has become Master of the Ocean.'[25]

Tirpitz made it clear that the build-up of the German Navy was aimed against Britain. In his masterly memorandum presented to the Kaiser on 15 July 1897, which Steinberg assesses as 'certainly the most remarkable document in the history of the German Navy,'[26] he had said:

> For Germany the most dangerous naval enemy at the present time is England. . . . Commerce raiding and transatlantic war against England is so hopeless, because of the shortage of bases on our side and the superfluity on England's side, that we must ignore this type of war against England in our plans for the constitution of our fleet. Our fleet

must be so constructed that it can unfold its greatest military potential between Heligoland and the Thames. . . . The military situation
against England demands battleships in as great a number as
possible.[27]

Admiral Sir Frederick Richards drew attention to the possibility that Britain
might face three powers and the Press expressed alarm. Beresford wrote to
the *Naval and Military Record* urging alliance with Germany. His reputation
was not enhanced by his pro-German views, but he was not alone.

The Russian fleet, too, was growing and the maintenance of the two-
power standard demanded a British programme increased from three
battleships, eight cruisers and four sloops to seven battleships, twelve
cruisers, twelve torpedo boats and four sloops. Beresford drew attention to
the mounting invasion scare and demanded a 'large fleet in the channel',
with suitable colliers, cold storage, distilling, ammunition and hospital ships.

Outside Europe, foreign policy was dominated by China. Britain in the
1840s had opened Chinese markets and other western powers followed. In
the Treaty of Nanking of 1842 Britain was ceded Hong Kong island, and
after the second Chinese War of 1856–60 the Treaty of Tientsin opened
up Peking and the Yangtse and ceded Kowloon to the British Crown.
Russia, Portugal, France and Japan promptly occupied Chinese territory.
Japan, claiming Korea, gained a clear victory over the Chinese, triggering
a scramble for concessions. In 1897 Germany took Kiao Chow and
announced she was building a naval base at Tsing Tao, Russia promptly
occupied Port Arthur. Britain now accepted a lease of Wei Hai Wei, which
she had previously declined. Britain's 'open door policy' had failed and
China was divided into 'spheres of influence' of which Britain's was the
Yangtse Valley.

'Beresford,' wrote Balfour to Salisbury, 'wants to go to China. . . . I failed
to discover in what capacity.' Salisbury's reaction was negative, so Beresford
approached the Associated Chambers of Commerce of Great Britain, who
agreed he should research the development of trade. With characteristic
egotism he wrote to Salisbury: 'If the Chinese Government will only
allow me to organize their forces in the Yangtse Valley and so give adequate
protection to trade and commerce, I believe capital will pour into the
country.'[28] He reached Hong Kong on 3 September 1898 and in just over
three months covered 5,000 miles, a great achievement in the terrain. He
collected data and met every influential British subject before starting home
on 9 January 1899 through Japan and the USA where he was received by
the President and Secretary of State; he spoke to the Chamber of Commerce
and Board of Trade in Chicago and the New York Stock Exchange. A month
after his return he completed a 500-page report, *The Breakup of China*, which
led him into areas far outside his mandate, including national, international,

racial and political matters, angering Russia and France. In a lengthy speech in the House he advocated the open-door policy, already extinct, floundering on, making innumerable speeches until Salisbury was provoked to say: 'I am afraid CB is an ass!'[29] But soon he returned to naval subjects, expressing faith in water-tube boilers, on which, as he had never served with them, he was hardly qualified to speak, provoking Percy Scott's remark:

'In the Navy we knew he was not a sailor, but thought he was a politician; in the House of Commons, they knew he was not a politician, but thought he was a sailor.'[30]

6

UNRULY MEMBER

Simultaneously with his nomination to the Hague Conference, Fisher was offered the appointment of Commander-in-Chief Mediterranean, taking with him his flagship *Renown*. Though this was the top sea-going appointment, he had aimed at First Sea Lord and was disappointed and angry that Lord Walter Kerr was chosen. Fisher was now 58, only 16 months younger than Kerr, and by the time Kerr retired would be 63 and unlikely to succeed him. He shook his fist and said, 'I will get there yet in spite of them!'[1] Fisher's habit of shaking his clenched fist to stress a point, as a gesture of determination, was well known; King Edward once said to him, 'Will you kindly leave off shaking your fist in my face?'

Kerr was an unoriginal thinker, had little creative imagination and tended to resist change. But the uninspiring appointment was aggravated by the simultaneous relief of Sir Lewis Beaumont as DNI by Reginald Custance, newly promoted rear-admiral, whom Marder calls 'brilliant',[2] a verdict few would agree with, and in November 1900 Goschen was succeeded by Lord Selborne, a lively man who quickly understood the naval problems of the day, but nevertheless, to Fisher's exasperation, the change brought all the difficulties of a politician learning a new job.

On arrival at Malta Fisher cut the tiresome protocol to a minimum. Normally all captains would call on the Admiral formally, the call later returned by the Admiral. Fisher sent for them all together and later the same day returned all calls, each lasting no more that three minutes.

Admirals customarily devised exercises personally, but, hardly more than stereotyped games, they had little relation to war. War plans were almost non-existent and when war threatened no one had any idea of the Admiral's intentions, frequently including the Admiral himself. This was partly inherited from the days of sail, when self-supporting ships were dependent on weather, compelling last-minute decisions. Nelson had not hesitated to sail from the Mediterranean to the West Indies in pursuit of the French. All round Fisher were the consequences of the long peace; admirals and captains whose minds had stagnated, had no experience of war and gave it no thought; admirals promoted because they reached the top of the captains' list, where they had arrived due to nepotism and social connections. Yet promotion was believed to confer the ability to deal with strategic and tactical problems. One historian has said, 'The Victorian Navy performed adequately the tasks demanded of it', but between 1815 and 1914 little *was* demanded of it and we have no idea how it would have performed if things had been otherwise. Until arrival at the rank of captain there was no chance, and even then little, of an officer being asked his opinion or given the opportunity to study war; he was seldom consulted and did not expect to be. Higher training of officers was negligible; there was no staff college and most officers believed that tactics and strategy should be left to the admirals. Fisher recognized that more stripes did not give him a monopoly of brains and immediately formed a 'committee' of officers of all ranks and branches. The older, out-of-date captains he omitted, some greatly slighted, exemplifying the tactlessness which made him enemies. He would have done better to have included them and gently ignored their unhelpful views.

He told the 'committee' that at The Hague German admirals had told him British battleships were obsolete, as they would all be sunk by torpedo craft. He dryly observed that this idea was fallacious and invited officers to contribute to tactics, especially defence against torpedo craft, and their offensive use. 'At last [younger officers] felt that they were themselves part of a profession that extended beyond mere seamanship and the thinking officers began to debate with enthusiasm how best to operate a fleet. From this Fisher drew an immense fund of information, ideas and innovation.'[3]

He began a programme of inspections; not the formal walk round, a few words with the odd rating chosen at random. Inspection meant the ship went to 'General Quarters' and was exercised in quick succession – 'out torpedo nets' – 'in nets' – 'fire quarters' – 'abandon ship', all so rapidly that the ship was left in an exhausted state of disorder. But if officers failed to show enough energy they paid the penalty. A commander was sent home that evening and on arrival was transported to a new appointment in a hot climate. A lieutenant in command of a destroyer was on the way to China as a watchkeeping officer the next day. But promising and energetic officers were pressed forward. 'Favouritism is the secret of efficiency!' was one of his maxims. But zeal and intelligence were his criteria; nepotism he abhorred.

Waking in the night, he jotted ideas on paper at the side of his bed. He rose at 4 am and started planning future exercises in the minutest detail. His flag lieutenant led a dog's life. Delay in hoisting signals was not tolerated and if ships were slow to respond a three-pounder gun drew their attention. One ship, misunderstanding an order, started on the wrong course and was instantly signalled, 'What the devil are you doing?' The offender primly made: 'Please repeat third word'. From every yardarm and masthead of the flagship came the word 'Devil, Devil, Devil, Devil'. When the fleet 'wheeled' about a small cruiser, the manoeuvre was bungled, and Fisher made to the cruiser, 'Manoeuvre well executed'. She, of course, was required to do nothing. He gave regular lectures to the officers, covering tactics, strategy and preparation for war, demonstrating his grasp of contemporary naval and political problems, stimulating interest and discussion. He invited captains and gunnery lieutenants to a lecture at Admiralty House, Valetta, on a Saturday morning; some did not accept and were *ordered* to attend the next day, Sunday. But his inspiring lectures were followed by animated discussion and soon he was obliged to restrict attendance.

> The principal officers of the fleet should be acquainted with the whole scope of the probable war operations and *saturated* with the views of their Commander-in-Chief so that they know what best to do next if one step goes wrong. They must also be prepared to provide against unforeseen contingencies. . . . What is the vital principle of war? It is the same afloat as ashore. To bring the preponderance of force to bear on a proportion of the enemy before it can be reinforced. Nelson at Cape St Vincent, the Nile and Trafalgar, and Napoleon in the field. Prayer for the unready and unpracticed fleet! –

> Give us peace in our time, O Lord![4]

His lectures were masterpieces. 'You must also read,' later wrote Lord Esher to his younger son, Maurice Brett, 'Fisher's notes for his Mediterranean Fleet lectures. They are a model.'[5] In six months Fisher's fleet was transformed to a standard never before known in the Victorian Navy.

But to universal amazement, including, apparently, Beresford, in December 1899 he was appointed Flag Officer, Second-in-Command, Mediterranean Fleet, flying his flag in *Ramillies*. After his limited service as a lieutenant, early promotion to commander by Keppel's favour, he had served in only one ship as second-in-command, before returning to another Royal Yacht. He commanded the tiny *Condor* in which he made his name and was promoted captain. As fourth Naval Lord, having proved unable to cooperate with other members, he had failed to convince them of the very real merits of his views on staffs. He had served the minimum time in command of *Undaunted* and in the Medway Dockyard Reserve to ensure automatic promotion to rear-admiral. His total service since gaining lieutenant's rank was 14½ years, of which 6½ were in Royal Service or as flag lieutenant; his total seagoing service, other than in Royal service, was 5½ years; many a lieutenant had longer and better experience at sea. He was almost the junior admiral; there were thirty-five rear-admirals senior to him and only four junior. Why, then was Beresford chosen for this cherished appointment? It was not on grounds of experience or seniority, nor because he showed great promise as an admiral. He had quarrelled with his Royal patron and the Queen still regarded him with disfavour, Nor can Fisher have asked for him, for although the two remained on reasonably unruffled terms for a few years yet, Fisher often showed amused contempt for the political admiral. There can be only one explanation: he was as much a nuisance in Parliament as in the Navy, creating work in answering his more embarrassing questions. The politicians could get rid of him by pushing him back into the Navy.

Clearly Fisher did not want Beresford. In his first three months, the latter complained, the C-in-C gave him nothing to do. He did not consult him, nor was he invited to the first three meetings to discuss preparations for war. Exclusion of the newcomer was tactless and Beresford might have benefited. But Fisher was very conscious of Beresford's suave tongue, the influence he commanded as an itinerant MP and confidant of men of influence, which would inhibit plain speaking and re-establish the very spirit he was trying to eradicate.

Inevitably Beresford's appointment created problems. He started to complain at once, protesting bitterly that his flagship happened to be refitting and he was obliged to take a house in Valetta. He could have transferred his flag temporarily to another ship, and in any case he retained his house for the rest of his appointment, making it a great social centre, outshining his less wealthy C-in-C. Each struggled to control his feelings. Beresford's appointment had been much publicized before his departure; he was dined by the London Chamber of Commerce and it was said he was going to teach the fleet tactics, for which he had devised new methods. The fleet waited, breathless, for the inevitable clash. The newcomer was received cordially, but one morning he landed his boat's crew on the Corradino parade ground and made a signal to the fleet that he would welcome any of the captains who wished to see some tactics. 'Linked together with a tack-line, in order to keep them in station, the men executed the evolutions of a fleet in obedience to signals,' he wrote.[6] Evidently this was his 'new method' of teaching tactics, which was somewhat ridiculous, since a man can turn on his heel, whereas a ship takes some minutes. Beresford became a laughing stock and Fisher seized his chance, making a signal to Beresford's flag captain demanding to know why men had been landed at the Corradino without permission, contrary to standing orders. Beresford explained that the omission was his, and Fisher put him firmly in place. This is said to have cleared the air, but their relationship was little more than an armed truce. Fisher unwisely sent Beresford a note asking why the *Morning Post* could have referred to 'The Mediterranean Fleet, under the command of Lord Charles Beresford', who sarcastically replied, 'From the enclosure you have sent me it appears that the British public are accustomed to the name of Lord Charles Beresford, but as yet ignorant of the name of Sir John Fisher. I would suggest that the remedy lies entirely in your own hands.'[7] Such hubris is perhaps unique in the annals of the Navy. Friction increased when the fleet was entering Grand Harbour and *Ramillies* missed her buoy, backing and filling while the fleet waited outside. Exasperated, Fisher signalled Beresford, 'Your flagship is to proceed to sea and come in again in a seamanlike manner.' Beresford was deeply offended. Chatfield, who was clearly anti-Fisher, called it a 'lamentable example of bad leadership',[8] and Roskill 'tactless, even insulting'.[9] But if Fisher had suggested to Beresford that he give the order, the latter would probably have taken the opportunity of publicly defying the C-in-C. Nor could Fisher ignore such ineptitude; similar signals were common and it would have been 'a lamentable example of bad leadership' if he had made an exception of a flagship. Chatfield believed the incident responsible for the rift between the two men, but it clearly had deeper origins. More offensive was Beresford's signal when *Theseus* was ordered to a Turkish port to collect mails, instead of the junior cruiser, as customary. With heavy sarcasm, he made a signal in plain language for all to see: 'I regret that after the good work *Theseus* has done under my command during the recent exercises, she is not to be allowed to take part in the regatta,' When Fisher yielded, he turned the knife: 'I am glad that after the good work *Theseus* has done under my command, the Commander-in-Chief has seen fit to allow her to take part in the regatta.'[10] The repetition of the words 'under my command' was deliberate.

Fisher may have tried to rid himself of his subordinate, for according to Beresford: 'I was approached as to whether I would accept the command of the Australian Squadron. Considering that the appointment would not afford the opportunities I desired of learning how to handle a fleet, I intimated my preference for remaining in the Mediterranean.'[11]

Fisher wrote to his wife: 'We finished the first part of our manoeuvres yesterday. They were quite splendid and everyone is delighted with themselves. Beresford came on board to tell me he had made up his mind now not to re-enter Parliament, but to remain out here with the fleet his whole time! as he had learnt more in the last week than in the last forty years!'[12]

Fisher offered a prize of a gold cup, valued at 50 guineas, (nearly £3,000 today) for an essay on tactics, especially the employment of torpedo vessels. The young Royal Marine officer, Maurice Hankey (later Lord Hankey), serving in Beresford's flagship, entered and was placed equal with four others including Bacon, 'just promoted captain at a very early age on account of his numerous writings on naval matters.'[13] To the dismay of those who had disdained to enter, Fisher invited all the competitors to a 'banquet (not a dinner mind you)' in the flagship to express his congratulations and thanks. 'It . . . will make my opinion more worthy of consideration with Lord

Charles,' wrote Hankey, 'when he does me the honour to ask it as he has done on several matters.'[14] Fisher repeated the competition the next year, when Hankey gained third place, foreshadowing his future stature. He was then working on a study of *Warfare on the Littoral*, believing the Royal Marines should be employed primarily in amphibious warfare, not fulfilled until the Second World War. Beresford was impressed and seized Hankey's ideas: 'The Second-in-Command is working up a case for the Marines for his next Parliamentary campaign and I have had to collect many statistics for him.'[15]

Beresford dined a Russian admiral at Corfu, gave a dance at Fiume and entertained the Greek Royal family to dinner at Piraeus. On Christmas day 1900 his guests included Princess Amelia of Schleswig-Holstein and the Earl and Countess of Annesley, while the following year the Duke and Duchess of York (later King George V and Queen Mary) lunched with him. He visited Tetuan and stayed with the Bey. Hankey wrote to his wife: 'I have translated correspondence for the Admiral in Spanish, French, German and Italian during the past week. I shall probably be on his staff at Taranto, when we are paying an official visit next week. . . . We have been hobnobbing with Austrian Dukes and Princes, guests of Lord Charles.'[16] After lunching the Duke of York, Beresford wrote to his former friend, now King Edward VII who noted scornfully to his son that he was 'honoured by a lengthy epistle from Lord CB, who seemed as usual much in evidence during your stay'.[17]

Fisher was concerned at the weakness of his fleet which might be opposed by a combined French and Russian one. Since 1831 Russia had attempted to gain control of the Dardanelles and access to the Mediterranean. In 1833 she gained exclusive right of passage through the Straits enabling her to threaten Britain's route through the Suez Canal to India and the land route through the middle East. France attempted to establish bases on the north African coast. After 1870 France and Russia again saw the advantages of cooperation against Britain and an association took place in 1891, followed in 1895 by an alliance. With French support the danger of a Russian *coup de main* against Constantinople was real and in that event the French Fleet at Toulon was available for action against Britain in the western basin of the Mediterranean. Hopkins, Fisher's predecessor, had repeatedly drawn attention to the dangers and his fleet was divided into two, one based at Gibraltar and the other at Malta, a strategic disadvantage of which he was acutely aware.

But Custance wrote: 'The wants of the Mediterranean Fleet have been repeatedly pressed upon the attention of their Lordships by the C-in-C. The Home Fleet has no such advocate, but it is believed that the manoeuvres have shown that the necessity of practice and frequent exercise together of its battleships, cruisers and destroyers is important if it is to be on a par with the formidable German force which is being rapidly developed in the North Sea.'[18]

Custance's views were prescient, but premature. Germany's naval plans were in the early stages and she was not yet a threat to Britain. Fisher believed his problem more immediate; the French Fleet at Toulon, including nine battleships, had reached a new efficiency and could easily be reinforced from Brest. Fisher's eleven battleships were, he thought, inadequate to deal with the Alliance and his nearest reinforcements were two thousand miles away. He inundated the Admiralty with letters.

But he could not restrain his impetuous subordinate, who in June 1900 sent him a long report, precisely reiterating Fisher's views but giving an appearance of originality. And he sent a copy to Salisbury. In a patronizing covering note to Salisbury, he said his report was in no way critical of Fisher; 'Sir John is an able clever man and, as he is responsible, he is certain to see the weaknesses that I perceive . . . whether he has written home on these points I do not know as, beyond an agreement in conversation that the fleet is not strong enough out here, we have not written or discussed the matter,'[19] which was palpably untrue.

Beresford raised many other matters with Fisher, all well known to the latter; the inadequacy of coal stocks and ammunition, the advantages of oil fuel, the need for a breakwater to protect the Grand Harbour, the advantage of nucleus crews for ships in reserve, improved wireless communication and the desirability of a naval War College, all of which Fisher had long pressed. Beresford suggested that he should take responsibility for all training, a trap Fisher was hardly likely to fall into. Without consulting Fisher, he invited a number of politicians and journalists, prominent members of the Navy League, to visit the fleet. Fisher, presented with a *fait accompli*, obtained retrospective Admiralty approval. The party included the *Daily Mail* naval correspondent, Arnold White. Three years earlier James Thursfield (later Sir James) had written to Fisher asking for his son, a cadet in *Britannia*, to join Fisher's flagship, beginning a correspondence that gave Fisher Press support, while keeping him anonymous. Now Beresford introduced him to White and the two men took to each other at once and he fed White and Thursfield with information. But Fisher was discreet, constantly reminding them not to mention his name and was careful not to reveal confidential matter. The partnership did much to expose naval weaknesses. On 6 November 1900 Fisher wrote to White: 'I wish specially to ask you to go on reiterating . . . the paragraph 'Wanted, Fleets on a war footing'. That is the pith of the whole matter. . . . the Mediterranean and Channel Fleets should be kept organised for war in every detail, . . . it's criminal folly not to do so. There would not be time to mobilise ships and hire auxiliaries to be brought into play! The vital blow would have been struck!'[20] Again, on 16 February 1901: 'The French say they will be off Malta from Toulon in thirty-six hours after the declaration of war. . . . In how many hours, pray will . . . <u>our</u> reinforcements reach Malta, or even Gibraltar, <u>after</u> the outbreak of war? Not one vessel will be sent <u>before</u> the declaration of war <u>for fear of precipitating matters</u>.'[21]

Beresford was of a different mind. He confided to his private notebook, 'Arnold White ought never to have lauded Fisher and myself. It creates irritation among our brother officers', but to an enquiry from White whether Fisher's fleet was strong enough, he craftily replied: 'It would be most improper and prejudicial to discipline if I were to give you details as to why I am so anxious as to want of strength and of proper war organisation of the fleet in the Mediterranean. I have communicated my views in strong Anglo-Saxon language to the properly constituted authorities. My duty and business out here as Second-in-Command are simply to obey orders to the best of my ability, not to offer criticisms which might become public.'[22] This was published in the *Daily Mail*.

In the House of Commons Beresford's conduct was questioned and Arnold-Forster, Parliamentary Secretary, replied, 'There is nothing to show that [his letter] was intended for publication, and it seems highly improbable that the rear admiral would have taken a step so contrary to discipline'.[23] White immediately wrote to Arnold-Forster accepting responsibility, and received a reply: 'The rights and duties of an officer holding a high command are strictly limited by the rules of the Service. Lord Charles, was and must be wrong, while his flag is flying, to set an example which he would be the first to condemn if followed by an officer under his command.'[24]

A reduction in the First Lord's salary was then moved. White published an article in the *National Review*, titled *A Message from the Mediterranean* and published his letter to Arnold-Forster in *The Times*. A further question was asked to which Arnold-Forster replied: 'The Admiralty understand that the letter was a private one, written without any idea of its being published, and that its publication was unauthorised. . . . It has not been thought necessary to call upon the rear-admiral for an explanation.'[25] Unless Beresford committed a specific disciplinary offence there was little he could do and disciplinary action against a rear-admiral with a national following and great influence demanded an offence of the first magnitude.

That Fisher was suspected of passing information to White is evident, for he wrote to the journalist: 'I have been paid the great compliment of a letter from Lord Goschen to say that there is a strong Mediterranean flavour in your writing; and that you might have been supposed to have seen all the public and private letters I have been writing to the Admiralty ever since I assumed command of this great fleet,' and in a postscript he wrote, 'Please do not put anything about me in the papers, or allude to me in any way, as it will do more harm than good and spoil my work.'[26]

Fisher was embarrassed and concerned. He wrote to Fawkes:

Many thanks for your letter of June 21st which has just arrived, and its enclosure about Beresford's letter to the *Daily Mail*. . . . So far as I am personally concerned, it will of course be obvious to you that I have nothing whatever to gain by kicking the shins of the Admiralty! So that the articles (of which, by the way, I have only seen a portion) are certainly not written in my interest and only serve to aggravate instead of smoothing and facilitating. . . . I am sorry words and phrases of mine are quoted, as you mention, but with a large fleet like this the admiral cannot hide his views, and mine, as you know are very strong.[27]

His protestations of innocence were not wholly honest; it was White's use of his own language that betrayed him.

It has been claimed that Fisher's reluctance to consult Beresford was attributable to self-interest, and that he was equally indiscreet and un-principled as the latter, to whose activities he objected in order to appropriate the limelight. His pains to ensure his name was kept out of the Press deny this. His frequent marking of letters *BURN* or 'For your eyes only' have been claimed to be insincere, but he cannot be blamed if his injunctions were ignored and he often said he preferred 'to work like a mole – underground'.

Beresford outwardly gave Fisher support in his reforms and in his note-book listed twenty improvements the C-in-C had achieved. He approved of Fisher's lectures and discussion with officers. The gunnery of the fleet had vastly improved. But above all Fisher 'has made the fleet a fifteen-knot one without breakdowns, in place of a twelve-knot one with breakdowns.'[28] In a letter to Fisher, possibly referring to his success in gaining reinforcements for the Mediterranean, he wrote: 'Bravo, and again bravo! The fleet, the country and the Empire will owe you a lasting debt of gratitude; you will have saved us all. What a confession after six years of this Government: evidently it is now a case of the civilians at the Admiralty being on our side against the naval experts.'[29]

But his hypocrisy was revealed by Fisher's Chief of Staff, Captain George King-Hall, who wrote that he acted 'like a kind of buffer'. For behind his back Beresford denigrated Fisher, who wrote memoranda to Beresford, tact-lessly, sometimes brutally worded, that King-Hall did not send on, recognizing the likely reaction. Beresford came to see him frequently, always maligning Fisher, 'which I had to discourage'. He noted in his diary on 22 October 1901, 'Beresford detained me for half an hour, more or less, having a hit at the C-in-C, ending up by saying he was an Asiatic'.[30] Beresford used his social position, wealth and influence to overshadow Fisher. 'Beresford was "news", again and again stealing the limelight from his Commander-in-Chief,' wrote Peter Kemp.[31] Fisher was an ambitious man; he wanted to be First Naval Lord, not merely for personal satisfaction, but because he sincerely thought he, and he alone, had a grasp of the future needs of the Navy. Vain, perhaps, but true. Yet sometimes he considered abandoning his career, especially when an irresponsible correspondent of *The Times* suggested Beresford as First Lord on Goschen's retirement.

Fisher arranged for exercises with the Channel Fleet, under A.K.Wilson, appointing himself chief umpire and giving Beresford command of the Mediterranean ships. Beresford recorded in his notebook that the exercises 'taught admirals lessons they ought to have known as lieutenants. The forms generally approved in the Service were shown to be useless and dangerous. Even the best place for an admiral to command his fleet in action was unknown. The things now improved and in process of improvement should have done so long ago.' (*Sic*)[32] This note demonstrated Beresford's unrealistic outlook. He deduced that admirals should have a close knowledge of signals and read them personally. Colomb's *Manoeuvring Book* contained 14,000 signals for changing formations. Tryon had ignored it.

Fisher wrote to Selborne, 'Both Wilson and Beresford handled their squadrons most admirably.'[33] But Beresford pre-empted any outcome by ensuring that the newspapers reported that he had out-manoeuvred Wilson. Fisher wrote: 'Everyone is very angry with CB at the paragraphs put in the paper about his beating A.K.Wilson, which is so stupid of him, and is not true. And of course it gets up the backs of the Channel Fleet, which we had avoided. He really is incorrigible.'[34] And again: 'You are right about our friend. The tongue is an unruly member, *especially when it's an Irish Member.* . . . The worst of it is that he puts *all* his friends in the wrong box also, as they are obliged to disown him when he makes exaggerated statements. The best thing he can do is to keep quiet for the present; but I fear he won't and will flounder further.'[35]

By July Fisher had been damaged by publicity and he now believed his career would come to an end when he hauled down his flag. 'I had a long letter from Beresford [at home on leave] this morning telling me his news from England. He says the whole Cabinet is most furious over the Mediterranean Fleet agitation. . . . It certainly has done away with the idea of my going to the Admiralty! Nor do I think it likely that I shall get anything else after this. However, I feel that I have done the right thing, and I daresay I shall get along all right on half-pay.'[36]

At last, in February 1902, to Fisher's relief, Beresford hauled down his flag. He was elected unopposed as MP for Woolwich, intending to continue his campaign for naval reform, and Fisher wrote to Fawkes: 'I have written a letter to CB, of which I have kept a copy, to prevent him in any way, either quoting me or using my name in any way in his approaching campaign. His intentions are no doubt good, but, as you have heard, "Hell is paved with good intentions"; and I much fear he will put his foot in it and spoil by injudicious speech the great good he undoubtedly could do in educating outsiders for the good of the Navy.'[37] But, whatever he wrote to Fawkes, he saw the advantage of a prominent naval officer in Parliament and wrote to Beresford at the end of the month suggesting how he should approach the debate on the Naval Estimates, which he headed:

> *Private. No one to see this letter except your own self!!!!* You should repeat Dilke's unanswerable arguments. 'We must go into a naval war with ships ordered 4 or 5 years before that war was declared. You cannot build ships in a hurry with a supplementary estimate.' *It is simple madness to underbuild.* You cannot improvise battleships, cruisers and destroyers. . . . No, what we want is an *additional naval member of the Board of Admiralty absolutely disassociated from all administrative and executive work and solely concerned in the* **PREPARATION OF THE FLEET FOR WAR.'** Battenberg has invented a magnificent name for him – THE WAR LORD . . . *to have a Von Moltke on the Board. . . . All the other Lords have too much to do. . . . Battenberg would really be the man for the billet.* The Director of Naval Intelligence is in too subservient a position. . . . I am sure I can rely on your discretion not to haul me into the matter. . . . Consult Thursfield before you make out your speech. . . . *Indeed I should ask him to revise your speech were I in your place.* He knows how to put things to the British public.[38]

This appears closely to coincide with Beresford's proposal when Fourth Sea Lord, foreshadowing the later position of Chief of Staff. But Fisher's anxiety for the appointment of a 'War Lord' was concerned primarily with the state of his own fleet. At any time until the *Entente Cordiale* of 1904 war with France was a possibility and he knew his fleet was not strong enough. '*I maintain it to be a cardinal principle (that should never be departed from) that the Mediterranean Fleet should be kept constituted for instant war,*' he wrote to Selborne. 'Instant readiness for War' had already become one of his maxims.

But Fisher agreed with Custance that Germany was the real enemy. He wrote to Thursfield in November, 1901; 'Personally I have always been an enthusiastic advocate for friendship and alliance with France. They never have and never will interfere with our trade. It's not their line and really we have no clashing of vital interests. . . . The Germans are our natural enemies everywhere! We ought to unite with France and Russia.[39]

Though perhaps resentment had an influence, he had little faith in Kerr, who busied himself in minutiae.[40] Writing to Thursfield, he said Selborne 'is far more alive to the great issues at stake than his chief naval adviser'.[41]

Fisher complained that Kerr was amazed to find on his return from six weeks' leave that five new destroyers reported to him as ready when he left were not ready when he returned. 'Who has been hung? Who has had one single word of censure?' asked Fisher.[42] Kerr lacked Fisher's iron hand.

Selborne and Joseph Chamberlain invited Fisher to write to them, of which he took full advantage. He wrote voluminously with his customary hyperbole. 'If at times I express myself very strongly, I hope you will forgive me.' His persistence bore fruit. Selborne visited Malta, ostensibly to inspect the new breakwater for protection against torpedo attack. He was accompanied by Fawkes, Kerr and Custance. 'I hope I shall be able to hold my own,' wrote Fisher, 'though it's going to be four to one.' He was; most of his proposals were approved, despite the stubborn opposition of Custance.

Beresford afterwards said Fisher explained 'in the most masterly manner the necessity for reinforcing the Mediterranean and increasing stocks of coal and stores'. But Sir Charles Walker, a senior civil servant, later Fisher's secretary, relates: 'Jacky locked them in his cabin with himself only, and from what he told me later, he indulged in some pretty plain speaking (I think his animosity to Custance dates from this time).'[43] This seems likely, for earlier he appears to have respected Custance's opinions,[44] but now recognized his weaknesses; his stubborn belief that he was the only one who understood naval strategy, that steam, steel, torpedoes, mines and gunfire had done nothing to change it. He was a believer in tradition to the exclusion of material progress; he scorned the 'materialists'. But tradition can become a substitute for thinking. Custance was a leading member of the 'historical school' round which gathered all the reactionary officers who were out of their depth with the new technology.

But Beresford had missed the most important subject of discussion – the creation of an embryo naval staff which created much of the animosity between Fisher and Custance. Beresford had wanted the staff to be under the Intelligence Department and Custance saw enhancement of his status. Fisher wanted to train prospective staff officers, for which a Staff College was needed. On 30 July 1901 he wrote to his wife: 'I have had another great point conceded by Admiralty in the establishment of a Naval War College, which I urged ferociously when they were at Malta. I feel sure Lord Selborne was convinced, but the others would not have it at any price, and now it is announced! Of course [Kerr] and [Custance] can both make matters very inconvenient for me, inasmuch as I don't get replies to small matters which don't go to the First Lord. However, it can't be helped.'[45] This hardly supports Roskill's view that Fisher 'considered training for staff duties to be quite unnecessary'![46]

Details of the scheme were soon announced. The course was compulsory for selected captains and commanders and included preparation of a plan of operation in some particular theatre, the attack and defence of fortified places in this theatre, lines of communication and logistics during the operation, British and foreign trade routes, tactics, naval history and international law.[47] This ambitious course was to be completed in nine months. Perhaps Custance was converted, for on 17 October 1901 he praised it, but demonstrated his hatred of Fisher: 'Fisher is very active in the Mediterranean, but much of the advantage which should be derived from it is lost on account of his want of grasp of fundamental principles and desire to run himself to the front at any price. It is a depressing and melancholy spectacle.'[48] And three months later he wrote: 'Fisher has made a great effort to get into the Admiralty as Second Sea Lord, (*Sic*) but has, I trust been defeated. The way in which he takes in most people is extraordinary, seeing how superficial and time-serving he is.'[49]

For Custance of all people to charge Fisher with superficiality is ironic. His limited understanding of strategy and tactics, which he could not relate to changing times, was demonstrated in his book *Naval Policy: A Plea for the Study of War*, a masterpiece of sophism. But he was right about Fisher angling for the job of Second Naval Lord; he wrote to Fawkes about it, but added that he would be glad to accept the appointment of C-in-C Plymouth.

Battenberg, Custance's assistant, commissioned the new battleship *Implacable* in September 1901 and joined Fisher in the Mediterranean. Fisher thought him one of 'perhaps the two best officers in the whole British Navy' (the other being May) – a compliment he had paid to several other officers! Fisher jumped at the opportunity to discuss staff and planning matters, sending him a succession of memoranda, 'to be treated as strictly private. . . . I do this in view of your remark of yesterday, "Is there no means of opening Lord Selborne's eyes?" '[50] Among these was one headed *War Plans*, suggesting the possible contingencies: War with France; War with the dual Alliance (France and Russia); with the Triple Alliance (Germany, Italy and Austria); with the United States; a German-American alliance; a Russian-American alliance; with an Eastern Triple Alliance (Russia, Japan and China). He added: 'It goes without saying that there should not be loss of an instant of time on the outbreak of war from the enemy adopting an unexpected plan! There should be no possible fresh plan that the enemy could devise which had not been thought out and considered beforehand.'[51]

This long document proves three important points. First Fisher was not opposed to a Naval War Staff, as has been so often claimed; indeed he prepared the paper to make the point. Second, he was far from the 'materialist' he was claimed to be by the pseudo-intellectuals of the 'Historical School' and, third, he was not ignorant of strategy and tactics, he was no 'mere constructor' as he was afterwards described; his thinking on strategy and tactics was deep and thorough.

Battenberg replied at length that under Custance the Intelligence Department had made great strides. A 'Defence Division' had been added dealing with plans of campaign and strategy for peace and war. But to make plans for all probable and improbable events would be wholly beyond the powers of the NID. Under Custance the NID had 'invaded every department of the Admiralty' and 'had its say' on all matters of importance. With a dilatory man like Kerr at the head of affairs, unsurprisingly, Custance had moved to fill the vacuum. But Battenberg continued: 'Still the Department is carefully labelled "purely advisory" and if the civilian element *can* "short circuit" it, it occasionally does so. The time has come when . . . the well digested, focused opinions of the many and versatile brains at work . . . cannot be lightly brushed aside or ignored. . . . [The head] should be a member of the Board, second only to the First Sea Lord (the Commander-in-Chief) but that officer's first assistant. *Preparation for War* in every particular should be his charge.'[52]

Battenberg had laid bare the problem of a naval staff. All were agreed on its necessity; but to whom should it be responsible? If he were a member of the Board its head would become responsible in practice to the civilian, political First Lord. Hindsight makes the solution easy: the First Naval Lord should be Chief of the Naval Staff, with a deputy, *responsible only to him*, and not a member of the Board, and with a mechanism by which the expert views of the staff as approved by the First Naval Lord, could be conveyed direct to the Cabinet and not filtered by a politician with other motives.

On 25 February Fisher sent two papers to Selborne which should finally dispose of the myth that he opposed a war staff. They were *On the increasing necessity for a General Staff for the Navy to meet War Requirements* and *The Strategical Distribution of Our Fleets*, in the first of which he wrote: 'We must have a very much larger department than the present Intelligence Bureau at the Admiralty with its associated small though excellent Greenwich College Class for Strategical Instruction. We have a magnificent model to work upon and to guide us! The Great German General Staff, the admiration of the world and the organiser of the greatest victories of modern time is absolutely applicable in its ideas and its organisation to meet all the needs of the Navy. It is essential that our "Fighting" Admirals should also be "thinking Admirals".'[53]

Fisher was promoted Admiral on 2 November 1901. Impressed by his visit to Malta, Selborne, in a light-hearted letter on 9 February, 1902, offered him the appointment of Second Naval Lord. But he added a caution: 'If we ever differ, as in the natural course of events we probably occasionally shall, no one off the Board must ever know of our differences. . . . So long as we do not resign, our solidity to the Service and world outside must be absolute.'[54]

The following May Custance exposed to Bridge his enmity toward Fisher: 'The worst thing I know of is the advent of Fisher with all his wild, superficial ideas. No man has less grasp of principles. Beresford is as mischievous as he can be, but is losing prestige rapidly.'[55]

On hearing of his appointment Fisher wrote to White: 'It's plain to anyone that Lord Selborne has got his head the right way by his Parliamentary statement. . . . I do hope Beresford will be circumspect in his speech; he has a magnificent opportunity on 14th March; but any indiscretion or exaggeration will be seized on, and the red herring thus provided will be used to draw the public off the scent.'[56]

Fisher and Beresford shared some opinions; they had discussed the naval staff problem numerous times, and Beresford now ventilated them in Parliament. But, fed with information by Custance, he abandoned restraint. To the London Chamber of Commerce on 14th March he recommended Fisher as 'War Lord'. Fisher was furious. He had already given much thought to his personnel reforms and looked forward to his new position. He wrote to Selborne: 'I am very sorry about Beresford's extravagances. He promised me he would be circumspect and judicious. He has been neither, and has personally annoyed me very much by praising me, which invariably reacts in "envy, hatred, malice and all uncharitableness", and recommends me for "War Lord", a berth I do not wish for (even if it were created), as I prefer to be Second Naval Lord to anything else (even to First Sea Lord) (*Sic*) *because* . . . the most serious questions of all appear to lie in the province of the Second Sea Lord (*Sic*).'[57]

On 28 March he wrote to Lord Spencer:

> *There is a great deal in what Beresford urges*, but he exaggerates so much that his good ideas become deformities and are unpractical, and his want of taste and his uncontrolled desire for notoriety alienates his brother officers! He promised me faithfully (for we have always been good friends) that he would be circumspect and judicious in what he was going to say in public. He has been neither! . . .
>
> He is a first rate officer afloat, no better exists in my opinion (which is a good deal to say!) and in the two years he has been under my command he has never failed once to do everything he has been ordered, cheerfully and zealously, and *has always done it well*.[58]

Whether Fisher's avowal of friendship and praises for the operational skill of the political admiral were sincere is doubtful. He probably felt it necessary not to exhibit antagonism. But Beresford was involving himself in public arguments. Admirals Penrose Fitzgerald and Vesey Hamilton described his pronouncements in the Mediterranean as 'subversive of all discipline' and 'contrary to the best traditions of the Navy'. Beresford wrote to *The Times* replying to 'ignorant and childish attacks' on him and untruthfully claimed he had written with the knowledge of the C-in-C.

The Times gave a guarded welcome to his re-election: 'We need not consider too closely . . . whether the gallant admiral is the ideal "Member for the Navy". We might desire a man of less exuberant and impulsive oratory and . . . of greater sobriety of judgment and expression.'[59] It then referred to his letter to the *Daily Mail*: 'We do not know how far he was responsible for that untoward publication, and we would fain believe that he was not responsible for it in any way; but in that case he must have shown

82

scant judgment in selecting a correspondent who could not be trusted not to disclose a private letter, neither intended nor suitable for publication.'[60]

Beresford would have been wiser to have left the matter. But not he. 'The publication of that letter was a very grave mistake, but all blame (which I own is thoroughly deserved) . . . should be laid on my shoulders as the person solely responsible.'[61] Inevitably, Arnold-Forster, having accepted White's assurance of Beresford's innocence, which the latter had not contradicted, was accused of misleading the House. Beresford had to make a personal statement, admitting his responsibility. 'It was insinuated that I should have written home and told the authorities this. I conceive I ought not to do anything of the sort, unless the authorities asked me, because there was nothing in my letter about the strength of the fleet that I had gained through my official position. I am, however, prepared to receive any punishment the authorities choose to award me for not having complied with the regulations.'[62] The first part of the statement was evasive and inaccurate, the penultimate blatantly untrue and the final sentence a cynical challenge to the Admiralty. The *Daily Mail* was indignant and demanded an explanation from White, who wrote: 'Mr. Arnold-Forster's answer in the House of Commons is both contrary to facts and also to written evidence which he knows me to possess. I await an apology from Mr. Arnold-Forster for making a statement in the House on 9 July, [1901] which was untrue.'[63]

This was soon forthcoming. Arnold-Forster had accepted White's admission of responsibility. Beresford had, he said, followed with offensive charges against him although he held in his hand a letter in which Beresford had denied any offence. 'I did not rise in my place, because the letter was marked "private", and when I asked the noble Lord if I was at liberty to state what he had told me, he refused. Only after I had written telling him that this was intolerable did he accord me the permission I needed.'[64] Arnold-Forster then quoted the relevant passage:

> On the basis of Mr. White's letter, published in *The Times* of 6 July, you were perfectly justified in making the statement that he was responsible for publishing my letter. I told him he could do what he liked with it when he asked me if he might publish it, because there was nothing in it that trespassed on confidential reports. But I was absolutely wrong to do this. The Admiralty never asked me 'whether directly or indirectly I had caused the publication, etc.' Had they done so, I should have told the truth, with the probable result that I should have been ordered to haul down my flag. But why should they have asked me the question, after Mr. White's letter?[65]

Arnold-Forster pointed out that Beresford's letter to *The Times* was written almost three months after he had hauled down his flag, whereupon Beresford admitted responsibility for the position in which the

Parliamentary Secretary had been placed, claiming that the latter wished to make extracts from a private letter, from which false impressions could be adduced. 'The only passage I desired to omit,' came the reply, 'was one so offensive to Mr. White that I thought the noble Lord would not wish me to publish it.'[66]

Beresford rambled on, attempting to embark upon a dissertation about the Mediterranean Fleet: 'When I went out to the Mediterranean I found the fleet dangerously weak.' But the Speaker put a stop to it and he continued his incoherent explanation, once again inferring that he had been the driving force in improving the fleet: 'I do not regret writing my letter, because the fleet was in a very dangerous position with regard to its fighting efficiency. Between June 1900 and June 1901 there were few additions made to the fleet.' Again the Speaker stopped him. 'I have been driven to mention these things,' he continued, but at last he realized he was not to be allowed to make a speech and ended with a futile apology, far too late to undo the damage he had done himself, finally admitting White had several letters authorizing publication.[67] Unashamed, he spoke at length on the Navy Estimates, making a thinly veiled attack on Fisher:

> I want to call attention to the want of organisation and the lack of efficiency. . . . There are thirteen battleships there now as against ten last year. Those thirteen are ready to fight. . . . Stores are now 80% better. The fleet then in the Mediterranean would have exhausted its coal stocks in a few weeks, no provision having been made for war. . . .
>
> What did the responsible authorities in the Mediterranean say about all this? I was not responsible; I was exceeding my duty in mentioning it at all; I was only the Second-in-Command and was there to obey. But members know that in both services, officers have continually to threaten to resign to get things put right.[68]

There is no evidence that at any time Beresford threatened resignation. Arnold-Forster rose and neatly demolished him.

> The noble Lord told us that it was due to his representations that the Mediterranean coal supply was increased. What actually happened? At the end of 1899 the Commander-in-Chief called attention to the fact that the stock would not be sufficient. On 5 February 1900 an additional supply was sanctioned by the Admiralty, four days before the noble Lord hoisted his flag. He has also suggested that, because of some agitation, more battleships were sent to the Mediterranean. But those battleships were not built in six months; they were laid down three years before, and were sent to the Mediterranean when they became available, in pursuance of Admiralty policy.[69]

7

THE ICONOCLAST

Fisher returned to the Admiralty on 5 June 1902. He wasted no time. Within minutes he sent the first pages to the printer of the preamble of the new schemes of training and entry of officers.[1] Selborne's decision was opportune, for matters of personnel were in turmoil and needed sorting out.

Among current problems was the status of 'civil' officers, especially engineers. Early paddle vessels were never intended as warships and their engineers were no more than mechanics, men of little education and less refinement, with no rank or rating. It was hardly surprising in the Victorian atmosphere of social distinction that a gulf existed between them and the 'military' officers. As the complexity and importance of ships' machinery increased, a far better trained and educated man was needed and soon a higher standard of education was demanded for engineer officers than for deck officers. In 1875 the Cooper-Key Committee recommended that engineer officers should belong to the military branch, with equality of rank, pay and promotion.[2] When the Royal Naval Engineering College was opened in 1880, they were recruited from a social level, comparable with deck officers.[3] But recruitment was always a problem. An engineer officer's job was necessarily a dirty one and no matter how learned, any profession that involved coal, oil and ashes was unlikely to appeal to Victorian middle-class gentility. The disdainful attitude of the deck officers to engineers was not surprising and was exacerbated as steam displaced sail and the practical work of the deck officers declined. They no longer controlled the sails and could stand back and adopt a detached role. Imitating the habits of the more aristocratic Army, they introduced expensive wines into naval messes and entertainment became more lavish. More and more officers joined the Service from aristocratic families. A high proportion had titles, and those without aspired to rub shoulders with them. 'Those naval officers born with blue blood were as conscious of it as their cousins in the House of Lords. Aboard ship they lost no opportunity of superimposing naval pomp on their own basic magnificence.'[4] Remnants lingered even between the world wars. 'A roll-call of the officers of HMS *Queen Elizabeth* in 1928 would have sounded like a courtly assembly of the olden time. More than a polo team might be raised among the peers on Sir Roger [Keyes]'s staff. Even the midshipmen, hand-picked like the rest . . . included two lords, a baronet and an earl's son.'[5]

The Service would have benefited if, on the introduction of steam, the deck officers had accepted the training necessary to supervise the running and maintenance of machinery, but such duties were thought of little importance and it would have been absurd to expect them to do so before the introduction of the screw propeller, when it was too late; the new branch was established. Adoption of the Cooper-Key Report stopped short of military status, and by then there were additional aspects. The deck officers smelt competition.

Meanwhile the large numbers of men needed to man the guns were only intermittently required to handle the sails, and other duties had to be found, resulting in even greater concentration on ships' cleanliness and appearance. Commanders vied with each other for the beauty of their paintwork, polished brass and white decks. Officers often spent £2,000 from their own pockets in beautifying their ships (about 5½ years pay!). This was the avenue to promotion and once an officer reached captain's rank, promotion to full admiral was assured. The authority of the deck officer, his control of all the doings of the ship, the certainty of his future, created an attitude of complacency and superiority and he made every effort to ensure the powerlessness of the engineer officer was maintained. For at least the last twenty years of the nineteenth century a huge agitation took place for improvement in the status and powers of the engineer officers. The level of discontent grew to unacceptable proportions and was much discussed in the national Press. Recruitment almost dried up.

When Fisher arrived at the Admiralty the situation was already serious; as far back as 1871 he had written that the engineer was 'the coming man'.[6] The shortage of engineer officers of the quality needed had coincided with the greatest expansion and technological development the Navy had experienced. Agitation spread throughout the country, meetings were held by the professional institutions and the Press made increasingly vehement comment. Fisher wrote to Selborne: 'We want, for the good of the Service, to get rid of this discontent and increasing soreness. It is for this reason that I hope, at some early stage of our discussion after the holidays, you may be able to say something explicit before the next session opens, when the enemy will open fire, so I hear.'[7] A few days later he wrote to Arnold White: 'My programme . . . has been described as a "damned big pill to swallow"! But I have retorted that if not swallowed soon, it will shortly be so damned big that they won't be able to swallow it at all! This remark has induced conviction and *not* the soundness of the arguments for reform.'[8]

Fisher recognized that there were two problems. Technological advances in engineering and weaponry demanded an officer of much greater intelligence, technical awareness and scientific education than before. The dilettante officer was no longer acceptable and improvement in the position of engineer officers was essential if progress was to continue.

There was another problem. Royal Marines were carried in all the larger ships as detachments available to carry out limited operations at short notice. They had always taken part in the daily running of the ship, but properly regarded themselves more as soldiers than sailors. Marine officers had too little to do, many were bored at sea, limited accommodation could not be wasted on unproductive officers and their talents were wasted.

In six months Fisher produced a scheme to solve these problems. His solution seemed revolutionary to his contemporaries, though it was a logical step. Indeed, it proved too revolutionary and subsequent events largely negated Fisher's efforts, though experience in the twentieth century led in 1956 to an even more far-reaching reorganization.

HMS *Britannia* was the training establishment for naval cadets from 1859, but at the end of the century a college was built at Dartmouth, and when Fisher took office the building was already fast progressing. The scheme, known as the Selborne-Fisher Scheme, was announced on Christmas Day 1902.[9] Its main object was the amalgamation of the deck and Engineering branches. Cadets would enter Dartmouth between the ages of twelve and thirteen, would be trained together until they reached the rank of sub-lieutenant, when they would be distributed between the two branches and the Royal Marines.

> The result aimed at is, to a certain point, community of knowledge and lifelong community of sentiment. The only machinery which can produce this result is early companionship and community of instruction. These opportunities will be secured by a policy of:-
>
> > One system of Supply
> > One system of Entry
> > One system of Training.[10]

The specialization of an officer was shown by a letter after his rank in the Navy List, (E), (G), (N), (T), etc. to denote engineering, gunnery, navigation and torpedo. The curriculum at Dartmouth was to include a very high proportion of engineering. But amalgamation was not complete, for an engineer remained an engineer and a marine a marine. Specialization was 'definite and final', though engineer officers and marines were available for bridge watchkeeping or general duties and the deck officer could lend a hand

87

in the engine room. But the objective was not interchangeability; it was to give deck officers a scientific education to understand new weapons and equipment daily becoming available and at the same time to train engineers in the skills of a sailor so as to build up that 'lifelong community of sentiment' Fisher so clearly saw necessary. The appointments of Admirals Superintendent of the Dockyards and Controller of the Navy were to be filled exclusively by engineer officers.

Fisher early gained the support of Selborne, but had a hard task to convince his naval colleagues on the Board. He wrote to his son:

> I've got through the biggest part of the big scheme I have been working on since June 10th last, and Lord Selborne seems very pleased; But I think the rest of my colleagues look upon me as a sort of combined Robespierre and Gambetta![11]

After one session he told his private secretary, 'My dear Walker, I did not think admirals could be so rude to one another'.[12] But even grudging approval of the Board did not end his problems. King-Hall recorded in his diary the petty objections to the scheme. Egerton, then captain of *Vernon*, opposed it:-

> [Fisher] led him into his room, then shook his fist at him, saying:- 'If you oppose my education scheme I will crush you'. Fisher was beside himself with rage – Egerton kept cool and refused to be bullied into agreeing with Fisher that torpedo lieutenants could be made in three months. Soon afterwards Fisher became C-in-C at Portsmouth. . . . Fisher made himself as disagreeable as possible. . . . When the three months elapsed, Egerton refused to sign the certificates of the Torpedo Lieutenants that they were competent, and Fisher managed to keep Egerton waiting eighteen months before he hoisted his flag. Arbuthnot, who also opposed him, has never hoisted his flag.[13]

There were forty-five captains above Egerton in the 1902 *Navy List* and the junior rear-admiral was four years senior to him, so he was not kept waiting long! The length of time required to train a torpedo lieutenant might be a matter for discussion, but not for opposing the whole scheme.

Support came from the King 'He gave me his unfaltering support right through, unswervingly, though every sycophantic effort was exhausted in the endeavour to alienate him.'[14] The Prince of Wales (later King George V), wrote: 'I call it a grand scheme and wish it every success. No doubt it will be severely criticised, especially by the *old ones*, who are too conservative for our modern days. . . . I consider the whole scheme a splendid one.'[15]

Opposition came from diehards, and 'prehistoric admirals' suffered apoplexy, like Admiral Edward Field, who had joined the Navy in 1841, was promoted captain in 1869 and had never been employed since, steadily promoted on the retired list. Admiral Sir Arthur Moore wrote to his brother about this 'dreadful revolution. . . . It is likely that the Commander (Engineering) will be next in seniority to the Captain. If the latter is disabled in action, the former must leave his engine room at high speed, to go on deck and handle . . . the ship, at possibly a critical moment.'[16] He had overlooked the fact that engineering specialists were not intended to take sea-going command, but his view was typical of the hasty judgments of that generation of naval officers.

But opposition was not confined to out-of-date admirals. Admiral Sir Herbert Richmond, as late as 1919, was to write to Carlyon Bellairs, (a former Lieutenant who, after a disagreement with Fisher, had retired, entered Parliament and become one of Fisher's influential enemies), 'The engine-room artificers . . . say that they get as good a training in the *Fisgard* as the old engineer cadet used to get; that several have received commissioned rank; that they have done their work efficiently and are better practical engineers than the Osborne-trained youth – why then should [they] not be allowed to be the engineer officers of the Navy? They want an engineers' mess (isn't it funny to see it all coming round again?) and promotion up to the highest ranks.'[17] Such a concept demonstrates ignorance of the needs of the Navy, the necessity for professional status for engineer officers and the difference between the artificer and the professional engineer. It represents a reversion to the middle of the nineteenth century.

Beresford declined to lead the opposition. As usual he had got wind of the scheme and on 8 August attempted in the Commons to pre-empt Fisher's initiatives: 'I earnestly hope the Parliamentary Secretary will be able to tell the House that the grievances of the engineers have now passed the long continued stage of consideration.'[18] Interviewed on its announcement, he said, 'The strongest opponent of the scheme will acknowledge that it is a brilliant and statesmanlike effort to grapple with a problem upon the sound settlement of which depends the future efficiency of the British Navy. . . . Naval officers [will] have an opportunity of adding to their professional attainments the essential knowledge of marine engineering. . . .The present status of naval engineer officers could not continue. . . . The abolition of distinction regarding entry has settled this point once and for ever.[19] He wrote to Fisher; 'In 20 years' time naval officers will wonder how a steam navy could possibly be run and administered by an executive who knew nothing whatever about steam.'[20]

Support came from younger, more progressive officers, even Custance! Among politicians, Goschen opposed it, but 'Arnold-Forster called it the most colossal work he had ever heard of.'[21] Later he said it was 'one of the greatest reforms that had been undertaken for the Navy in past years' and Arthur Lee (later Lord Lee of Fareham) said the results of Fisher's policy were 'a Navy greater in strength and efficiency, better manned and equipped, better trained and educated in every way, and more ready for instant service' than ever before. Julian Corbett wrote an article in the *Monthly Review* praising the scheme and, though the *Naval and Military Record* was at first opposed, it suddenly changed its view and found it 'impossible to praise too highly'.

But the scheme grossly underestimated the engineering profession. The existing engineers, with a better general education than their deck contemporaries, then spent five or six years studying it, while the cadet in *Britannia* spent only two years there, and at 16 his general education ceased, which created opposition from the existing engineer officers.

Fisher increased the training at Dartmouth to four years, cadets entering at 13. The syllabus included 1,346 hours of engineering, 1,023 on science, including electricity, while general education took 3,222 hours, leaving only 249 hours for seamanship and 258 for navigation. For the deck officer there was too little stress on the last three, while the scientific education was inadequate to provide engineers of professional standing. After his time at sea, the sub-lieutenant who elected for engineering did six months at Greenwich, followed by six months at Keyham which it was claimed would be enough, in view of the volume of engineering instruction at Dartmouth. Thus there were valid reasons on both sides for disputing the merits of the scheme; both engineers and seamen would be inadequately trained.

The existing engineer officers were to be allowed merely to fade out, just as the old navigating officers had in the nineteenth century. Secretly, Fisher promised the old branch that they would be incorporated in the new scheme later. He obtained changes in their designation and they became engineer-rear-admirals, engineer-captains and so on, but retained their non-military status and their juniors, the lieutenants (E), appeared before them in the *Navy List*, among the deck officers.

But the historian who wrote (*in the 1990's!*) of the 'devotion' Fisher 'inspired in the engineers whom he rescued from second-class citizenship' is far off the mark. They are all long dead! Since 1902 entry has been identical. The present author, for example, qualified for any of the branches existing between the wars, deck, engineer, paymaster, Royal Marines (and Sandhurst or Cranwell).

In the event the Royal Marines never entered the scheme at all, partly because of quiet but determined opposition from the Corps, though Hankey enthusiastically supported it, as did Major General Sir George Aston, then a Major RMA at the Admiralty, and partly because volunteers from Dartmouth were almost non-existent.

But the new College at Dartmouth was designed for a course of only two years, now doubled in length and including engineer and Royal Marine candidates, aggravated by the expanding Navy. Extra accommodation had to be found so Fisher persuaded the King to make available Victoria's old home on the Isle of Wight, Osborne House.

The selection of officers was confined to those whose parents could afford £1,000 for their sons' education (about £53,000 in the 1990s) which restricted it to about 3% of the population. 'Is it wise or expedient to take our Nelsons from so narrow a class?' asked Fisher.[22] Indeed Nelson himself would have been unable to join the Navy in the latter years of the nineteenth century.

But the *Naval and Military Record* said in 1910: 'We should view with great apprehension any attempt to officer the fleet at all largely with men of humble birth'. This was not snobbery. A naval officer must, even today, be a gentleman, whatever his origins, and naval ratings held those of humble birth with little respect; they saw them as one of themselves and 'out of their station'. They were as much snobs as the officers, fond of serving under men of distinguished background. Moreover, standards of personality and character were important and 'diplomatic' work undertaken by officers on foreign stations required that they should be able to hold their own with the highest levels of foreign society.

But Fisher disagreed 'on the far higher ground of efficiency'. Ability was not confined to the well-to-do. He wanted no fees at Dartmouth. This was not the last time he was to show liberal views and the King often chaffed him as a Socialist.

But Fisher's reforms were not confined to officers. Since introduction in 1868 the rating of Engine Room Artificer had been recruited from adult skilled craftsmen. Unaccustomed to naval discipline, they found it hard to adapt to a restrictive life. Skills and abilities varied; though each had completed an apprenticeship as fitter, boilermaker, coppersmith, for example, knowledge of theoretical engineering was limited. A craft-trained man had no knowledge of how triple-expansion engines worked, much less how to detect malfunction or keep them in the fine adjustment necessary; he might never have seen one. ERAs had to be trained as technicians as well as craftsmen. Even Fisher did not recognize this, as his reference to 'engine-driving' shows. But he fully understood the need for men accustomed to naval discipline from an early age. On 28 March 1903 an Order in Council created the rating of 'Boy Artificer', entering at the age of 15. In the same month twenty-six boys joined *Algiers*. They were trained in the Steam Reserve Factory, later to become the Mechanical Training Establishment.

The navigating branch, gunnery and torpedo training also came under his scrutiny. Descendants of the feudal 'masters' had remained a separate branch with ranks of navigating lieutenant, staff commander and staff captain, most learning at sea as masters' mates, until in 1873 military officers took over navigation. The numbers of the old branch decreased until in 1879 they were replaced by lieutenants (N), though entries into the old branch continued until 1893, the last staff captain retiring in 1913.[23]

But methods remained crude; at the turn of the century a young officer produced the first 'speed and distance table', showing distance run at various speeds. However obvious, this was considered so great an advance that the Admiralty issued it to all ships.

When Fisher was C-in-C Mediterranean, his fleet had met the Channel Fleet in Lagos, and a navigating officer, Henry Oliver (later Admiral of the Fleet Sir Henry) unburdened his mind to Fisher. Oliver and Lieutenant Herbert Richmond discussed the matter and prepared a joint paper. In 1903 Fisher selected Richmond, just promoted commander, as his naval assistant, who showed him the paper. He immediately formed a committee which included Oliver and Richmond, to make proposals for the navigating branch. Richmond wrote in his diary: 'It really is wonderful to have a man at the head of affairs who can take the matter up as Fisher has, who is absolutely approachable and ready to listen to suggestions and act on them'.[24] In only a few months Fisher established a navigation school in the old cruiser *Mercury*. An Admiralty Circular of 15 June 1903 affirmed 'Lieutenants (N) will in future be placed on exactly the same footing as regards executive command and ship duties generally as Gunnery and Torpedo Lieutenants.'

Fisher's huge correspondence with Selborne covered many other subjects, Boys' Training Ships, technicalities of gunnery, the gunnery and torpedo schools, the promotion of fifty warrant officers to lieutenant, tactics, strategy and a host of more minor matters. But his tenure was short. When he had been only four months in office, he wrote to his son:

> I think it is quite decided that I go as Commander-in-Chief at Portsmouth on August 28th next and Captain Tyrwhitt, who is now Lord Selborne's Private Secretary and was my Flag Captain, says Lord Selborne tells him privately he is determined I shall come back as First Sea Lord when Sir Walter Kerr goes.[25]

Officially, the reason given for Fisher's early departure was that he was required to supervise the institution of the new course at Osborne. This is not convincing for it would be as easy to do so from London, with more authority. He disliked serving with Kerr and it was undesirable to move straight from 2nd to 1st Naval Lord. Certainly he needed the money; the C-in-C's pay was £4,000 p.a, about double that of the Second Sea Lord. But he was anxious his departure should not be misunderstood and sought Thursfield's advice. 'Admiral Heneage told a friend of mine lately that the members of the Board were all at loggerheads! *He knew this for a fact!* and Fitzgerald has said *they hope for the best* when I am got out of the Admiralty!'[26]

After a short leave at his beloved Marienbad he hoisted his flag at

Portsmouth on 31 August 1903. He threw himself into activity immediately on arrival. 'I find no end of slackness in all directions,' he wrote to his son. But he was enjoying himself. 'I really don't think I shall care to leave here, it's so delightful not being in an office all day and being able to have a fling at ship work.'[27] 'It's curious that every place I go there seems more to do than the last.'[28]

At Portsmouth he became the driving force behind submarines, which were now being taken seriously. In a speech at the Royal Academy banquet in October 1903 he said:

> We require a fearless, vigorous and progressive administration open to any reform and never resting on its oars – for to stop is to go back – and forecasting every eventuality. I will just take two instances at hazard. Look at the submarine boat and wireless telegraphy. When they are perfected we do not know what a revolution will come about. In their inception they were the weapons of the weak. Now they loom large as the weapons of the strong.[29]

Two types of submarine had been developed in the United States, but opinions were divided on their practical value. A.K.Wilson's unfortunate description 'Damned un-English' has repeatedly been taken out of context to suggest that *all* naval officers opposed submarines, and many did. In 1900 five vessels of the Holland design were ordered from Vickers, Sons and Maxim. At Fisher's suggestion, Bacon, then a captain and torpedo specialist, was placed on the Controller's staff to supervise experiments. 'I knew nothing about submarines; no more did anyone else,' he wrote.[30] On the surface they were propelled by petrol engines of 120 horsepower, with internal mechanical sparking plugs which gave endless trouble. The danger of petrol fumes and carbon monoxide from the exhaust was so great that the Engineer-in-Chief, Sir John Durston, refused to have anything to do with them when powered by petrol engines. Sir William White, Director of Naval Construction, would have nothing to do with them in any form. Submerged, they were blind, navigation relying on dead reckoning. Propelled under water by batteries driving electric motors which sparked badly, there was always danger that petrol fumes would be ignited; when charging, the batteries gave off explosive gases and explosions were not uncommon. White mice were kept in cages to indicate accumulations of carbon monoxide. (I wonder why they were white?).

Safer heavy oil engines (diesel engines), invented by Richard Hornsby and Sons in 1891 were not used. Bacon visited Hornsby's and found the weight too great, but does not appear to have pursued the development of lighter engines. It was some years before they were adopted for larger submarines. The early Hollands were too small for seagoing work and before the last was complete Bacon obtained authority to build larger vessels with engines of

500 horsepower, batteries of double the capacity, aiming at a speed of eight knots underwater and twelve on the surface. A conning tower was provided and Bacon pressed the development of a periscope.

The five Holland boats were hazardously brought to Portsmouth, most of the way under tow and Bacon took them on a passage round the Isle of Wight. Three broke down before they passed the Spit Fort and only one got as far as Cowes.

Meanwhile, the engines of A1, the first larger boat, developed only 320 horsepower, giving her just ten knots, so a new design was put in hand, while the trials of A1 continued for six months.

> Hot bearings, scored liners, red-hot pistons, fouled sparking plugs, burnt-out plugs, white-hot induction pipe, all came along. . . . Day after day, night after night, week after week, month after month, trials went on with failure following failure. . . . All the time the hulls of the boats on the stock were growing . . . and still no engines.[31]

Despite all this Fisher and Bacon, almost alone, saw the change the new vessel would bring. Fisher recognized at once that the submarine compelled revision of fleet disposition and revolutionized naval warfare. But the 'historical school' disparaged submarines. Beresford had been promoted vice-admiral in October 1902 and given command of the Channel Squadron, resigning Parliament after less than a year, and hoisting his flag in *Majestic* on 17 April 1903. He now described submarines as 'Fisher's toys' and said that a machine gun 'would soon put paid to them'. Yet he later claimed to have proposed building two experimental vessels and that the five Holland boats were purchased at his suggestion.[32]

Bacon's responsibility to the Controller did not inhibit Fisher, for the boats were based at Portsmouth under his command. But the ridicule directed at them forced him to work discreetly to convince the Board, especially the First Lord. 'I am working subterraneously about the submarines and there are already "upheavals" in consequence.'[33]

In October 1903, having witnessed the new boats exercising, he wrote a paper entitled *The effects of Submarine Boats*, which he prefaced: *These remarks can only be fully appreciated by those who witnessed the flotilla of Submarine boats now at Portsmouth, practising out in the open sea.*

> There is this immense fundamental difference between the automobile torpedo and the gun – the torpedo has no trajectory: it travels horizontally and hits below the water, so all its hits are vital hits. . . . The Submarine Boat which carries this automobile torpedo is up to the present date absolutely unattackable. When you see [surface ships] on the horizon, you can send others after them to attack them or drive them away! You can see them – you can fire at them – you can avoid

94

them – you can chase them – but with the Submarine Boat you can do nothing! . . .

It must revolutionise Naval Tactics for this simple reason – that the present battle formation of ships in a single line presents a target of such length that the chances are altogether in favour of the Whitehead torpedo hitting some ship in the line. . . . [But the single line ahead survived.]

It affects the Army, because, imagine even one submarine boat with a flock of transports in sight loaded with some two or three thousand troops! Imagine the effects of one such transport going to the bottom in a few seconds with its living freight!

Even the bare thought makes invasion impossible! . . .

It affects the existence of the Empire because . . . we are in peril now by having only 20 per cent of our very minimum requirements in Submarine Boats, because we are waiting for perfection! . . . We strain at the gnat of perfection and swallow the camel of unreadiness!

We shall be found unready once too often.[34]

His suggestion of abandoning the single line ahead, which he had advocated strongly in the past, was a good example of his adaptability to changing conditions His views were reinforced by trials carried out against the iron-clad *Belleisle*. Heavily reinforced under the hull, she was sunk in Portsmouth harbour in seven minutes by one torpedo.

Long afterwards, in April 1918, Hankey, Secretary of the War Cabinet, wrote to Fisher: 'Last night I dined with Lord Esher. He showed me letters of yours dated 1904 describing in detail the German submarine campaign of 1917. It is the most amazing thing I ever read; not one letter only, but several.'[35]

But though Bacon's reports were being taken more seriously, he and Fisher were fighting a lonely battle. In January Fisher wrote, 'Satan disguised as an Angel of Light wouldn't succeed in persuading the Admiralty or the Navy that in the course of some few years submarines will prevent any fleet remaining at sea continuously, either in the Mediterranean or the English Channel.'[36]

Despite his view that submarines should be outlawed as pirates, Wilson suggested manoeuvres between the six available boats and the Home Fleet under his own command. Fisher persuaded the Admiralty to agree.

Two of Sir Arthur's ships were 'sunk' and the battleship *Empress of India* only saved itself by moving off at high speed. None of the submarines was successfully attacked, though unhappily A1 was sunk with all hands in collision with a liner leaving Southampton. (She is now at the Submarine Museum, Gosport.) But Fisher had made his point. The Prince of Wales

95

wrote to him of the enormous future for submarines, advocating building more at once.

Throughout his time at Portsmouth, Fisher put a great effort into publicizing the Navy and particularly submarines, by inviting many prominent men in public life to visit him as guests. In February the King came and the next month the Prince of Wales spent a week at Admiralty House with all his family.

Although the Controller, Rear Admiral W.H.May (afterwards Admiral of the Fleet Sir William), did nothing to obstruct Bacon, there was little enthusiasm on the Board, compared with Fisher's almost schoolboy passion for submarines, and his deep thought about their development and employment: 'It's astounding to me, *perfectly astounding*, how the very best amongst us fail to realise the vast impending revolution in naval warfare and naval strategy that the submarine will accomplish!' He went on to describe the escape of *Empress of India*, from a torpedo launched by a submarine

> of the 'pre-Adamite' period, small, slow, badly fitted, with no periscope at all . . . and yet this submarine followed that battleship for a solid two hours under water coming up gingerly about a mile off every now and then (like a beaver) just to take a fresh compass bearing of her prey, and then down again! Remember that this is done (and I want specifically to emphasise the point) when the Lieutenant in command of the boat [was] out in her for the first time in his life on his own account and half the crew never out before either! Why it's wonderful! And so what results may we expect from bigger and faster boats, and periscopes more powerful than the naked eye (such as the latest pattern one I saw the other day), and with experienced officers and crews, and with nests of these submarines acting together? . . . In all seriousness I don't think it is even *faintly* realised – *The immense impending revolution which the submarines will effect as offensive weapons of war.* When you calmly sit down and work out what will happen in the narrow waters of the Channel and the Mediterranean . . . it makes your hair stand on end![37]

It seems surprising that he should have to press the matter on the Admiralty, who should surely have been taking the initiative, and his foresight is impressive. He even predicted the German wolf-pack system of the Second World War.

A few days later, frustrated, he wrote: 'I have had a reply to my letter to him from my dear friend the Controller of the Navy. It is plausible but damnable. This is what he (in effect) says: "Yes, I fully admit all you say, but we are very busy now perfecting the type of submarines! Just you *wait* patiently till we get our new 'B' type, and then we'll order submarines in shoals! *Don't* hustle us! Plenty of time!" *Give peace in our time O Lord!*'[38]

Fisher can be criticized for his impatience. It might be better to await experience to incorporate improvements in the B' type before ordering large numbers, but the key lies in the words 'Plenty of time!' 'Some people,' he continued, 'think you can go round the corner and buy a submarine like a pound of sugar! *There will be no time for anything!* War will come like the Day of Judgment! Suddenly! Unexpectedly! Overwhelmingly!'[39] But at this juncture even Fisher saw submarines as part of the operational fleet rather than commerce raiders.

But after the disasters of the South African War a Commission of Enquiry under Lord Elgin had investigated its conduct. Lord Esher and two others had signed a minority report highly critical of the War Office, which had grown like Topsy, with ill-defined responsibility, over-centralization, overlapping between the Commander-in-Chief and Secretary of State for War and vague terms of reference which allowed escape from blame when anything went wrong. Since Waterloo the Army had been organized only for colonial wars. Wellington was Commander-in-Chief in 1827–28 and from 1842 until his death in 1852 at the age of 83, adhering to the belief that soldiers should be recruited from the gutter and wealthy gentlemen alone were capable of command. Lord Hardinge followed and altered nothing. In 1856 command passed to the Duke of Cambridge, a stiff-necked, diehard cousin of the Queen. Not until 1871 did Gladstone abolish purchase of commissions and introduce promotion by selection, steadfastly resisted by the Duke, who remained in office for 39 years, though latterly his position was a mere sinecure, his long absences hardly noticed. He was succeeded in 1895 by Wolseley, who found his post so emasculated that he called himself 'a fifth wheel in a carriage',[40] and in 1901 by Lord Roberts, already in his 69th year.

The Elgin Commission reported in 1903. The War Office had recognized that khaki uniforms were needed, yet the only reserves were scarlet and blue; the Lee-Enfield rifles were wrongly sighted, their bullets apt to strip in the barrel; there were virtually no reserves of horses, saddles or horseshoes and the cavalry sword, still regarded as an essential weapon, was quite useless, with only eighty in reserve; there were no plans, no maps and no staff officers. In the belief that it would take only three months for the dashing British Army to deal with a few rustic farmers, only rudimentary preparations were made. The minority report said: 'Only an extraordinary combination of fortunate circumstances, external and internal, saved the Empire during the early months of 1900 and there is no reason to expect a repetition of such fortune if, as appears probable, the next national emergency still finds us discussing our preparation.'

Victoria's name never appeared in the *Navy List* and on his accession Edward ordered that he should be shown as head of both services. St. John Brodrick, (later Lord Midleton), Secretary of State since 1900, and Roberts

97

showed remarkable determination to resist reform, opposing the abolition of the post of Commander-in-Chief and Esher's proposals for a General Staff.[41] Fisher wrote to Selborne from the Mediterranean, 'Mr. Brodrick will never reorganise the British Army unless he begins *ab ovo* and does away with the Sergeant-Major principle, and that the British Army is to be disorganised for six months out of the year for the leave season.'[42] The King called the War Office a 'mutual admiration society' and demanded it should be organized on the lines of the Admiralty. Roberts was convinced by Esher, whom Balfour chose to accomplish reform.

Esher, then aged 52, had been private secretary to Hartington. For five years an MP and for seven years secretary to HM Office of Works, he was more outstanding for the positions he refused – editor of the *Daily News* and the *New Review*, undersecretary of the Colonies, Governor of Cape Colony, biographer of Disraeli. Now he refused the War Office, and later the GCB and Viceroyalty of India. His superlative use of words, philosophical argument and logic were inescapable. A favourite of Queen Victoria, a friend of Edward VII, he was passionately interested in Defence. He had access to all the ministries. Hankey wrote:

> He had a finger in every pie. Neither Balfour nor Campbell-Bannerman, nor Asquith could dispense with him at the Defence Committee. For ten years he hardly missed a meeting. . . . To the secretariat he was an invaluable friend. Were we short of work, he would walk into some Government Department and get some question referred. If we had difficulty with some Minister he would smooth it out. . . . His influence was immense and it was always exercised with wisdom and restraint.[43]

Balfour and the King met Esher at Balmoral to persuade him to accept the War Office, which he vigorously refused. 'So I made my counter-proposal,' he wrote, 'Balfour should appoint Commissioners to carry out the WO changes – the commissioners to be myself, Fisher and Brackenbury [General Sir Henry, Director General of Ordnance].' The King now sounded out Fisher's views at Balmoral, where he cross-examined him over several days.

Fisher passionately believed the two services should work together in amphibious warfare, 'an Army and Navy Cooperative society'. To ensure nothing was overlooked and for discussion with Balfour, the King asked him to write his views as memoranda, one of which suggested a single Minister for both services – a Minister of Defence – and a complete supersession of all the 'old gang' in the War Office. '*These valuable papers are to be very carefully kept for future guidance,*' minuted the King.[44] Esher supported this view: 'A Minister of Defence – yes. A Ministry of Defence – no.'[45] Fisher would hardly have anticipated the emasculation of the heads of the services and the chaotic state of Defence of the 1990s. His fight to wrest control of gun design and supply from a preclusive War Office had awakened him to the dangers of a Ministry of Defence. Cyprian Bridge wrote to the second Lord Fisher in 1921:

> He was greatly interested in the agitation started by some people who knew little or nothing about the Navy or of its history, to set up what was to be called a 'Ministry of Defence'. This was to mean in practice putting the Admiralty under the War Office – a silly and indeed mischievous suggestion which your father helped us, who foresaw its dangers, to defeat.[46]

Esher's proposal was accepted and Arnold-Forster became Secretary of State for War, to whom Balfour suggested the committee should consist of Esher, Fisher and Sir John French, which Arnold-Forster enthusiastically supported, later suggesting Fisher should be chairman. 'His rank, experience and great force of character will fully justify this.'

Fisher believed that for an island race expenditure on the services was unbalanced. Army estimates had risen from £18m in 1895 to £30m in 1901, compared with £36.9m for the Navy, though the Army did not bear the costs of ships. He believed the total budget could be restricted to £60m with a 'Navy 30% stronger and an Army 50% more effective' which would 'clip *eightpence off the income tax*'.[47]

Selborne was greatly upset by Fisher's appointment without consulting him and instructed him to refuse. Battenberg warned Fisher of the 'endless ill-feeling and bitterness amongst the soldiers' if a sailor were to reorganize them, and was supported by Drury, Second Naval Lord, and May, controller. Fisher asked Arnold-Forster to 'pitch him overboard', but the latter would not hear of it, writing to Balfour, 'I am quite certain that no name will command as much confidence with the public as Sir John's.' Balfour sent a telegram to Selborne which did little to mollify his injured pride and he wrote to Fisher, as the latter put it, that '*the Board will expect me to fulfil all my duties at Portsmouth.* It's as much as to say: All right, serve on the Committee, but, by Jove, if we find you away from the port we'll rub your nose in it!'[48] French's appointment was dropped and Colonel Sir George Clarke (later Lord Sydenham) substituted, largely because he was progressive, favouring a maritime defence policy, though he tended to be opinionated.

It was understandable that the Army objected to a sailor telling them their business, especially as Fisher seldom concealed his contempt for army officers. 'I always explained to them that I was Lord Esher's facile dupe and Sir George Clarke's servile copyist, thereby avoiding odium personally (I was getting all the odium I wanted from the Admirals).'[49]

Fisher was the leading light of the 'Dauntless Three' as the newspapers dubbed them, (though Campbell-Bannerman called them 'Damnable,

Domineering and Dictatorial'). Esher was on holiday and Clarke Governor of Victoria, so the first meeting was delayed until early in 1904 by which time Fisher had completed a draft report and recommendations, which were accepted virtually intact by Esher and Clarke. Because of Selborne's views, most of the meetings took place in Portsmouth, so the War Office concluded, with some truth, that they were 'being reorganised at Admiralty House, Portsmouth'.[50]

Fisher believed there was no hope of competing with the huge continental armies; Britain's intentions were entirely defensive, the Empire more than satisfied any territorial ambitions and she had no interest in expansion in Europe.

> The Regular Army . . . should be regarded as a projectile to be fired by the Navy. The Navy embarks it and lands it where it can do most mischief! Thus the Germans are ready to land a large military force in the Cotentin Peninsula in case of war with France and my German military colleagues at The Hague conference told me that this comparatively small military force would have the effect of demobilising half a million of men who would thus be taken away from the German frontier. . . . Instead of our military manoeuvres being on Salisbury Plain . . . aping the vast continental armies, we should be employing ourselves in joint naval and military manoeuvres embarking 50,000 men at Portsmouth and landing them at Milford Haven or Bantry Bay.[51]

He was already organizing exercises on these lines. On 5 January 1904 he wrote, 'I yesterday sent all my plans to French for embarking the whole of his First Army on Monday 27th (full moon), at Portsmouth, and he is coming here with his Chief Staff Officer, Sir Frederick Stopford, next week, and we land them like Hoche's army in Bantry Bay'.[52] He later appended a note, 'The War Office stopped this'. The Army was determined not to cooperate in such exercises, which anticipated so brilliantly the operations of the Second World War and the Falklands Campaign of 1982.

The choice of Fisher for the Esher Committee led to his becoming one of a small group of seven who influenced the Sovereign and on whose support they in turn depended. They included Mrs George Keppel, a discreet and influential Liberal, whose special relationship with the King was accepted by the others, Sir Ernest Cassel, Sir Charles Hardinge, an undersecretary at the Foreign Office (later Lord Hardinge of Penshurst, Viceroy of India), Louis de Soveral, the cosmopolitan Germanophobe Portuguese Minister in London, Esher, Knollys and Fisher. The last three became a close group who dined regularly together at Brooks's, under the acknowledged leadership of Esher, to exchange views.

Esher knew the proficiency of the War Office at dismissing any proposals for reform and insisted that all the recommendations of the committee should be acted on, subject only to the approval of the Prime Minister, who agreed.

Fisher summarized in simple terms the spirit of the Army officers of those days in a letter to Knollys: ' "Pastime and leave" take the first place in a Military Officer's thoughts and his profession comes second, and it's "bad form" to study it or to talk of it! . . . But are we not better without these idlers who never intend to spend their lives in the Army, but only to make a convenience of it for social purposes or personal advantage?'[53]

His view was unwittingly supported by Violet Bonham-Carter, who described how the young subaltern, Winston Churchill, having decided to leave the Army and devote himself to writing and politics, returned all the way to India 'to discharge his last military duty, the winning of the polo tournament, and then to send in his papers and leave the Army.'[54]

Esher wrote: 'There are no first-rate lieutenant-generals, except French. He is developing so fast that in a few years he will be the Fisher of the sister service. . . . If he had a quarter of your intellect . . . we could reform the Army as well as the W.O.'[55] And, writing to Haldane in 1905, he remarked, '[The Army] . . . is officered by a caste with caste prejudices.'[56] The following year he was to write to Knollys, 'There is not one man in the Army Council and very few among the Directors at the War Office who has ever attempted to think about the work they have to do, before they were appointed to their present posts.'[57] And again to the Duchess of Sutherland, 'There is a very bad time coming for soldiers. . . . I fear that proficiency in games or in the hunting field will not help our poor lads much when they have to face the carefully trained and highly educated German officers.'[58]

Fisher attacked the regimental system because officers were not transferred from regiment to regiment for cross-fertilization and selected for promotion on merit, but were obliged to await a vacancy in their own regiment, resulting in the certainty that incompetent officers would in their turn rise to high rank. The words 'Carry on, Sergeant-Major' he saw as depriving young officers of the opportunity of gaining first-hand experience. In the Navy the officers told the petty officers what to do and how to do it; in the army the reverse was true.

The Esher Commission presented its first report on 11 January 1904:

> At the outset of our enquiry . . . we were driven to the conclusion that no measure of War Office reform will avail unless it is associated with provision for obtaining and collating, for the use of the Cabinet, all the information and the expert advice required for the shaping of the national policy in war and for determining the necessary preparations in peace. Such information and advice must necessarily embrace,

not only the sphere of the War Office, but those of the Admiralty and the other offices of State.[59]

The Defence Committee of the Cabinet formed in 1895 had no specific functions, no regular meetings and no minutes, its membership confined to politicians. In December 1902 it was renamed the Committee of Imperial Defence and in March 1903 reorganized by Balfour under his own chairmanship, with the First Sea Lord, Commander-in-Chief of the Army and the Directors of Military and Naval Intelligence co-opted.

The Esher Commission continued, 'A committee which contains no permanent nucleus and which is composed of political and professional members, each preoccupied with administrative duties widely differing, cannot, in our opinion, deal adequately with the complex questions of Imperial Defence.'[60]

The Commission proposed a permanent secretary, under whom there should be two naval officers, two military officers and two Indian officers, with, if possible, one or more representatives of the colonies. The permanent secretariat should consider all questions of Imperial Defence, collate information from all departments, prepare documents for the Prime Minister and Defence Committee, furnish advice on defence matters and keep records for the Cabinet. Esher and Fisher saw eye to eye. At last some coordination could be achieved between the Cabinet, the Admiralty and War Office.

The Secretary of State should be placed in the same position as the First Lord and all submissions to the Crown made by him alone. The office of Commander-in-Chief was to be abolished and an Army Council instituted, similar to the Board of Admiralty, consisting of four military members and three civilian under a Minister reporting to Parliament. The First Military Member would be responsible for operations, the second for personnel, the third for supply and the fourth for armament. One civilian would deal with civil business and another finance. Fisher proposed Sir John French as First Military Member, 'because he never failed in South Africa', Smith-Dorrien as second, Plumer as third and Slade as Fourth. Few of his nominations were accepted, but the trio agreed that all the old men should be cleared out.

I know we are all three agreed that 'new measures require new men'. . . . It is only by the agency of young and enthusiastic believers in the immense revolution that must be carried out that our scheme can bear fruit . . . every one of the 'old gang' must be cleared out, 'lock, stock and gunbarrel, bob and sinker'.[61]

The committee's final report was approved by the King on 26 March 1904. Roberts was summarily dismissed. But within the War Office many worked against the scheme, especially the Director of Military Intelligence,

Lieutenant-General Sir William Nicholson, (later Field Marshal, First Baron), who had great influence and believed in the predominance of the Army and unimportance of the Navy, which he thought incapable of preventing an invasion. Fisher intimated to Esher that he would not be prepared to go to the Admiralty if Nicholson remained. 'I think it better to let you know at once what my views are.'[62]

Nicholson was packed off to Manchuria as Chief British Military Attaché with the Japanese Army. But he was back in the War Office in 1905 and Chief of the General Staff in 1908. He had his revenge as a member of the Dardanelles Commission.

Clarke wanted the committee to remain permanent, but Fisher, Esher and the King opposed him in view of the resentment it would cause in the Army, and, at Fisher's forceful suggestion, Clarke became Permanent Secretary of the CID.

The King 'highly praised the work of the committee', with which Arnold-Forster 'could only cordially agree'. He was impressed by Clarke 'and of course, immensely by Fisher'.[63]

Opposition mounted against Fisher's appointment as First Naval Lord, which was widely known. Sir Frederick Richards, so shocked at the new education scheme, attracted a bevy of reactionary senior officers. Beaumont, Fisher's commander in *Bellerophon*, who had served with him in *Excellent* and the Admiralty, joined the opposition. King-Hall recorded that Beaumont 'is endeavouring to prevent Fisher from returning as First Sea Lord [*sic*] but as I told Rice, there is not much chance of his doing that.'[64]

Noel recorded in his diary that he had bicycled over to Hurlingham Court to see Richards and in 1911 wrote to Selborne reminding him of an interview he had had with him before taking up the China Command and asserting that had Selborne heeded his opposition to Fisher's appointment, a view supported by those he called the most reliable men in the upper ranks of the Service, the country would not have been brought to a position he claimed was deplorable, even perilous.[65] Selborne's reply was curt. Had Noel had his way, Britain's naval position would certainly have been 'deplorable' and his judgment of the 'most reliable men' is questionable. Ten years earlier Fisher believed him 'eminently gifted but he will very soon be too old!'[66]

Fisher was by no means enthusiastic about the appointment. He wrote to Esher in April, 1904, 'I'm not so awfully keen on going there, and I don't want to be stuffed down Selborne's throat!'[67] Again, in May, 'And I hope to pick up a job somewhere.'[68] It was uncertain whether his appointment would be ratified; he expected opposition from politicians and conservative elements in the Navy to the massive reforms he planned, so support was essential from Selborne, who, reasonably enough, wanted to know their full extent. Much discussion between them followed, with great probing from the latter. Fisher drew up his schemes in detail and submitted them to his 'committee' who revised them considerably. He then asked 'the one with the most facile pen' to revise his draft. 'My print herewith contains words and phrases not meant for ears polite, it's only meant to sledgehammer your own seven brains; so therefore write a calm and dispassionate précis for me to give to the First Lord.'

Selborne visited Portsmouth frequently and finally on 13 and 14 May made his formal offer, leaving a lengthy *aide memoire* placing their discussions on record, especially reduction in the naval estimates which had risen from £23.8m in 1898–99 to £36.9 (55%).

When Selborne visited Malta in 1901 Fisher had pressed vigorously for the establishment of a Naval War College. On 9 June Selborne sent Fisher a further *Memorandum respecting additional problems to be dealt with and Questions to be taken up*, of which a significant passage was:

> 4. The NID must work out plans of campaigns in every possible naval war – against France, against Russia, against France and Russia, against Germany singly or in any combination, against the United States, etc.[69]

Fisher's appointment was announced on 20 June, much to the alarm of the Syndicate of Discontent, as Fisher dubbed the out of date officers and civil servants who objected to change merely because it *was* change. Yet, despite all this detailed discussion, on 28 July Fisher wrote to Esher, 'Selborne has been trying to draw me, but I've steadfastly declined to say a word or write a line until I am installed. . . . I've got the preamble of my new scheme ready! It's 31 pages of foolscap!'[70]

But Esher wrote, 'Jacky fusses because he thinks he will have fights with Selborne and he wishes for the advent of a new Government. But it is always six of one and half a dozen of the other with these people; and although just now he gets sympathy from Spencer and E.Grey, if *they* were in office, he would get sympathy from Selborne and would have to fight the others. Sympathy is a cheap article.'[71]

Later that month however Fisher wrote:

> Selborne came here and was so cordial and responsive that I have made the plunge, and with *immense* success. He has swallowed it all whole . . . and he has agreed to all the new blood I want. Of course everyone will say I've 'packed' the Admiralty with my creatures (Very sorry, but I can't help it.) Selborne has also agreed to my being President of a Committee to devise new types of fighting ships. I explained to him that I had got the designs out of what had to be; but it was politic to have a committee of good names, and then Tommy Bowles and others will fire away at them and leave me alone.[72]

So it was not only his 'scheme' of which he feared emasculation, but the *Dreadnought*. But he used the word 'design' loosely; he was concerned only with the armament, speed and armour of the ship, and would leave the technical details to the appropriate departments.

Immediately on his arrival at Portsmouth he had started to 'pack' the Admiralty with efficient officers who had his trust. King-Hall recorded in his diary on 15 October 1903:

> Angus MacLeod [Rear-Admiral, later Admiral Sir Angus] told me that he had been offered Queenstown and that Barry [Captain, later Rear-Admiral], one of Fisher's men, was to succeed him [as Director of Naval Ordnance]. There is no doubt that Fisher has got MacLeod out of it in order to put Barry in. . . . Lord Walter Kerr seems quite helpless, and . . . the Admiralty is practically run by Fisher (though C-in-C Portsmouth), Battenberg [then Director of Naval Intelligence] and Tyrwhitt [Captain the Hon. Hugh].[73]

8

FIRST SEA LORD

Fisher took up his appointment on 20 October 1904, though he wanted to do so on Trafalgar day ('a good fighting day'). That evening he handed his detailed plans to Selborne, who returned them the next day with his approval and only minor modifications.

He persuaded Selborne to restore the old title 'Sea Lords' dating back to the 17th century 'which some silly ass some hundred years ago altered to "Naval Lords"', a trivial change all naval officers would applaud. But his other schemes were far from trivial. Rumours had spread, and on arrival he was confronted with opposition that would have daunted a lesser man. The whole Board (except Selborne), the Treasury and all the reactionaries opposed him. Recognizing the odds, he had negotiated with Selborne a redistribution of his duties in relation to the other members, including Selborne himself. As the senior professional officer he was to be responsible for the efficiency of the fleet, preparation and readiness for war, larger questions of maritime policy and warfare, fighting efficiency, organization and mobilization of the fleet, control of intelligence, hydrographical and ordnance departments and, to facilitate his reorganization, 'distribution and movements of all ships in commission or in reserve', which was to become of great importance both then and ten years later.

The new terms were immediately criticized, enabling a First Sea Lord to interfere with the work of his colleagues, which was perfectly true. Fisher was described as autocratic, but he never interfered if duties were properly conducted and did not obstruct his sweeping plans. He believed the First Sea Lord was *princeps inter pares* and the system worked with new efficiency and vigour. He never differed with other Board members in writing, but discussed papers with them and arranged for minutes to be amended by agreement. Otherwise he left decisions to his colleagues and often signed papers without reading them.

Fisher's reforms having already been agreed with Selborne, the cooperation of all departments was essential. 'It will be a case of *Athanasius contra Mundum,*' he wrote to Arnold White, 'very sorry for Mundum, as Athanasius is going to win!'[1]

Sir Philip Magnus believed that without the King's support Beresford and his adherents would have overthrown Fisher before his reforms were complete.[2] When in 1904 Fisher complained that he had wasted five hours with the King, who 'can't grasp details', Esher responded: 'The King will not go into details, for his life is too full for that, but he will always say to himself, "Jack Fisher's view is so and so, and he is sure to be right". I don't think you need trouble about HM for he will always back you.'[3]

Direct access would have been unconstitutional and unacceptable to the politicians, so Selborne arranged Fisher's appointment as First and Principal Naval ADC. The King demurred, but was persuaded, the connection proving of great value. The two men became extremely close, Fisher relying increasingly on the King for support and encouragement, exemplified when, in March 1905, dissatisfied with Government policy, Fisher sent the King a copy of an impulsive letter of resignation, adding that he had been offered the chairmanship of Armstrong-Whitworth at a salary of £10,000 a year (£½m in 1990s). The King, with quiet wisdom, dissuaded him and, later that year, awarded him the Order of Merit.

Fisher returned to the Admiralty at a critical moment. International relations were in disarray. Russia and Japan were jockeying for position in the Far East and Britain mistrusted the Franco-Russian treaty. The King did not share this; he had proposed an *Entente* with France as early as 1866, and Fisher, recognizing the German threat, advocated friendship with France, writing to Arnold White in 1902 about 'a society I believe called the "Entente Cordiale".'[4] France remained hostile, and when the King on his own initiative and against the advice of Lansdowne, Sir Edmund Monson, the British Ambassador, and the Foreign Office, had made his State Visit to Paris in 1903, with no Government Minister in attendance, he had been greeted as he drove down the Champs Elysée with cries of '*Vive Marchand!*', '*Vive Fashoda!*' and '*Vivent les Boers!*' But the next day at the Hôtel de Ville at Vincennes the King made a short but effective speech in excellent French, ending, '*Je puis vous assurer que c'est avec le plus grand plaisir que je reviens à Paris, ou je me trouve toujours comme si j'étais chez mois.*' The mood changed and at a State Banquet President Loubet mumbled a poor speech, the King, responding clearly, without notes and with an accent like a native, was greeted with a loud ovation. Thus the way had been paved for better relations with France, though not yet an alliance or even an *Entente*.

Britain had cultivated friendly relations with Germany, to which there was little response. Treitschke, a Prussian professor of history in Berlin, of great influence in Germany, was virulently anti-British, pointing to the British possession of one fifth of the habitable globe 'by theft. By what right? By the right first of craft, then of violence. . . . As long as England, the great robber-state, retains her booty, the spoils of a world, what right has she to expect peace from the nations?'[5] Germany was an academic country and Treitschke's influence was strong.

In the time of Roon and the elder Moltke, when the question of enmity to Britain was discussed, the response was always, 'Is it possible to land an army on English soil? And bring it safely back again with its plunder to the shores of the Elbe and the Rhine?' Hemmed in by the sea to the north and south and by Russia and France in the east and west, Germany, with an expanding population, wanted colonies.

The accession of the ambitious Kaiser Wilhelm II in 1888, his dismissal of Bismarck in 1890 and the appointment of the expansionist Von Bülow as Chancellor in 1900 heralded the introduction of the *Weltpolitik*.

> The wave-beat knocks powerfully at our gates and calls us as a great nation to maintain our place in the world – in other words to pursue world policy. The ocean is indispensable for Germany's greatness; but the ocean also reminds us that neither in it nor across it in the distance can any great decision be arrived at without Germany and the German Emperor. – Wilhelm II.[6]

Professor Callender believed that Mahan's book changed the course of history, comparable with *Uncle Tom's Cabin* and *The Origin of Species* and he compressed Mahan's doctrine into the single sentence, 'He who is master of the sea, is master of the situation'. The Kaiser became one of Mahan's greatest disciples, recognizing that German domination of Europe and the world demanded domination of the sea. In Von Tirpitz he found a Minister of Marine who supported this view. The draft Navy Law contained details of Germany's vast increase in population, foreign trade, fishing industry, commerce and heavy industry since 1871. Imports had more than doubled in the ten years 1861–71 and exports nearly trebled, despite falling prices. Germany's merchant fleet had grown from 82,000 tons in 1872 to nearly 10.4 million in 1897; from 147 ships to 1,127. Population had increased by 30% and even the flow of emigration had dwindled from a peak of 221,000 in 1881 to a paltry 33,824 in 1897.[7]

The first German Navy Law appeared in 1898 and the second in 1900. They announced that Germany must have a battle fleet so strong that 'even for the adversary with the greatest sea-power, a war against us would involve such dangers as to imperil his position in the world'. There could be no doubt against whom this policy was directed, for then Britain possessed fifty-four battleships and Germany only fourteen. 'German colonies and trade were to provide the excuse for the "fighting' fleet" which alone could make the Kaiser "master of the situation". The War Lord's frequent references to "shining armour", "the mailed fist", and the "rattling of the sabre in its sheath", left the world no reason to doubt that Prussia remained loyal to the ambitions of Frederick the Great.'[8]

Tirpitz was the first to recognize that a powerful fleet between Heligoland and the Thames would minimize the danger of a sudden attack by Britain and could be used as a political instrument against her. This was his 'risk theory', both offensive and defensive, a political weapon and a deterrent.

During the debate on the Navy Law of 1898 the socialist August Bebel said in the Reichstag: 'There is, especially [in] this house, a large group of fanatical anglophobes, made up of men who want to pick a fight with England and who would rather fight today than tomorrow. But to believe that with our fleet, yes, even if it is finished to the very last ship demanded in this law, we could take up the cudgels against England, is to approach the realm of insanity. Those who demand it belong not in the Reichstag, but in the madhouse.'[9] He was greeted with prolonged laughter.

Fisher, at The Hague conference had drawn the senior German officers into disclosing much of the Fatherland's plans. But at the turn of the century he and the King were probably the only ones fully to recognize the dangers ahead, despite the retrospective claims of others. Fisher wrote to Arnold White in August 1902: 'The German Emperor may be devoted to us, but he can no more stem the tide of German commercial hostility to this country than Canute could keep the North Sea from wetting his patent leather boots! It's inherent. Their interests everywhere clash with ours, and their gratitude for all our beneficence to them is nil! It is a fact that in Hong Kong a body of German merchants assembled to drink champagne in gratitude for our reverses in the Transvaal; looking thereby to German Ascendancy there through Holland, which they intend to annex.'[10]

Archibald Hurd wrote in 1902: 'Germany is a serious menace in the "home seas". . . . The growth of the Kaiser's Fleet has already suggested the danger of our resting satisfied with the present Two-Power standard. . . . If, as a nation, we accept this measure of strength, in less than a decade Germany will hold the balance of power in European waters. The Kaiser and his people appreciate the old truth that sea-power is synonymous with commercial power.'[11]

'Our only probable enemy,' Fisher wrote to the Prince of Wales, 'is Germany. Germany keeps her *whole* fleet always concentrated within a few hours of England. We must therefore keep a fleet twice as powerful concentrated within a few hours of Germany.'[12]

Relations with France improved. The visit of the King was followed by the return visit of President Loubet, which cemented the rapprochement the King so earnestly desired. Germany's warlike aims began to be more generally recognized. Von Bülow himself later admitted they had considered an attack on Britain during the Boer War, 'but we should have found neither strength, nor means nor leisure to proceed with the building of our Navy as we have been able to do'.[13] Richmond records that Von Bülow had reported General Von Plessen's view that Germany must have 'not only Denmark in her hands but also Holland and her Colonies, if for nothing more than the urgent need for coaling stations.'[14] Yet a Liberal Foreign Minister was tempted by the attractions of appeasement. On 9 January 1906 Sir Edward Grey wrote to Campbell-Bannerman:

> In more than one part of the world I find signs that Germany is feeling after a coaling station or a port. Everywhere we block this. I am not an expert on naval strategy, yet I doubt whether it is important to us to prevent Germany getting ports at a distance from her base; and the moment may come when a timely admission that it is not a cardinal object of British policy to prevent her having such a port may have a great pacific effect.[15]

Almost immediately on arrival at the Admiralty Fisher was struck down with 'flu, just as a crisis was breaking. In 1898 Russia had occupied Port Arthur and in 1902 the Anglo–Japanese Alliance was signed. Negotiations between Russia and Japan broke down and on 8 February 1904 Admiral Togo, in command of the Japanese fleet, torpedoed the Russian fleet off Port Arthur and invaded Korea. In October the Russian Baltic Fleet under Admiral Rodjestvensky sailed for Japanese waters and on the day Fisher joined the Admiralty stumbled on a flotilla of British fishing smacks off the Dogger Bank which they assumed to be Japanese torpedo boats and opened fire. What they imagined the Japanese were doing in the North Sea or how they got there remains a mystery, though they subsequently claimed to have been warned by Germany of the presence of torpedo boats. Vice-Admiral Sir Charles Drury, Second Sea Lord, deputizing for Fisher during his illness, was brought the news one Sunday evening by a *Daily Mail* reporter. He got in touch with certain Cabinet Ministers and believed that the action being taken would lead to war. He went to Fisher who rose from his sick bed and demanded admittance to the Cabinet meeting, representing his views so strongly that they were accepted and war was averted.

Beresford, in command of the Channel Squadron, was at Gibraltar. A.K.Wilson, in command of the Home Fleet, brought it to Portland to prevent the Russians returning to the Baltic, while Beresford was ordered to intercept them. Rodjestvensky's four battleships took shelter in Vigo, but the second division, under Rear-Admiral Fölkersam, were due at Tangier. Beresford awaited them at Gibraltar, intending to order Fölkersam to anchor inside the mole. Should he refuse, Beresford would attack them with four of his battleships at a range of 5–6,000 yards. 'It appeared to me that this would only be chivalrous under the circumstances. If the Russian ships had commenced to knock my ships about, I would have engaged them with the whole 8 Channel Fleet (*Sic*) battleships.'[16]

Fölkersam had three battleships and five cruisers, probably a match for four battleships, though they were so loaded with coal and stores that their upper-deck guns could not have been worked, and the fight would have been 'murder'.[17] These proposals were reported to the Admiralty after the event when Battenberg and Fisher were outraged at the use of only half the battleships. Battenberg minuted : 'If this statement became public property, the taxpayers would probably enquire why they were paying for the other half.'[18] And Fisher wrote: 'Lord Nelson's dictum was "the greater your superiority over the enemy the better" and he was a chivalrous man'.[19]

Selborne decided that Beresford should be informed that his proposed action 'could not have been justified on any grounds and least of all on those of sentiment. . . . Their Lordships would expect and require you to make use of the whole of the force at your disposal.'[20] But, typically, Beresford came back with a tortuous explanation in an attempt to justify himself. 'Is comment necessary?' asks Marder. But Beresford in his memoirs, wrote, 'The misunderstanding arose because the Russian admiral did not proceed to the nearest British port and explain the circumstances'![21] Surely a somewhat unrealistic attitude when war threatened! Immediately Rodjestvensky reached Japanese waters his fleet was destroyed by Togo at the Battle of Tsushima.

Fisher's brief from Selborne to reduce the Navy Estimates presented him with an apparently insoluble problem – how to reduce expenditure and yet enhance the power of the Navy, which both saw as essential. But 'Like Napoleon, he was that very rare bird, the fighting man who considers the taxpayer'.[22] But he also recognized that the slothful administration of the Navy impaired its efficiency. 'Reduced naval estimates are no sign of reduced naval efficiency,' he wrote to the Prince of Wales, 'On the contrary swollen estimates engender parasites both in men and in ships, which hamper the fighting qualities of the fleet. The pruning knife ain't pleasant for fossils and ineffectives, but it has to be used, and the tree is more vigorous for the loss of excrescences.'[23] Though funds would always be limited, he believed the politicians would eventually see the white water ahead and authorize them, when his slimmed-down, healthier Navy would grow only in effectiveness. 'The defect of the previous system was that there was no authority that could tackle questions from the standpoint of the fighting efficiency of the fleet, and it must be remembered that it is for this sole purpose that the Navy Estimates exist!'[24]

Fisher worked all hours, including Sundays, uninterrupted in the empty building. He went to bed at 9.30 pm, rose between 5 and 5.30 am and often at 4 am. He worked for about two hours before breakfast, meals taken hastily when opportunity arose, and often went without a midday meal. In January

1905 the King wrote to him: 'Admiral Sir John Fisher is to do *no* work on *Sundays,* nor go near the Admiralty, nor is he to allow *any* of his subordinates to work on Sundays. By command. Edward R.'[25]

But things did not run smoothly, the Cabinet always questioning his reforms. 'We have got a crisis on with the Cabinet,' he wrote in January 1905, 'and we are to meet them at 3.30 today. I hope my colleagues will stand firm. They are both a bit wobbly.'[26]

In forwarding his proposals to Selborne he had listed his unofficial committee at Portsmouth, and continued: 'This is the *modus operandi* I suggest to you. If these proposals in their rough outline commend themselves to you and our colleagues on the Board, let me have these seven, assisted by Mr Boar (who is a mole in the Accountant General department) and secretly these eight will get out a detailed statement supported by facts and figures for consideration before we take a step further!'[27]

In many respects the nineteenth century changes in the Navy were too fast and too great to be digested. Most senior officers had joined when sail was the prime mover. Ships and living conditions were little different in 1854 from those of 100, 200, or 300 years earlier. Recruitment had changed little, though the Press-gang had ceased in 1815. An attempt at continuous service introduced in 1853 extended only to 7,000 men and ships still had to advertise locally to enter men. Fisher's first ship, *Calcutta,* had remained in Falmouth for six months trying to raise a crew, and this in wartime. The education of officers had improved little; many despised what they called the 'matériel' approach. Wemyss, for example, 'openly confessed' that 'technicalities bored him'.[28] But that generation suffered more than their fair share of change and the human belief that during one's youth the world was as it should be, and natural resistance to change, led them to question all change. All through Fisher's Service life he had noted and thought over every new development and related it to others, so the picture was whole. He sought the solutions and knew he was one of very few. He intensely disliked yes-men and always listened attentively to others, his eyes fixed on the speaker, his lips parted, taking in every word and never interrupting, so that he garnered a huge volume of information in his incredibly retentive memory. Collating details, he was able to judge with almost infallible accuracy the views expressed, and if after discussion he rejected them, it was on a sure foundation and he would tolerate no further opposition. Obstruction from self-interest he demolished mercilessly; far from suffering fools gladly, he refused to suffer them at all. Major General George Aston, then a major in the Admiralty, wrote: 'He was like a sort of steam roller, and anything you wanted to get forward you could hang on behind with the certainty that it would progress. If you disagreed with him it was another matter. You could neither steer nor put the brakes on the steam roller if you thought it was moving in a disastrous direction.'[29]

Fisher saw what had to be done before the Armageddon he so clearly foresaw and knew he was the only one who could or would do it, and there was little time left. All his major reforms were interconnected, each dependent on the others, like a game of chess. But at first sight none could be achieved until others were completed.

The average commission lasted between four and five years, ships remaining on foreign service from commission to commission, their crews only changing when another ship joining the station could bring out replacements in grossly overcrowded conditions like those in *Donegal*, thirty years before. (A lieutenant was posted abroad for a five-year commission three months after his wedding, at the end of which he was again sent abroad for four years within six months of his return; in ten years he had had nine months with his wife.) Many officers preferred to remain on half-pay for long periods, while ratings tried to find other employment when their ships paid off and were reluctant to sign on for continuous service. When ships were commissioned, officers were out of date after years ashore and men unskilled. Fisher reduced the length of a foreign commission to two years. But this meant more men were on passage to and from foreign stations and the cost led to opposition.

Wooden ships had been kept in service as long as the timbers were sound (*Victory* was already 46 years old at Trafalgar) and the practice was continued when steam and steel replaced sail and wood; none thought of ships as obsolete before they were worn out. The Reserve Fleet was crowded with them. They were the conception of their designers, naval tacticians having little say about them, despite the rapid advances in warfare which made it all the more necessary that they should be fashioned for a purpose, instead of being built to the vagaries of their designers and then uses found for them. Many of the old ships were out of date, their guns of inadequate range, their protection insufficient and unable to keep up with a modern fleet. Even if they had not been outgunned and outranged, they could never have got near enough to the enemy to attack. Yet there were many such ships in full commission abroad. In war they would be useless and would have to be paid off; yet they cost money to man and maintain. The Foreign Office liked to have ships visiting other countries to 'show the flag', and as long as the paintwork and polish were brilliant, few recognized that the ships were useless and the expense unjustified.

The Dogger Bank incident, occurring within days of his arrival, presented Fisher with an opportunity. The Public demanded 'War with Russia' and Battenberg related that Fisher dictated to him a message to all Cs-in-C and Senior Officers abroad:

War with Russia is imminent. Concentrate your fleet at Station Headquarters. Pay off immediately, all standing, the following ships

113

[here followed a list of all sloops and gunboats]. Send home [crews] by first packet and wire date of arrival in England.[30]

Battenberg continued: 'By the time these parties arrived home we had enough officers and men for the scheme, which was put into execution. It was on this brilliant scheme that the fleet was first manned under the test Mobilisation of July 1914 and then went into the war. [Battenberg was First Sea Lord at the time]. . . .The C-in-Cs at regular intervals sent plaintive telegrams asking when these crews of paid-off ships might be expected back again. . . . No replies were ever sent.'[31]

Thus was the deadlock broken. Lord Cawdor, who had replaced Selborne as First Lord, said in his explanatory statement to the Navy Estimates of 1906:

> A great naval war [the Russo–Japanese] has given us a practical demonstration of the comparative values . . . of different classes of ships. . . . One point of great moment is that by keeping these older ships we do not in any way affect the question of reduction of new construction. The retention of twenty out-of-date *Orlandos* [obsolete cruisers, some less than fifteen years old] does not do away with the necessity for the construction of a single modern, fast armoured cruiser.[32]

This was almost a direct quotation from a paper by Fisher headed *A Lesson from the Far East* which continued, 'For years Russia has been patching up and renovating useless old vessels at enormous expense, and we now see of what practical value these ships are when face to face with a modern fleet. . . . They could neither fight nor run away, and their presence has involved the whole of the squadron in disaster.'[33]

154 ships were paid off, ninety to be scrapped, thirty-seven retained for possible auxiliary use in war and twenty-seven retained but not to be maintained. Apoplectic admirals fumed in their clubs and swore Fisher was the ruination of the Navy. So he was, if the Service was a yacht club. Stephen King-Hall gives us a glimpse of service on the Cape Station in 1913, even after Fisher's purge had long taken effect: 'There were three ships in the squadron. . . . They were all in the last stages of decay and slackness . . . as ships of war they were useless, but as conveyances for "showing the flag" they served their purpose. They were symbols of the majesty and might of Britain.'[34]

Dockyards and bases were so choked with useless ships that little room was left for the active fleet, and it was contemplated to spend £13m on extensions, which were now cancelled, while the saving in personnel enabled Fisher to take his next step. The Reserve Fleet was divided into a Fleet Reserve and a Dockyard Reserve. Ships in the former were supposed to be ready for sea and in the latter were those under refit. But though the first group were maintained by a central pool of manpower and might be ready for sea in a material sense, (though in fact they seldom were), they would have to be manned, ammunitioned and stored on the outbreak of war. The new ships' companies gathered from peace duties in harbour ships, from the training schools and from the Reserves, would hardly know their way about, know nothing of the eccentricities of guns and machinery, the men unknown to the officers and the officers to the men. When ships were brought forward for annual manoeuvres, breakdowns of machinery and equipment were common. The months required to 'work up' with a new ship's company hardly met the speed of events Fisher foresaw. His dictum 'instant readiness for war' was the code by which he planned and he introduced the 'nucleus crew' system which meant that the officers and men essential for fighting the ship were available on board: the captain, gunnery officer, gunlayers, sight-setters, torpedo officer, engineer officer and enough engine room ratings familiar with the ship to take her to sea for a short time and actually operate with the fleet. The first-line ships even included paymasters and medical officers. The hewers of wood and drawers of water could come later. Each division of the Reserve Fleet was maintained at one of the home ports under a rear-admiral, the whole being placed under a vice-admiral, whose title was changed from that of Admiral Superintendent of Naval Reserves to Admiral in Command of the Home Fleet. The ships went to sea periodically for a short time to gain practice in steaming, using armaments and handling the ship.

Battenberg wholeheartedly approved: 'Then Fisher's genius invented the Nucleus Crew system (to carry out which all useless "War Junks" had to be paid off), which has turned out a brilliant success.'[35]

Since Trafalgar the disposition of British fleets was based more on the protection of land masses and on foreign trade than on the strategic deployment of the fleet. 'Oblivion to, or ignorance of, the fact that the security of the country against invasion is linked up with its ability to defend its trade, and that the Navy must be provided with flotilla and cruiser forces adequate to fulfil both purposes simultaneously, has more than once placed the country in jeopardy.'[36]

Britain kept one strong fleet in the Channel and another in the Mediterranean. Next in importance came that in the East Indies, to protect her most important possession, India, while the lesser fleets and squadrons were allocated to China, North America and the West Indies, the Cape, the Pacific and the south-east coast of South America. During the long peace fleets had acquired a classification 'into degrees of relative importance, and this priority in strength has been reflected in the rank and capabilities of the admirals selected to command them. So much has this been the case that today an admiral is apt to look on a definite number of

115

ships under his flag as a *right* rather than a *strategic exigency*.'[37]

The build-up of the German fleet necessitated the strengthening of British fleets in home waters. Fisher did not later 'hit on the idea' to silence his critics, as elsewhere suggested; it was a major, if not *the* major part of his scheme.

I.   Every fighting ship in reserve must have a nucleus crew.
II.   The reinforcements for the fighting fleets and squadrons must be collected together while in the reserve at the most convenient ports and be placed under the Flag Officer who will take them to their war stations, and this Flag Officer to understand he will be shot like a dog in case of any inefficiency in these ships in war.[38]

The [old] Home and Channel fleets have been reduced to eight battleships and two third-class cruisers only, as they are nearest to the home reserve.

The reserves at home have been grouped into squadrons of about four to six ships, so that on outbreak of war they will complete to full complement and go to sea, to whatever destination they are intended for, as complete units, under the admiral or commodore told off for them in reserve, who will form part of the nucleus crew of the squadron.[39]

The above extracts are from *The Scheme*, placed before the Cabinet by Selborne on 6 December 1904, only seven weeks after Fisher's arrival.

The advent of steam and telegraphic communication had diminished the necessity for isolated units abroad and the only gunboats remaining were those on the rivers of China and the west coast of Africa. Larger ships were withdrawn from the south-east coast of America and the Pacific, while the China, Australia and East Indies squadrons were left only with cruisers, their admirals being instructed to make plans for cooperative effort in the event of war. Their Commanders-in-Chief were deeply offended, especially Noel, now C-in-C China, who, overlooking (or disregarding) the change in circumstances resulting from the Anglo-Japanese alliance, wrote home protesting at the removal of his five battleships, sent as a temporary measure in response to Russia's similar action and no longer needed after Tsushima.[40] On return on hauling down his flag he 'used such violent language' to Fisher 'that his acceptance of the Nore greatly surprised me. To have a mutineer in high command would soon lead to awkwardness!'[41]

These redeployments were largely completed early in 1906 and the reorganization in European waters continued. The strongest possible fleet was kept close to Germany and the old Home Fleet, renamed the Channel Fleet, was increased to fourteen battleships with six armoured cruisers. The improved relations with France permitted reduction of the Mediterranean Fleet to nine battleships, with four armoured cruisers, while the old Channel squadron was transferred to Gibraltar, to be known as the Atlantic Fleet, available to reinforce the Channel or the Mediterranean. This was not only a strategic measure: 'During the 12 months ending 30 June 1904,' wrote Fisher, 'the ships of the Home Fleet, the Channel Fleet and the Cruiser squadron were in Portsmouth dockyard for over 30 per cent of the year! Disorganised and unfit for sea! See what this means! A battleship costs over £100,000 a year for its upkeep, irrespective of repairs, but it's not the money waste! *It's the efficiency waste! Every day these fleets and squadrons are not together they are deteriorating.*'[42]

Esher vigorously supported Fisher. On 1 March 1906 he wrote to Campbell-Bannerman:

> The Board of Admiralty found a system of fleet distribution dating back to 1805. They have distributed the fleet in a manner suitable to the conditions of 1905. The lesson that evolution in mechanical science leads to economy of time and labour has filtered very slowly into the minds of those responsible for naval administration. Now the lesson has been driven home and the present Board of Admiralty can justly claim that they are abreast of modern requirements and at the same time have lightened very considerably the annual burden upon the taxpayer.[43]

Removal of ships from foreign stations made possible the re-establishment of the two power standard in home waters, though its definition was increasingly difficult. Greater fire power, endurance, speed and effectiveness of armour outmoded mere counting ships. Tsushima had increased Britain's margin over Russia; she now had fifty-six battleships and forty-five armoured cruisers compared with a combination of forty-six and fourteen for Germany and Russia and forty-nine and twenty-six for France and Russia.

Reduction of foreign stations enabled Fisher to close the naval bases at Halifax, Jamaica, St. Lucia, Ascension, Trincomalee and Esquimalt. A small force of Royal Marines was kept at Ascension to man the defences and Gibraltar was enlarged as a repair base for the Atlantic Fleet. The retired admirals developed a deeper hue of purple.

Fisher cut deeply into the tail to sharpen the teeth, installing more efficient accounting procedures in the Royal Dockyards (many of which were adopted by private yards) constituting the Chief Constructors and Chief Engineers 'Managers', with financial responsibility and appointed a Director of Dockyards reporting to the Controller. He reduced the total workforce by 6,000 half-employed men, reorganized the system of storekeeping, drastically reducing the stock of stores that could readily be obtained from 'trade'. 'There is only so much money available for the Navy. If you put it into chairs that can't fight you take it away from ships and men who can'.[44]

He reorganized the Royal Naval Reserve, so that officers and men went to sea in commissioned ships, instead of exercising in hulks with obsolete weapons. He formed the Royal Fleet Reserve of fully trained ratings who had left the Navy. He reorganized the 'Fleet Train' of ammunition, store, distilling, hospital, cable, repair ships and dispatch vessels.

Though it was necessary to keep their ships together for exercising, grandeur and self-importance played a prominent role, the whole fleet entering dockyards for maintenance simultaneously, while ships' companies went on leave, always at the same time of year. This not only offered the best moment for an enemy to strike, like Fisher's complaints in the Esher Committee about the Army, but confronted the dockyards with an overwhelming burden of work, to be left afterwards with men under-employed. In future each ship was taken in hand successively.

As a corollary to the Selborne-Fisher Scheme, he pressed forward the rank of Artificer-Engineer, (later Warrant Engineer) to assist the Lieutenant (E) in charge, and provide watchkeeping officers, affording promotion for Engine Room Artificers. But the most consistently praised of his reforms, the creation of the rating of Mechanician proved least successful. Like his contemporaries, he believed 'engine driving' required no theoretical knowledge. There was at that time little chance of finding among the stoker ratings men of sufficient calibre. This was a curious blank in Fisher's mind; he claimed ERAs were recruited for what he called their 'toolsmanship' and should be wholly employed in repair and maintenance, replacing them in their watchkeeping duties by mechanicians. But repairs cannot be carried out on running machinery and ERAs would be unemployed at sea. Even Fisher thought the advent of turbines would demand 'some 50 per cent less Engineer Officers'. Quite the contrary; the exacting nature of turbine-engined ships demanded higher professional attainment and probably more of them.

All these measures resulted in dramatic economies. Hitherto each Admiralty department prepared its own estimates independently, without regard to others, for example, the Vote under the Admiral Commanding Reserves, amounting to £420,600; but the provision of batteries, drill ships etc. for the Reserves, which came under other votes, amounted to £476,000. Duplication in the dockyards led to unnecessary accumulations of stock; 10,000 chairs were stored in various establishments. In the Hydrographic Department the supply of charts to the public and foreign governments showed a loss of some £70,000 a year.

In November 1904 Fisher formed a Committee on Naval Estimates, which sat daily under his chairmanship, rendering its first report in 22 days. His economies resulted in a reduction of the Navy estimates of £3.5m for 1905–06 (actually nearer £5m due to a built-in escalation of £1.5m) compared with nearly £37m the previous year (9.5%) and the total reductions in the years 1905–08 were £5.47m or nearly 15%. Such economies carried the politicians with him, and enabled him to promote his even greater reforms.

Like Beresford, he believed that the system of promotion left aged and incompetent admirals in responsible positions. Younger men were needed: 'No Admiral ought to be at sea after 55 and I ought to be put on half-pay *at once*! . . . The increasing age of our Admirals is appalling ! . . . Let us have favouritism back again, and Nelsons at 40 winning the battle of the Nile instead of Sir Methuselah Buggins and the other old fossils coming along!'[45] He repeated his views on the incompetence of admirals, expressed to Selborne from Portsmouth: 'We can't have a redistribution of our fleet until we rearrange our strategy. . . . *How many types of ships do we want?* This is quite easy to answer if we make up our minds *how we are going to fight!* Who has made up his mind? *How many of our admirals have got minds?*'[46]

Fisher's attention was not confined to these matters. Until the last quarter of the nineteenth century, the naval rating, wholly dependent on his officers for his well-being, accepted his position with resignation. During the 1880s death benefit societies for petty officers were set up to aid their widows. The normal method of drawing attention to grievances was by petitions or memorials presented to the Admiralty or through Members of Parliament, and the benefit societies became embroiled in them. Combinations of naval officers and ratings had been specifically prohibited in 1860. Many of the societies had nevertheless petitioned for improvements, but did so through civilians, not subject to the Naval Discipline Act. In the 1890s the Warrant Officers' Society (formed in 1792) under the notable leadership of Henry Capper, a gunner, pressed for reforms aimed at promotion to commissioned rank. He had many articles published in service journals, gaining some support. In 1891 an 'earnest Appeal' was unsuccessful and Capper wrote anonymously to the *Naval and Military Record*, proposing that representation in Parliament should be achieved by supporting sympathetic MPs in naval constituencies. The MPs had no better success and in 1893 Capper proposed an amalgamation of the warrant officers, stokers, painters and chief petty officers and, later, that the warrant officers should contribute to the strike fund of the National Sailors and Firemens' Union, representing the Merchant Navy. In 1894 he proposed that his society should affiliate to the London Trades Council. These efforts created antagonism, sympathisers recognizing the unacceptability of trade unionism in the Services and Capper's efforts attracted few men, both through fear of the consequences and good sense.

James Woods, a petty officer who transferred to the Coastguard Service in 1890, became involved in petitions to improve coastguard pay, and in 1897 accepted the editorship of a journal entitled *Hope; The Coastguard Gazette*, adopting the pseudonym 'Lionel Yexley' and turned the little leaflet

119

into a journal for the lower deck, In 1898 he purchased his discharge and changed the name of the journal to *The Bluejacket and Coastguard Gazette*, subsequently shortened to *The Bluejacket*, with remarkable success in combining moderation with representation of the viewpoint of the lower deck. 'A moderately conducted bluejacket's paper, by and for bluejackets, is a necessary safety-valve for bluejackets' feeling and we can only tell our readers to trust us and stick to moderate methods.'[47] Yexley added that though reforms might not come speedily, they must not 'resort to other methods'. Lower deck complaints were not against the officers, but against the politicians who opposed lower deck aspirations. Reactionary officers agitated for the suppression of *The Bluejacket*; some commanding officers prohibited its sale in their ships. Nevertheless it prospered, advocating improvement in victualling, promotion and moderation in punishments, improving its image by supporting Fisher and Scott, who were pressing for modernization, especially in gunnery. It circulation grew and by 1904 was 20,000. But after a quarrel with the paper's proprietor, Yexley resigned.

The spread of Socialism, then regarded much as Communism is today, was having an effect on discipline. In the five years before Fisher's accession there had been seven incidents classified as mutiny, resulting in punishments of up to five years' hard labour. Between 1899 and 1911 there were over twenty such incidents, most having little importance. But more significant was a case at Portsmouth Barracks in 1905 when the fire party was being mustered by an arrogant lieutenant, B.St.G.Collard, later to gain notoriety as the central figure in the *Royal Oak* Courts Martial of 1928, hopelessly mishandled by the Commander-in-Chief, Sir Roger Keyes. Collard looked back in nostalgia at the old ways and it was unfortunate that he should be confronted by an individual called in the Navy a 'lower deck lawyer', though perhaps this was inevitable one day. Collard considered the mustering was being sloppily carried out and ordered the answer to the roll-call to be made correctly in the then Service fashion, 'Here, Sir, please'. The man concerned, Acton, answered quite deliberately, 'Here'. Collard ordered his name to be called again, and Acton again answered 'Here'. However tactless Collard may have been, Acton was justifiably charged and punished. But a year later at 'evening quarters' a heavy rainstorm caused some men to break ranks and run for shelter. Collard recalled them, then formally dismissed them. As they dispersed, he heard mutterings of resentment and recalled the men concerned to fall in again.

In the Victorian Navy it had been customary, when an officer wished to address a group of sailors, to use the term 'On the knee!' This meant that all men would drop on one knee, so that the officer, standing, could both see and be seen. The order had largely fallen into disuse, perhaps considered degrading. In a situation already delicate, Collard ordered 'On the knee!'

1. HMS *Calcutta*, Fisher's first ship.

2. John Fisher, Midshipman, aged 14.

3. Acting Lieutenant aged 19. (In those days a Lieutenant wore only one stripe).

4. The Battle of the Peiho River, from an old print.

5. HMS *Coromandel*, Fisher's first command.

6. HMS *Marlborough*, Beresford's 'ship of happiest memory' (IWM).

7. HMS *Warrior*.

8. Beresford as Flag Lieutenant.

9. Lady Brooke.

10. HMS *Inflexible*.

11. HMS *Condor*.

12. *Inflexible* at Alexandria. Note the topmasts and yards removed.

13. The Armoured Train.

14. 'In the Navy we thought he was a politician'.

15. Fisher as C-in-C, Mediterranean.

16. Lord Charles Beresford as a Rear Admiral. (By courtesy of the National Portrait Gallery).

17. The anniversary of Trafalgar. Nelson leaves it to Fisher.

THE ANNIVERSARY OF TRAFALGAR

NELSON (*in Trafalgar Square*): "I was on my way down to lend them a myself, but if Jacky Fisher's taking on the job there's no need for me to b nervous. I'll get back on my pedestal."
Nelson looking up Sir John Fisher on his first day as First Sea Lord. Trafalgar Day, 1904

18. Admiral of the Fleet Lord Fisher, GCB, OM, about 1907.

19. The King, in confidence with Fisher.

20. *Pall Mall Gazette* cartoon of Fisher's fight for the Navy Estimates, 1908.

21. Strube cartoon of the scrapping policy.

ORIGINAL DREADNOUGHT PROPOSAL

PLAN

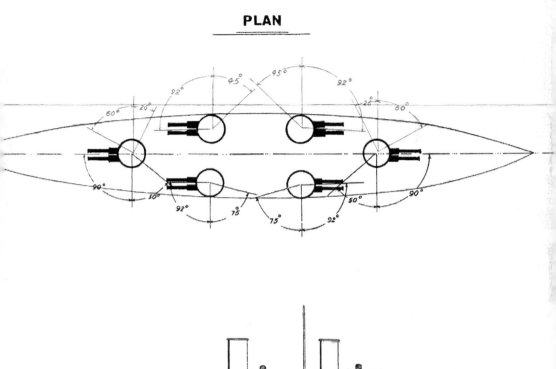

ACCEPTED DREADNOUGHT DESIGN

A

PLAN.

22. The *Dreadnought* design.

23. HMS *Dreadnought* going to sea for the first time.

24. Beresford's Mediterranean Fleet at Malta, 1906.

25. Admiral Sir Percy Scott.

26. Beresford as C-in-C Channel Fleet, with his staff, 1907. *L to R front row:* Sturdee, Beresford (with Kora), Henry Pelly, Flag Captain. *Back row:* Herbert Gibbs, Flag Lieutenant, Fawcett Wray, Flag Commander, John Keys, Fleet Paymaster, Charles Roper, Signal Lieutenant.

27. *Punch* cartoon of the dispute between Beresford and Percy Scott, with the Kaiser's untimely arrival.

28. HMS *King Edward V11*, 'a flagshippy flagship'.

29. The front cover of *The Tatler*, March 31, 1909. "BEWARE OF THE (BERESFORD) BULLDOG – HE BITES! The above photograph shows Sir 'Jacky' Fisher, the Admiralty 'boss' wearing an expression of the deepest and most touching melancholy. This we have endeavoured to explain by the introduction into the picture of an old sea dog who has just had his bone taken away. The question now is, 'Is Sir John a dreadnought – or isn't he?'"

30. 'The Commercial
     Traveller'. A cartoon
     in *Vanity Fair*, 1899.

31. A wartime placard of Fisher including a photograph of Epstein's bust completed
    in 1916.

Few of the men had ever heard the order and all refused it despite its repetition, but at last all but one man complied. Collard showed a modicum of tact, dismissing the men and explaining privately to the individual concerned the origin of his order and taking no further action.

But the Press got hold of the story and, with characteristic distortion, Collard was said to have addressed Acton angrily, 'Go down on your knees, you dirty dog, and learn your manners!' Collard had made himself ridiculous and was greeted with the cry 'On the knee!' whenever he appeared. Finally one night a drunken sailor called it out and three hundred men wrecked the canteen, then setting off towards the wardroom. The Guard was turned out with fixed bayonets, while the rioters smashed everything in their way throughout the night. This was repeated the following night and Collard was court-martialled for giving an unauthorized punishment to Acton, using abusive language and making an improper use of the order 'On the knee!'. So out of date was the order that several members of the Court had never heard of it. Collard was found guilty on one charge, but general slackness in the Barracks was primarily to blame. The damage done to the Navy was immense and suspicion of subversion arose. Fisher changed the Commodore, the Commander and some of the junior officers.

Many naval officers associated Yexley with subversion and considered him a mere agitator. More blamed Fisher, asserting, somewhat curiously, that his reforms had undermined discipline! The historian who claims 'men got fed and clothed in the Navy, which was more than could be guaranteed ashore' should look again. The pay of an able seaman had hardly changed in fifty years and in the first decade of the century was 1s 7d a day (under 8p or 55p per week; about £36 per week in 1990 equivalents). This was not supplemented by much in kind. Food was better than it had been, but quite bad enough. Refrigeration was new and diet consisted largely of salt meat. The three meals a day were sparse, breakfast consisting of bread and cocoa at 5 am. Messes of about twenty men chose a 'cook of the mess' in rotation, who was responsible for drawing food to the value of the ration allowance, preparing meals and taking them to the inadequate galley for cooking by remarkably inexpert cooks. If the full ration allowance was not used a sum was paid in lieu, known as 'mess savings', and in messes dominated by those wishing to save, men were seriously undernourished. Mess savings were also used to supplement diet from the ship's canteen, run for profit by private contractors, largely unregulated. Contracts were granted by commanding officers who frequently left it to the master-at-arms, who often accepted bribes. *The Bluejacket* claimed in 1900 that a trader had offered £700 per annum to supply a canteen and in 1906 an officer's wife was said to have demanded that her furniture be sent to Malta in return for a contract. In the age of paintwork and polish, when officers paid for extra varnish and gilt, when ratings were as proud of their ship as the officers, the canteen was

121

expected to supply free cleaning gear and stores, paid for by higher prices.

Yexley ran a campaign for improvements in victualling, taken up by other journals. When soldiers on passage were issued with meat from HMS *Ramillies*, questions were asked in Parliament about salt beef dated 1893 and the answer indicated this was normal. What was unacceptable for the Army was normal in the Navy! The *United Services Gazette* called for a Parliamentary committee and in 1900 a committee under Vice-Admiral Ernest Rice interpreted the high proportion of food turned down in pursuit of mess savings as evidence of its adequacy and described the standard in the fleet as 'unnecessarily high'.

Men were obliged to buy their own uniform and it became more elaborate and expensive. Kit musters were an obsession with some officers. They were carried out by the Ship's Police and taken to absurd lengths to comply with exact dimensions, involving substantial expenditure, and men were often prepared to pay a consideration to the Master-at-Arms to save expense.

Fisher was always keenly interested in the lower deck and studied with care their every concern; not for nothing was he universally known as 'Jacky'. Yet during his fifteen months as Second Naval Lord he appears to have failed to grapple with questions of victualling, uniform and low rates of pay. But when Yexley surrendered the editorship of *The Bluejacket* he entered into partnership with Gerard Meynell, a director of the *Westminster Press*, whose wife, Esther Hallam Moorhouse, a naval historian, was a close friend of Fisher. Yexley and Meynell started a journal called *The Fleet*, sold for two pence monthly and declared it represented the whole cross-section of ratings. From the first issue Yexley sent a copy to Fisher, who contributed a personal message to the July 1905 number, wishing it success, tactfully placing it in a recognized, semi-official position and removing any potential antagonism between the journal and officialdom. This convinced the naval rating that the First Sea Lord was ready to listen, defused possible trouble and encouraged men to air their grievances in *The Fleet* bringing their feelings into the open and keeping him in touch with the lower deck. If he had depended on 'the usual channels', reports passing through captains, admirals and commanders-in-chief would have been 'slanted', perhaps unconsciously, by the views of reactionary officers. At that time it was a quite new and brilliant move, though of course he was derided and denigrated by those who thought *The Fleet* a scurrilous rag.

Later, Oswyn Murray, then Assistant Director of Victualling, (later Secretary of the Admiralty) invited Yexley to discuss the problems of messing and wrote:

> Please go on criticising us to the full, for it does us good. Above all, let the men know through *The Fleet* that if only they show a strong desire

for reform, they are certain in these days to carry the Board of Admiralty with them.[48]

A few weeks later Fisher asked Yexley to meet him at his home to provide more information about corruption in canteens. Yexley thought Fisher did not understand the resentment caused by the provision of cleaning gear at the expense of higher prices, but stressed the matter. 'He did not reply, he just stiffened; his eyes opened until they became as round as saucers, and they looked at me with a kind of fixed glare. I could only liken them to one of the great cats at the zoo who gave the impression of being about to spring.'[49]

Fisher made his own enquiries and the next week again met Yexley, who realized he had won an ally. A committee was formed under Rear-Admiral Spencer Login. The official rations were valued at 10d a day (£3 in 1990s) and Yexley proposed that this should be divided into a standard ration of 6d and a messing allowance of 4d to be spent in the canteen at the price they were allowed for mess savings. The Login Committee agreed, paymasters were given greater control to deter corruption and a 'general messing' scheme was tried out in the new *Dreadnought*. A canteen inspectorate was formed and a list of acceptable contractors maintained at the Admiralty, who, in October 1909, took over the award of contracts. The result was an increase in mess savings equivalent to a rise in pay of about 16%. Yexley also campaigned for free uniform, but, as an alternative, advocated reduction in the cost by the withdrawal of unnecessary or unserviceable items, reducing the cost of a sailor's uniform from £9 5s to £6 5s.[50]

Discipline and punishment also came under Fisher's scrutiny, though much criticism was due to misunderstanding of the difference between the Army and the Navy. A ship might be on detached duty for many months at a time and the commanding officer had to have powers of punishment without recourse to trial by court martial. His powers therefore greatly exceeded those of the equivalent in the Army, where a court martial could usually be readily assembled.

The regulations were supplemented by Standing Orders for the ship and individual departments. The outsider described as 'trivial' orders that men were not to go over the lower boom with their trousers turned up, that they were not to lean on the forecastle rails, that cap ribbons were to be worn with the letter 'S' of HMS *Royal Sovereign* over the nose, and that kettle lids were not to be used for kneeling on. All these orders were based on common sense. Going over the lower boom so attired could result in trousers caught in projections; guardrails, designed for rapid dismantling, could collapse, resulting in a man overboard. The rule about cap ribbons was to ensure uniformity; it could hardly be left to individual taste! A 'mess kettle' was not the same as the shore article; it was a large vessel, the lid a convenient size for kneeling on and would soon become unserviceable if so used. Ill-informed agitation from outsiders caused unnecessary discontent.

Fisher and Yexley corresponded regularly, not only on welfare, but on defence policy. On 1 August 1909 Fisher wrote:

> Dear Yexley. . . .
>
> The *Observer* has hit the right nail on the head in its leading article recommending the 'Indomitable' type for colonial imitation, and not the small Beresfordian cruisers, which like ants will all be eaten up by one 'Indomitable' Armadillo, which puts out its tongue and licks them all up! . . .
>
> I asked the First Lord to see you some time back. I think he will shortly. I want him to get from you *first hand* all that the Bluejacket, the Marine and the Warrant Officer still lack![51]

Fisher earned and retained Yexley's confidence, which was reflected by the men of the Navy.

9

THE *DREADNOUGHT* REVOLUTION

Steam, mines, mobile torpedoes, bigger and better guns, increased ranges, breech loaders and fast destroyers brought about a state of confusion in naval tactics, but by the turn of the century they were beginning to crystallize. While in the Mediterranean, with advice on design detail from W.H.Gard, the Chief Constructor at Malta, Fisher reflected deeply on the ships of the future. He continued the work at Portsmouth, where fortunately Gard had moved. Fisher concentrated on armament, protection and speed. The new generation of ship must out-gun and out-run any other ship in the world; she must hit the target before the enemy could engage her and must be fast enough to ensure that he could not escape. But there were two dangers. Much emphasized by the 'Historical' school, the introduction of a new concept in large warships could reduce all navies to scratch and Britain's preponderance be lost. But if another country built the new all-big-gun fast battleship first, all older British battleships would be worthless; the US Navy had a design ready for a similar ship in 1902 (though it was not built until much later) and it could be surmised that Germany would work on the same lines. Fisher decided the latter was the greater risk; for Germany, Japan and Russia were thinking similarly. 'It is not without interest to learn from secret information . . . that a uniform armament of 12-inch guns for the future Russian and Japanese battleships has been decided upon as the outcome of the experience of these two countries in the war between them. The speed of their battleships will be 20 knots . . . the first desideratum in every type of fighting vessel is a greater speed than . . . the enemy's ships. It is the "weather gauge" of the olden days.'[1]

Long-range firing was more general in 1902, and in 1903–4 fire control and long-range firing experiments were successfully carried out in the battleships *Venerable* and *Victorious* at about 8,000 yards. In the Russo–Japanese war, the first major naval war since the Crimea, the British Naval Attaché,

Captain W.C.Pakenham (later Admiral Sir William) was in one of Togo's battleships at the Battle of the Yellow Sea and wrote that ranges of 20,000 metres seemed possible and 14,000 metres were 'reasonable'. At Tsushima he was again in Togo's flagship and confirmed this view. He suggested a battleship of 14,500 tons with six 12-inch guns and a speed of 21 knots. Fisher went further. His new ship was to carry the maximum number of the biggest available guns and must be built *first*.

But increasing ranges led to greater difficulty in determining them. In earlier days a ranging shot from one of the guns was, at a few hundred yards, a satisfactory way of gauging the range, but as ranges increased to thousands of yards it became impossible to judge where the shot fell. Much had been done to elaborate the science of gunnery, especially by Percy Scott. Even at the bombardment of Alexandria open sight directors had been used, with verbal transmission of director setting, but range was a matter of guesswork. The increasing use of directors had enabled guns separated over the length of a ship to be aimed on a converging path, so that all projectiles should arrive at a point. This could never be perfect, for minute discrepancies in guns and projectiles led to scatter, but it enabled a new system of ranging to be adopted. The range was first estimated, initially by eye, but in the last years of the 19th century the Barr and Stroud 4' 6" rangefinder was adopted, then a ranging salvo was fired. Ideally five projectiles were required for the separate splashes to be seen. When all fell short, the range had been under-estimated, while if it fell over, it had been overestimated; if some were over and some short, the range had been found and fire could then be opened with all guns.

The problem of ranging naval guns is complicated by the fact that, as opposing ships converge or diverge, range changes and the rate of change varies, even when ships remain on the same course. This is exacerbated by the change taking place during the time of flight of projectiles, by the rolling, pitch, heave and yaw of the firing ship. Much attention was paid to methods of measuring the enemy speed and course, and determining the enemy range at the time of arrival of the projectile. Some of the solutions offered, especially by those without seagoing experience or technical knowledge, were wholly impracticable. One of these was Arthur Hungerford Pollen, a lawyer turned journalist, who described himself as a 'naval correspondent' for *The Westminster Gazette* and the *Daily Mail*. He had never served at sea and had little scientific education, but by marriage became Managing Director of the Linotype Company, manufacturers of printing machinery. In 1900 he visited a relation in Malta and met a number of junior naval officers, who explained to him some of the many difficulties of naval gun-nery. He was invited by his cousin Lieutenant William Goodenough (later Admiral Sir William) to witness gunnery trials, when he was impressed by the poor showing of the 1889 battleship *Empress of India*'s old-style, breech-loading, 13.5-inch guns, manufactured when still under the control of the War Office, a design which involved returning the guns to a fixed heading to reload. Pollen compared the performance of these outdated guns with that of the smaller ones Scott had mounted ashore at Ladysmith, with which there could be no comparison, and determined to design equipment to ascertain the range, course and speed of the enemy in relation to the firing ship, from which the position of the enemy at the end of the time of flight could be calculated and mechanically relayed to the guns, a 'subject for which he had no possible qualification.'[2] With little mathematical knowledge himself – he later admitted his mathematics were 'not up to it' – he placed this problem in the hands of his technicians in the Linotype Company who suggested the use of simple trigonometry to ascertain range by placing two observers, one each end of the ship, so as to provide the largest possible base.[3] The basic principle was sound and had been applied since 1892 in the Watkins Position Finder, manufactured by Thomas Cooke of York, which then transmitted range and bearing to the guns by mechanical means. The first 'step-by-step' electric transmitter had been adopted as long ago as 1887, though only to transmit orders.

Fisher, when Commander-in-Chief Mediterranean, had introduced firing at 6,000 yards in HMS *Scylla* commanded by Percy Scott, and in the same year as Pollen's visit had carried out firing in five ships at 6,000 yards and in eight others at 5,500 yards.

In January 1901 Pollen wrote to Lord Walter Kerr, then First Sea Lord ('a family friend'), and offered his ideas to the Admiralty to develop. Kerr referred him to Selborne, who refused him an interview and suggested he should submit his proposals officially to the Admiralty. This he did the following month, receiving an immediate rejection. So he sent his 'prospectus' to a number of prominent naval officers, including Beresford, who appears to have been the only one to reply, and apparently without referring the matter to Fisher, his C-in-C, responded that 'The advantages claimed for your system, provided they can be realised, are undoubtedly of the greatest value . . . I think you have made out a very good case for being granted a trial of your system.'[4] In March the following year Pollen, associated with a self-employed engineer, Mark Barr, took out a patent on the apparatus and in May 1904 took out a further one on equipment he claimed took the two bearings simultaneously and transmitted them mechanically to a computing mechanism. But in 1902 Lieutenant Fawcett Wray had already invented a device by which the rate of change of range (the 'rate') could be calculated and the year previous to Pollen's application had invented the first 'clock'.

In May 1904 Pollen again proposed that the Admiralty should develop his system and was again rejected; he could hardly expect the Admiralty to do the development work on an apparatus on which he held a patent and all financial control! But Pollen turned to his father-in-law, Sir Joseph Lawrence, a Conservative MP, and through political pressure gained an interview with Kerr and May, now Controller, who informed him that no action would be taken without a complete description of the system in writing. Pollen again appealed to Beresford, now in command of the Channel Squadron, who, with little knowledge of gunnery himself, then formed a committee of gunnery lieutenants from his squadron to advise him. This extraordinary action without authority was effectively working against the Admiralty, who wanted to know whether Pollen had any good ideas they themselves could not develop. Advised by these officers, Pollen wrote a *Memorandum on a Proposed System for Finding Ranges at Sea and Ascertaining the Speed and Course of any Vessel in Sight*, which he sent to the Admiralty in November 1904. It was a pompously worded and arrogant paper which implied that he was dealing with fools, who had never heard of trigonometry (taught in depth at the long gunnery course and used extensively in navigation and nautical surveying). The Admiralty then formed a committee under Henry Oliver consisting of Lieutenant Thomas Crease, Captain Edward Harding, Royal Marine Artillery, and Captain B.J.W.Locke from the War Office, all of whom were expert gunnery officers. They met in December and, dissatisfied with Pollen's design, recommended rejection.

Pollen then started an extensive campaign. He wrote to everyone who mattered and many who did not, especially Beresford and Custance; with access to the Press in his journalistic role he gained vast publicity. But, recognizing there was more to fire control than he had imagined, he modified his proposals in a ponderous paper dated December, 1904 and entitled: *Fire Control and Long-Range Firing: an Essay to Define Certain Principia of Gunnery, and to Suggest Means for Their Application*, again putting forward his two-observer system, adding a 'change of range machine', which he claimed would register target range and bearing. He sent twenty-five copies of the paper to selected naval officers and again demanded that the Admiralty should develop his system at their expense.

Jellicoe became Director of Naval Ordnance in February 1905 and, advised by the members of Oliver's committee, who examined Pollen's proposals to overcome their objections, agreed to trials in HMS *Narcissus* which showed that, if a workable design could be manufactured, there were some prospects of success, and a set of his equipment was ordered for trial. In the meantime, however, Jellicoe and Percy Scott made criticisms of his methods, which resulted in further modifications by Pollen. Unfortunately for him, he was unable to design the change of range machine which he had promised. Even so, trials began in November at Portsmouth and Glengarriff in HMS *Jupiter* with the incomplete equipment. These exposed several fundamental design and manufacturing errors, especially his failure to understand the need to correct for yaw. Pollen therefore fitted a torpedo gyroscope driven by a spring mechanism, which only lasted for four minutes. Mark Barr had by this time parted company with Pollen, but luckily his technicians found a means of driving the gyroscope by compressed air.

In 1904 the Admiralty had, quite independently from Pollen, advertised for a range-finder of greater accuracy than the 4' 6" Barr and Stroud in current use. Almost simultaneously with Pollen's other problems Barr and Stroud produced the 9-foot rangefinder and Thomas Cooke of York produced a 10-foot version. As a result of these developments Pollen called off the trials in January 1906, to the great inconvenience of the Admiralty, and began a re-design of all his equipment. But in May he collected letters he had written to many naval officers and had them printed. He suppressed the recipients' names in some of these, but included Bacon, Beresford, Dreyer (one of the most advanced gunnery officers of his day), Fisher, Jellicoe, Kerr, Scott, Tweedmouth (the new First Lord) and A.K.Wilson. Throughout these letters Pollen adopted a posture of contempt for gunnery officers, whom he called 'amateurs'! Professor Sumida remarks, 'Pollen's call for a battleship with larger guns, higher speed and less armour may have caught the eye of Sir John Fisher, the First Sea Lord, whose views on capital ship design were quite similar'.[5] *Dreadnought* had been launched in February that year and the battlecruisers already designed.

By June Pollen believed he had solved his technical problems and again approached the Admiralty for trials. Jellicoe agreed to a trial of the gyroscope system provided agreement could be reached on the commercial terms, but 'Pollen's objective at this time was to persuade the Admiralty to accept responsibility for the manufacture of the AC [Aim Correction] instruments.'[6] Jellicoe refused to go further than to subscribe £4,500 (£¼m in 1990s) towards the cost of manufacture; few buyers of engineering equipment expect to meet the costs of development. Pollen now wrote a long history of his equipment to Tweedmouth, who naturally referred it to Fisher. At this stage Fisher optimistically expected the equipment could be properly developed and wrote over-enthusiastically to Tweedmouth, '*Pollen's invention is simply priceless* and I do hope we may hesitate at nothing to get ITS SOLE USE. We shall NEVER be forgiven if we do not! Jellicoe's arguments are so cogent and convincing that it's useless my enlarging on them!'[7] As Pollen's conceit and technical inexpertise became more apparent Fisher's opinion changed, but his view then had considerable impact, for the Admiralty agreed to a costly series of experiments, to subscribe to Pollen's development costs, to recognize him as sole inventor and if the system proved successful to pay him a sum of £140,000, (about £7½m in 1990s' value) for the monopoly, plus a royalty for each set fitted. A prototype Change of Range machine which Pollen had been unable to design for the *Jupiter* Trials was delivered in May 1906 and immediately he applied for a patent.

He now became even more audacious by entering the field of naval tactics. In October 1906 Custance wrote an article in *Blackwood's Magazine* and in *The United Service Magazine* entitled *The Speed of the Capital Ship*, in which he tried to denigrate the *Dreadnought*. Pollen protected his interests by opposing the views of Custance. His propaganda continued and he wrote numerous articles and papers, which he distributed liberally, until it became accepted by the lay public and the less intelligent naval officers that he was an expert in gunnery. In August 1907 Jellicoe was relieved by Reginald Bacon, and shortly afterwards Frederic Dreyer took over from Harding. Harding was said to have supported Pollen, Dreyer and Bacon to have opposed him. Dreyer had for long been involved in the problems of fire control and was a good choice to relieve Harding whose time was up. It has been claimed that Bacon, as a torpedoman, was opposed to gunnery, and Dreyer believed in manual methods of fire control. In fact, Bacon was a gunnery specialist and Dreyer a gunnery officer of distinction who had long worked on electro-mechanical means of control.

In November 1907 A.K.Wilson was asked to supervise further trials in HMS *Ariadne*. A gunnery officer, a recognised tactician and a mathematician, no better could have been chosen; Jackson told Pollen 'If [the system] can be broken, he will do it.'[8] He found the system was incomplete and told Pollen, 'You will have to explain to me some time or other, why on earth Admiralty should pay you £100,000 [£5.5m in 1990s] more than to Barr and Stroud or to any other maker of fire control instruments that have got to be used for your system'.[9]

Wilson then wrote to Pollen shrewdly asking for a 'written statement showing exactly what are the advantages you claim for your system as fitted in the *Ariadne*, and for which the Admiralty are asked to pay £100,000'.[10] Pollen was evasive and sent him a copy of his notes for a lecture he had been invited to give at the War College, Portsmouth. Wilson replied, 'I have read your lecture and it does not quite answer my question. . . . As far as I can see the only paragraphs in the lecture which refer to the apparatus which is fitted in the *Ariadne* are 17 and 18 and possibly part of 23. The rest, I understand, has not even been designed and . . . is not included in the £100,000.'[11]

During December 1907 and January 1908 trials were carried out between Pollen's gear in *Ariadne* and Dreyer's in *Vengeance*. Pollen consistently referred to Dreyer's system as 'the Wilson-Dreyer manual system'. It was neither. Wilson, renowned for fairness, was an independent umpire and had nothing to do with the development, which, utilizing the Vickers's clock and the Dumaresq, invented by Lieutenant John Saumarez Dumaresq in 1902, using a trigonometric slide, recorded the target course, speed and bearing and the change of range, rate and deflection, preceding Pollen's in origin. At the end of the trials it was plain that Dreyer's gear was at least as good as Pollen's, whose equipment cost four times that of Dreyer's. Pollen then attempted to force the hand of the Admiralty, threatening to sell his ideas abroad, demanding £300,000 (£16.5m in 1990s) for the monopoly, which even his relation, Moore, Bacon's successor as DNO, described as 'hush money'.[12] The Admiralty made it clear that they had no objection to his selling his equipment abroad and he sold to eight of the lesser navies, but the Germans were apparently not interested.

The story continues well into the war years. Pollen's Linotype Company was forced to merge with its American counterpart, leaving him without manufacturing facilities, obliging him to take over Thomas Cooke of York. After the war Pollen made a claim on the Royal Commission on awards to inventors, briefing a top barrister, Wilfred Greene, (later Lord Greene, Master of the Rolls), and was awarded £30,000, though this seems to be more for his efforts than his success. That 'The capability of the Pollen system was far superior to that of the alternative fire control system adopted by the Royal Navy for service during the First World War'[13] seems dubious; the evidence is hard to find. Despite his perseverance and propaganda, he never produced a workable version of his apparatus.

Fisher was very familiar with these problems and, like Scott, Jellicoe, Bacon and Dreyer, was immersed in them for many years. The gunnery problem led to the need for large numbers of guns of the same calibre so that the fall of shot was as nearly as possible the same. It would be unusual for the first salvo to find the range, so it was necessary to correct the range after the first and fire a second as quickly as possible. Reloading took time, so it was desirable to use only half the guns for the first ranging salvo, leaving the second half for the second salvo. By the time further corrections had been made, the first half of the guns would again be ready and, once the range had been found, all guns could be used continuously.

The next decisions were calibre and range. Pakenham said that when ships were being hit by 12-inch shells 'no one paid the least attention' to smaller shells. Moreover the accuracy of gunfire is much increased with heavier guns; the heavier the projectile at a given velocity, the more accurate at all ranges. Between 1899 and 1905 battleship design passed from the mixed armament of four 12-inch and twelve 6-inch of *Formidable*, through the four 12-inch, four 9.2-inch and ten 6-inch of *King Edward VII*, and four 12—inch, ten 9.2-inch and fifteen 12 pounders (3-inch) of *Lord Nelson* to the ten 12-inch and 27 12-pounders of *Dreadnought*, the last for defence against torpedo boats and destroyers.

Scott wrote, 'The mounting of only one pattern of gun was a most important innovation as regards fighting efficiency, and Lord Fisher deserves great credit for having introduced it. But alas, when he left office some years later he took his brain with him, and a brainless Admiralty started again to build ships with mixed armaments.'[14]

There has in recent years been denigration of Fisher on both sides of the

Atlantic. However obvious the statements, 'It is short-range firing that gives the maximum penetration of armour. In 1905 the thickest battleship armour could be penetrated at short ranges, but not at long ranges,'[15] this is simplistic, for what is the 'thickest armour'? It assumes the same weight and explosive power of shell. It ignores the well-known equation for kinetic energy[16] which is the reason for the use of heavier shells and larger-calibre guns which reduce loss of velocity at longer ranges.[17] It also ignores the fact that a shell hitting the enemy at an oblique angle has a greater thickness of armour to penetrate than if striking at right angles. Fisher had recognized the facts and this was why he adopted heavy guns.

Fisher did not confine his attention to the battleship. A need had arisen for a new type of ship to deal with German transatlantic liners designed for conversion into armed merchant cruisers. A new class of ship was needed with a margin of speed over the German liners and with gun range sufficient to prevent the enemy approaching within torpedo range. The speed was quickly decided as 25.5 knots, which gave the necessary margin. But the guns were the subject of long argument. Warship design is always a compromise between speed, which determines the weight of machinery, protection, which determines that of armour, endurance that of fuel, and armament. To build such ships solely for fighting AMCs was not economical and they must be capable of supplementing the fleet, though never intended to be part of the battle fleet. They were to be lightly armoured to achieve their high speed, so that they could dash in and harry enemy ships or operate as fast scouts capable of defending themselves. To do this they needed 12-inch guns. An advantage was the economy and flexibility of common gun design and ammunition for both types of ship. So a new concept was born and the new ships, at first called 'armoured cruisers', were clearly different from those existing.

Foreseeing events in the First World War, Fisher wrote in his war plans of 1906–7:

> The commonest aspect of our old naval wars is a British fleet endeavouring to force an unwilling enemy to action by an attack in general chase. It is superior speed that is the essence of success in such warfare, and no probable superiority in tactics can ever give so great an advantage as superior speed. . . . However venerable may be the maxim that the speed of a fleet is that of its slowest ship, it is not universally true. It is broadly true for a fleet trying to avoid action but for a chasing fleet it is the converse of the truth . . . for a chasing fleet the speed is that of the fastest ships. By their means – provided they have sufficient battle strength to hold their own for a while – a battle fleet of lesser speed can reach out and grasp the flying enemy by the tail, and hold him until it has time to get him firmly in its grip. For this

purpose no ship was ever designed so deadly as the 'Invincibles'. . . .
It is the very type that all the old men from Hawke to Nelson sighed
for, but never obtained.[18]

His ideas were to be proved at Jutland. He studied them in detail and then
submitted them to criticism by an unofficial committee of the 'five best
brains below the rank of admiral': Captain H.B.Jackson, Controller desig-
nate, a Fellow of the Royal Society, (later Admiral of the Fleet Sir Henry),
Jellicoe, Bacon, Captain Charles Madden, (later Admiral of the Fleet Sir
Charles), Lieutenant Wilfred Henderson (later Vice Admiral Sir Wilfred),
Gard and Gracie. Fisher infected his advisors with his enthusiasm, but both
political parties were devoted to economy and the two battleships *Lord
Nelson* and *Agamemnon* had already been approved with a mixed armament
and high superstructure, presenting a huge target, and more were planned.
If more were built, there would be little money for his future ships which
rendered existing ones obsolete. Once embarked upon, the new programme
must go ahead fast. So he asked Selborne to agree to the formation of an
official Committee on New Designs and in August wrote:

> About the Committee on new designs, I am also delighted with your
> approval! One thing I VERY SPECIALLY *wish you to do*: Not to take
> any step to lay down any fresh battleships, or that will in any way bind
> you to do so, until you have allowed me to set before you in detail in
> October next why we should hold our hands in this matter! . . . My *one*
> object is to entreat you not to allow us to be committed to lay down
> 'Lord Nelsons' *or anything else* until we have had a discussion next
> November.[19]

Later that month he received the cordial approval of the Prince of Wales:

> My Dear Sir John,
>   Many thanks for your letter and the preamble on new designs of
> fighting ships, which I have read with great interest and shall, of course,
> keep secret. I am sure they will be splendid fighting machines and I so
> agree with you about the increase of speed. . . . Of course the 'Snail'
> and 'Tortoise' classes ought to be abolished; they are utterly useless
> for anything. . . .
>   So you have actually disclosed all your proposals to Lord Selborne,
> and you must be relieved that he has taken it like a lamb. If you have
> him on your side, you will be all right.[20]

Many historians hostile to Fisher have claimed the committee was a device
to keep the syndicate of discontent at bay, but this is far from the case. It
was officially appointed in an Admiralty Letter dated 22 December 1904[21]
and included all the members of Fisher's committee with the additions of

Battenberg, Sir John Durston, Engineer-in-Chief of the Fleet, Rear Admiral Alfred Winsloe, commanding Torpedo and Submarine Flotillas, Philip Watts (later Sir Philip), Director of Naval Construction, Lord Kelvin, Professor Biles of Glasgow University, Sir John Thornycroft, and R.E.Froude, Superintendent of the Admiralty Experimental Works at Haslar, the foremost expert on hull form and speed. Henderson was appointed Secretary with E.H.Mitchell, Assistant Constructor, as Assistant Secretary. Discussion was deep and thorough, ensuring that well-considered proposals would result. But Fisher expanded the terms of reference to consider five types of ship: (i) the battleship, (ii) an armoured cruiser, (iii) ocean-going destroyers of 33 knots speed 'in average weather' and about 600 tons, (iv) coastal destroyers of about 250 tons and 26 knots and an experimental ocean-going destroyer aiming at 36 knots in average weather.

The principles of Fisher's concept were adhered to. The speed of the battleship was to be 21 knots, the guns to be 12-inch and as numerous as possible, with anti-torpedo craft guns only as secondary armament, and no big guns were to be mounted on the main deck which would have been unusable in heavy weather. The armour was to be 'adequate' and she was to be capable of using the docks at Portsmouth, Devonport, Malta and Gibraltar. The specification for the 'armoured cruiser' was similar, but the speed was to be 25 knots and the armour similar to that of the 'Minotaur' class armoured cruisers then under construction (6" side, 8" turret, and 1.5" deck).

The most intransigent problem was in the arrangement of the guns to avoid blast from one gun affecting the crews of another, which would have hampered the use of that turret. Nine different designs were considered for the battleship; originally Fisher wanted twelve 12-inch guns but was compelled by the limitations of design to reduce this to ten, in five twin turrets. In 1895 the Ordnance Committee had carried out experiments to ascertain the area in front of guns affected by blast, its distribution and pressures at specific distances from the muzzle.[22] Using cordite, the 12-inch gun created a pressure in the barrel of 7 tons per square inch and of 30 lbs per square foot at a distance as great as 150 feet in front of the muzzle, nearly a third the length of the ship. The committee concluded that it would not be practical to employ personnel within a sphere of 70 feet radius, with a centre 55 feet directly in line with the muzzle, greatly restricting arcs of training.

With increasing lengths of ships, traditional broadside fire, while still of importance, was no longer the sole requirement and an enemy might force an end-on engagement, particularly when 'crossing the T', so all-round fire was now of importance, even though superior speed gave the advantage in choosing the range and bearing. In the arrangement recommended by the committee three turrets were mounted on the centreline, while one was placed on each side, so that all but one turret could be used on each broadside while two, and in some circumstances three, could be used directly ahead or astern.

The anti-torpedo-craft armament of twenty-seven 12-pdr (3") QF guns was as widely distributed as possible to reduce chances of damage to numbers of guns by single enemy projectiles. Two conning towers were fitted, the after one as a standby in case of damage to the main one or the communication system and to accommodate the torpedo officer and signalman. The forecastle freeboard was 28 feet, enabling all guns to be used in almost any weather. The main armour belt had a maximum thickness of 11 inches, reduced to 6 inches at the forward end and 4 inches aft. The deck varied from 1.75 to 2.75 inches. An attempt was made to provide anti-torpedo measures, the magazine being kept high in the ship and protected by armour of 2" to 2.5" thickness. All main transverse bulkheads were un-pierced except for essential cables and pipes. Turbine main engines were early decided upon. The reciprocating engine had reached its zenith. Fisher's 14-knot fleet in the Mediterranean was, as Beresford had testified, considered a great achievement. Battenberg steamed six ships from New York to Gibraltar in 1905, but only three of them achieved an average speed of 18.5 knots, arriving with coal stocks almost exhausted and requiring extensive repairs.

HMS *Viper* of 1898, the fastest destroyer of her day, had been fitted with four turbines totalling 10,000 horsepower and on special trials achieved a speed of 36.5 knots. *Amethyst*, a triple-screw light cruiser, was under construction, while the French were fitting turbines to torpedo-boat G293 and the Germans in S125 and the cruiser *Lübeck*. But *Dreadnought*'s 23,000 horsepower was a leap forward, reducing weight, maintenance, vibration and engine-room complement, while saving fuel. But lengthy discussion took place on the problem of astern power, as it was believed this would be insufficient for ease of manoeuvring, especially in a squadron. Charles Parsons was invited to give evidence. His proposals were accepted after comparative trials between HMS *Eden*, a turbine-driven destroyer, and HMS *Waveney* of the same class with reciprocating engines, which showed the former to handle at least as well as the latter. In addition, Winsloe, Jellicoe and Madden carried out trials at sea in the turbine steamer *Queen*, on which they reported favourably. Froude also carried out extensive experiments at Haslar to determine horsepower and speed ratios. 'No greater single step towards efficiency in war was ever made than the introduction of the turbine,' wrote Bacon, 'Previous to its adoption every day's steaming at high speed meant several days overhaul of machinery in harbour. All this was to be changed as if by magic.'[23]

Coal capacity was to be 2,400 tons, giving the ship an endurance of 5,800 miles at economical speed and 3,500 at 18 knots. Oil fuel stowage was also provided as an alternative. The final outcome was a battleship of 17,900 tons, 490 feet long and 82 feet beam. She was named *Dreadnought*, in classic Fisher language.

For the armoured cruiser six designs were studied. As in the battleship, much argument took place concerning the arrangement of the guns, and, as the ship was intended to chase, using her speed to choose the range, it was desirable that she should be exceptionally strong in end-on fire and attempts were made to locate the guns at the extremities, abandoned due to the resulting excessive pitching. Consideration was given to reducing the number of guns to six but the saving in weight was not justified and the idea was abandoned. In the final arrangement one turret was mounted each end and one on each broadside, so arranged that all eight 12" guns could be trained on either broadside, though blast prohibited the use of both broad-side guns simultaneously on the same side. The 4" anti-torpedo-boat guns were distributed similarly to those of the battleship and the freeboard forward was 30 feet, again ensuring the guns could all be used in a seaway, the forecastle extended to abaft the broadside guns. The armour protection was 6" thick amidships, reducing to 4" forward and terminating abaft the after redoubt, where a 6" armoured transverse bulkhead was installed. The armour of the fore conning tower was 10" and the after one 6". The deck armour was 1.5" on the flat and 2" on the slopes. Turbine machinery was chosen and, though Parsons originally proposed 38,000 horsepower, she was eventually built with 41,000 on four shafts. She carried 3,000 tons of coal, giving endurance of 5,500 miles, and, like the battleship, could also burn oil. She was named *Invincible*.

In an addendum it was stated 'for an equal number of guns that can be fired on the broadside, the length of the line of battle will be exactly half.'[24] This point was important, for the longer the line of battle, the easier the target for torpedoes.

Though the terms of reference had included the three types of destroyers, the committee decided that design of these vessels was better left to the specialist firms and did not therefore make any proposals. They then divided into four sub-committees on 'General Details', 'Armament and Naval Details', 'Destroyers' and 'Submarines'. Jackson, Watts, and Durston were on all of them.

The Committee first met on 3 January 1905. It met eight times before the end of January. Its first report was issued in February. The speed with which the work was done was characteristic of Fisher, but the committee's work was exceptionally thorough. Moreover, he discussed the scheme with Sir Arthur Wilson, then in command of the Channel Fleet, whose opinion he valued, and Beresford, no doubt to satisfy his vanity and silence his poten-tial criticism. They both attended the Admiralty on 4 January and both agreed with the proposals.

This did not stop Custance attacking the scheme anonymously. He wrote in May 1905: 'The Committee on Designs . . . is an irresponsible body. Of fifteen members five hold responsible offices . . . the remainder are irresponsible, being either subordinate officials or non-officials, who, as no reports are to be published, will not have to face public criticism. It is an instance of the tendency not only to transfer the control of the *matériel* from the Controller to the First Sea Lord, but to undermine the authority of the other members of the Board over the general shipbuilding policy . . . on which largely preponderate specialists in questions connected with *matériel*, only a very small minority being unconnected with it. . . . Wide knowledge of the principles underlying the conduct of war are inadequately represented. . . . tactical and strategic requirements . . . should be the dominating factors in considering any design.'[25] He went on to argue that speed was of no value. 'Neither in practice nor in theory has it ever been proved that superior speed gives any tactical advantage, unless it be thought an advantage to be able to run away.'[26] He refused to believe that speed gave both the opportunity of choosing the range and the ability to manoeuvre into a strong tactical position, surely obvious to any intelligence. He believed in slow, heavily armoured ships with a mixed armament. The 'historians' were so blinded by the traditional invincibility of the Royal Navy that they despised and ignored modern developments, even including the director or any other of the gunnery innovations pursued by Fisher, Wilson, Scott and Jellicoe. Custance drew his arguments from Salamis, the first Punic War, the Dutch during the seventeenth century and a tortuous and confusing study of the Battle of Tsushima, concluding, 'The matérial school will forget that the great object in battle is to upset the moral equilibrium rather than to perforate armour. They will not understand that it pays better to defeat the crew and capture the ship than to sink her. The Russians alone are in a position to say whether a hail of 6-inch shell is more trying than less numerous 12-inch shell. The larger gun no doubt makes better shooting at long ranges, but at decisive ones – 5000 yards and under – the difference is not great.'[27]

Pakenham had said that when ships were being hit by 12-inch shells 'no one paid the least attention' to smaller ones, and the notion, in modern conditions, of capturing enemy warships in a major battle displayed Custance's unrealism when ranges had already reached 10,000 yards and those of 20,000 were contemplated. 'The conceptions of war held by the present naval advisors of the Government are fundamentally unsound . . . a disposition to exalt the ship above the man. . . . Fighting power is sacrificed to speed, which must be based on the idea not of fighting but of running away. . . . Both views are equally destructive of the true spirit and are opposed to the traditions of the Navy,' wrote Custance.[28]

To refute these arguments Jackson prepared a paper, which he marked

For the use of the Board only. 'Based on the average of the results obtained by the fleet in the 1905 battle practice,' he compared the weight of projectiles that would hit an enemy 'in 10 minutes if the rapidity and accuracy of fire from a pair of 6-inch, 9.2-inch or 12-inch guns equalled the average obtained in that practice' and gave the following figures: two 6-inch guns – 840 lbs; two 9,2-inch 2,812 lbs; two 12-inch 4,250 lbs.[29] A report in 1905 from the Director of Naval Intelligence, Captain Charles Ottley, remarked: 'The present war has indicated the necessity for radical modification of one feature at least, that is the nature of the armament to be carried, and we ourselves have been the very first to recognise this in our latest design of battleship and armoured cruiser. . . . If, as seems probable, the lesson is equally appreciated and acted on by other maritime powers, it is evident that all existing battleships will shortly become obsolescent. . . . We shall have no option, therefore, but to resume our building programme on the same relative scale at once . . . for, unless we do, our superiority will exist only in ships of small fighting value.'[30] To this Fisher appended a note: 'How glad we ought to be that we dropped our battleships and armoured cruisers last year! Why, they are now as obsolete as the Ark!'

The speed with which the programme was achieved was remarkable. The critical item was the gunmountings, so those intended for the 'Lord Nelsons' were appropriated. *Dreadnought* was laid down on 2 October 1905, only nine months from the first sitting of the committee, during which all the decisions were taken, design completed, drawings prepared, materials obtained and machinery built. She sailed for trials under the command of Reginald Bacon on 3 October 1906, a year and a day from laying down. The claim of the Beresfordites that this was achieved by forward ordering of materials, repeated by historians ever since, cannot be true, since the interval between approval of the design and starting work left insufficient time. The remark by one writer that 'it was two months after this much-vaunted time that she actually became ready for sea . . . a minor piece of trickery . . . a public relations coup' is ridiculous. All ships have to go through a period of trials and two months is minuscule compared with many.

Trials in home waters followed and problems arose. During full power trials the low pressure turbines, driving two shafts, developed a much higher proportion of the power than the high pressure ones, obviously an inherent design fault, but one capable of correction in future ships, justifying the decision to suspend future building until experience from *Dreadnought* was available. Bacon cut the trial from four hours to one, on the advice of his engineer officer, who feared overstressing might result. At speeds over fifteen knots the steering engine proved insufficiently powerful to return the rudder to amidships, driving the ship in circles until speed was reduced. This too could be rectified, so Bacon suffered the problem and did not report it, in case trials were suspended. These were completed in January 1907, when the ship was to proceed on stringent trials, especially of the armament. Fisher selected Dreyer as 'Experimental Gunnery Officer'. Gunnery trials were carried out at Aranci Bay, Corsica, and Dreyer wrote: 'It soon became clear that pre-dreadnought battleships would stand no chance against Dreadnoughts. With four twelve-inch turrets bearing, we could fire four-gun salvos every fifteen seconds, a loading interval of thirty seconds for each gun being obtainable with good drill.'[31]

Finally the ship sailed to Trinidad to try the machinery over long distances, and further gunnery exercises were carried out. *Dreadnought* proved herself, for she steamed home from Trinidad (twice the distance of Battenberg's cruisers) at an average of 17.5 knots, an unheard-of achievement for a battleship, and on arrival her main engines exhibited no defects whatever, in spite of the fact that for two days the ship mysteriously slowed down by about one knot and then picked up speed again, found on docking to be due to rudder plating partly torn off. While still attached, it slowed the ship, and when it ripped off, she speeded up again, which also explained the problem with the steering gear.

All the accommodation for officers was, contrary to custom, located forward to give them rapid access to the bridge and that for ratings aft, which gave rise to the belief among the ship's company that these newfangled turbines would cause vibration and that the arrangement was intended to maintain the officers' comfort. *Dreadnought* lacked the spaciousness of the old ships and some retrograde officers were more concerned with creature comforts than fighting efficiency:

> She was a very uncomfortable ship for both officers and men. The messdecks were small and cramped and, being aft, most inconvenient to the internal economy of the ship. . . . Cabins were small and distributed all over the ship, wherever room could be found for them. My first cabin was in one of the messdecks aft and a horrible place it was to live in. . . . One had to walk half the length of the ship to the officers' bathroom. My second was forward, all mixed up with the chain cables and the [emergency] diesel engine . . . whose vibrations made life in its vicinity very uncomfortable. . . . There was a good wardroom forward, very light and airy and on the upper deck; the Admiral's quarters on the deck below were also good. . . . I had been much more comfortable as captain of my assorted collection of torpedo craft.[32]

Fisher had taken a brilliant risk in *Dreadnought*. Had she failed, suspension of the building programme implied that Britain would fall behind other powers, but his judgment was vindicated and the effect was astounding. No battleship in the world could match her in speed, firepower, range or reliability; all others were outdated. The designs of her successors were already prepared and only needed modification in the light of experience in

Dreadnought. Now the battleships went ahead with great urgency, *Bellerophon*, the name ship of a class of three ships (*Bellerophon*, *Superb* and *Temeraire*) almost identical to *Dreadnought*, but displacing 18,600 tons, were laid down only two months after *Dreadnought* began her trials, with sixteen 4-inch guns as secondary armament to deal with increasing torpedo range. They were followed by the 'St. Vincent' class of three ships (*St. Vincent*, *Vanguard* and *Collingwood*) of 19,560 tons, a scaled-up version of the 'Bellerophons' with the calibre of their ten 12-inch guns increased from 45 to 50, giving a longer gunbarrel, range increased to 10,000 yards and greater accuracy. Then in 1909 came *Neptune*, 19,900 tons, the first British battleship to have superimposed turrets, one firing over another. The Committee on Designs had tried to introduce superimposed turrets in *Dreadnought*, but had been frustrated by blast problems later alleviated by changes in propellant which also allowed the two midship turrets to fire simultaneously on the same broadside. Almost identical were *Colossus* and *Hercules* of six months later.

But by 1909 the 13.5-inch gun was available, further increasing range and accuracy. They were fitted in the four 'Orion' class battleships of 22,500 tons (*Orion*, *Monarch*, *Thunderer* and *Conqueror*), their ten guns fitted in twin turrets on the centre-line. With 12-inch armour, they became known as 'super-dreadnoughts'. They were followed after Fisher's retirement by the 'King George V' class of four ships (*King George V*, *Ajax*, *Centurion* and *Audacious*) of 23,000 tons nearly 600 feet long with a beam almost 90 feet, then *Iron Duke*, *Marlborough*, *Benbow* and *Emperor of India* of 25,000 tons, 623 feet long and 90 feet beam. *Erin* and *Agincourt*, intended for the Turkish Navy, were commandeered at the outbreak of war, the latter with 14 12-inch guns in seven turrets.

Of the armoured cruisers *Indomitabl*e was launched first, on 16 March 1907, *Invincible* followed a month later and *Inflexible* on 20 June. Then came *Indefatigable* the name ship of a class of three (*Australia* and *New Zealand*) 18,750 tons, 26 knots. *Lion* (26,350 tons, 27 knots) was laid down in November 1909 and her sisters, *Princess Royal* and *Queen Mary* in May 1910 and May 1911 respectively, followed by *Tiger*, (28,500 tons, 29 knots) completed in October 1914.

Some of the armoured cruisers were larger and much faster than the battleships, and the Committee on Designs reported: 'The armoured cruisers are not comparable with anything existing; they are in reality, fast battleships'.[33] Further, they had very strong broadside fire and therefore 'it makes the armoured cruiser all the more qualified to lie in the line of battle.'[34] The last four had 13.5-inch guns and 9-inch armour, while the earlier post-Dreadnought battleships had 12-inch guns and 10-inch armour, so the statement was not wholly unreasonable. It was for this reason that the new ships were called battlecruisers.

140

But there was a fundamental flaw in the Committee's reasoning, for Fisher never intended the battlecruisers to lie in the line of battle. Their greatly superior range and speed enabled them to keep up with the enemy, yet to keep out of his range; most of the German battleships at Jutland had 11-inch guns, whose range was far less than that of the British ships. The British battlecruisers, if they had been operated as Fisher intended, could have stood off and shelled the German ships at their leisure. But visibility was low, Beatty allowed his ships to get well within range of the Germans, who, with their superior shells, inflicted considerable damage.

Destroyers, too, were progressing. Fisher's 'coastal' type was built virtually as he planned. The 1906 ships were 250 tons, oil-fired, turbine-driven, 4,000 horsepower and 26 knots, about the same as earlier ships, but the ocean-going 'Tribal' class of 1907 were of 850 tons, 14,500 horsepower, later increased to 1,000 tons and 15,500 horsepower, all having a speed of at least 33 knots, *Tartar* attaining 35.4 knots. Speeds remained similar until the war, but machinery weights were reduced from 64 pounds per horsepower to 33.6 in the M, N, O and P classes of 1913–15.

Fisher's bold decisions to build *Dreadnought*, to focus on the big gun, the turbine and oil fuel transformed the Navy. By 1914 turbines provided 53% of British horsepower and Britain was far ahead of Germany, the programme carried out in remarkable secrecy. When complete, *Dreadnought* was based at Sheerness; it was explained to the public that her size prohibited manoeuvring with existing ships. Each new ship joined her, gradually building up a new fleet, so that, as Mahan said, on Fisher's retirement '88 per cent of the British guns [were] trained on Germany'.[35] General Ellison, (secretary of the Esher Committee), wrote in 1926: 'The German High Seas Fleet and its harbours were now our primary objective. The abject surrender of the German Navy on November 20, 1918, was the crowning triumph of a policy ruthlessly and relentlessly pursued since 1904.'[36] The effect on Germany was profound. Confronted with a new type of ship, a long-range gun and new tactics, all her ships were obsolete except torpedo boats. The Baltic ports were too shallow for the new ships, while the Kiel Canal was both too narrow and too shallow, requiring dredging and widening, which was not completed for seven years. Fisher had written in 1906: 'An increase in the size of German ships will necessitate either widening or deepening the Kiel Canal, possibly both, and its approaches, and also extensive dredging operations in their naval ports. . . . It may, therefore, well be doubted whether Germany is at present in a position to make a sudden advance to ships of 20,000 tons.'[37] Germany's fleet had effectively been halved, since it was no longer possible for one fleet to serve both the Baltic and the North Sea. Moreover, foreign construction of all battleships was suspended for nineteen months while they pondered their new designs, and the revelation of *Dreadnought* diverted attention from the battlecruisers. Germany was able to devote neither her design capability or building capacity to them and it was not until 1910 that she had a single one. She was never able to make up the lead Britain had gained and, had she been the first to make the difficult decision, Britain would have had to scrap her entire battle fleet and start again, with Germany in the lead. It was Fisher's foresight that ensured victory in the long run.

But criticism of Fisher mounted. There were, of course, genuine doubters, but most came from disgruntled officers who saw the comfortable life of the nineteenth century steam Navy fast disappearing. To the journalists Beresford was a heaven-sent source of 'news'. Fisher's towering personality enabled them to whip up controversy to fill their columns. Former Board members joined the hunt, opposing reforms they had failed to introduce. But criticism came from other sources as well. Sir George Clarke, as Secretary of the CID, though scarcely qualified to express a view, opposed the construction of *Dreadnought* and begged Campbell-Bannerman to appoint a committee to reconsider building policy, with the circuitous comment, 'It should be an axiom of our policy never to lead in ship construction, but always to follow with something better'.[38]

Even Battenberg joined in; one of a number of admirals Clarke improperly corresponded with, he wrote to the latter: 'I do cordially agree with all you say, especially the fever which has seized hold of J.F. . . . also the senseless way in which he insults and alienates our senior men. . . . However, he shall have my views in season and out of season, from high and low altitudes, now that he has asked for them.'[39] Yet three months later he wrote to Fisher: 'Let your detractors do their worst; no one pays any attention to them'.[40]

Fisher had his firm supporters too: Selborne, McKenna, Esher, all the progressive naval officers, the journalists White and Stead and in the background, very discreetly, the King. Stead wrote:

> The most monstrous accusations were hurled against him, by men who were not worthy to black his boots. At the time when he was risking everything by his dogged determination to keep up the supremacy of the Navy, he was denounced as a traitor in the pay of Germany. . . . Those of us who knew the motive of these attacks could afford to smile. As for Fisher, he heeded them as little as if they were the icy spray which hurtles through the air when a destroyer is dashing at full speed through the waves.[41]

10

GOLD LACE AND GLITTER

When Beresford hoisted his flag in *Majestic* as Senior Officer, Channel Squadron (not as in his autobiography, C-in-C, Channel Fleet, which did not then exist, though later he held this command), he chose as his second-in-command Rear Admiral the Hon. A.G.Curzon-Howe, who had been promoted lieutenant for service in the Royal Yacht, to commander for services during the cruise of the two Princes and to captain for further service in the Royal Yacht.

In this appointment Beresford's vanity was demonstrated as never before. Oliver, fleet navigating officer, wrote: 'Crowds of MPs and newspaper men came to see him, and it was difficult to get access to him about Service matters, and anything arranged was forgotten as soon as you left him.'[1]

He boasted of his exercises, which differed little from those of his contemporaries: 'In the fleet under my command, the drills and exercises were particularly onerous; for it was a rule never to go to sea without practising some exercise or tactical problem.'[2] Yet one of his midshipmen, Oswald Frewen, a relation, wrote: 'The two squadrons [divisions] steamed parallel for hours . . . at ranges varying from 3,700 to 2,100 yards. I am perfectly certain that not one ship would have remained afloat after ten minutes.'[3] And Oliver said:

> The flag captain and I arranged how the squadron was to leave Lamlash; I was then to explain to the admiral, and Evan-Thomas (flag captain) was to go in later to see if he had forgotten, and, if so, explain it again. A copy was given to the flag-lieutenant in case the admiral's memory failed. When we weighed and went out in single line ahead, we steered to the eastward till the rear ship was clear of the entrance; a course signal was then to be made, but the impulsive admiral made the next signal: *Form single line ahead*. The rear-admiral signalled to

ask what the course was, and that infuriated Beresford. He had lost the flag-lieutenant's paper and got the squadron formed up in divisions in line ahead eight points [90°] off their course for Belfast. We lost half an hour over this and were late arriving.'[4]

Later, Evan-Thomas was sick; Beresford was laid low with gout, but told Oliver not to tell Curzon-Howe, but to take command. Approaching Berehaven Beresford reappeared. 'Some one let the cat out of the bag and a very angry rear-admiral came on board an hour later and he and Beresford were soon at it hammer and tongs . . . because the admiral did not wish to make public that he had gout.'[5] A midshipman remembered seeing him being carried by four Royal Marines to the bridge during another attack, 'looking very much like a Roman Emperor'.[6]

Beresford boasted to the admiral superintendent at Devonport, 'I have instituted a system by which the fleet [sic] carries out its own repairs and maintenance, using ships' artificers. This has saved the State a good deal, and keeps the ships efficient, compared with the old plan of leaving things until they got into a dockyard.'[7] This 'system' is quite inexplicable, since ship's staff had always carried out its own maintenance, even in the days of sail, leaving for dockyards only defects too great in magnitude or volume.

He wrote obsequiously to Selborne: 'I wish you could have seen the attack on Lamlash. The landing was splendid, all without warning, the two divisions on different sides of a grouse mountain eight miles apart 3,000 men and twelve guns, with bogs, fences, etc. between the hill and the shore. . . . We all learned a great deal.'[8]

Beresford carried out night action exercises without lights, with the result that *Hannibal* and *Prince George* were in collision and the Admiralty ordered dimmed navigation lights to be used in future, much reducing the value of the exercises.

In February 1904 Beresford transferred to HMS *Caesar*. The following month the Kaiser visited Gibraltar in SS *König Albert* and, as an honorary admiral in the Royal Navy, hoisted his flag in *Caesar*. He dined with Beresford, who characteristically arranged a great ceremonial. Boats of the squadron lined the passage between *König Albert* and *Caesar*, each burning a blue light, all orders passed in silence. 'After dinner, when it fell to me to propose His Majesty's health, and I stood up, glass in hand, as I said the words "Emperor of Germany", a rocket went up from the deck above, and at the signal every ship . . . fired a royal salute.'[9] As the Kaiser left the ship the German and British flags were hoisted on the rock and illuminated by searchlights, while 2,000 rockets were launched from the breakwater, bursting in an arch over the German ship. Beresford wrote to the King, but received only a formal acknowledgement from Knollys.

144

A few weeks after Beresford's mishandling of the Dogger Bank affair, Fisher's plans for the redistribution of fleets came into effect and Beresford's Channel Squadron became the Atlantic Fleet, he was elevated to Commander-in-Chief, and it was proposed that he should be appointed Commander-in-Chief, Mediterranean. The obvious choice was Wilson, highly regarded, one of the outstanding tacticians of his day, but Fisher wanted him for the vital appointment of Commander-in-Chief of ships in Home Waters. 'Beresford,' minuted Battenberg, 'trains the flag officers and captains under him. . . . What we want there is a C-in-C who will train and teach.'[10]

Beresford was not due for promotion to full admiral until November 1906 and his appointment to an important command is curious, for there were at least twelve flag officers senior to him, but we get a clue from his behaviour when told that he would be relieved in the Atlantic Fleet by Sir William May just one month short of the two years he expected to hold his command. He was infuriated beyond reason, King-Hall recording in his diary that he had written to May,

> that he would be glad to give him lunch or fight him, but he would not be superseded. Beresford then went to see Lord Selborne, who said he could do nothing, but referred him to Fisher. Fisher said to Beresford that all arrangements had been made for May to relieve him on the earlier date, and that he wanted Beresford to come on a committee. Beresford said he did not intend to be superseded, nor would he go on a committee. Fisher then replied: 'Well then, you will not go to the Mediterranean,' upon which all the pent-up wrath of years between the two men broke out, and Beresford said: 'You dare to threaten me, Jacky Fisher. Who are you? I only take my orders from the Board. If I have to haul down my flag on 7 February, I will resign the Service, go down to Birmingham, get into the House and turn out both you and Selborne. What is more, I will go to the Mediterranean, and I will not go on a committee.' More words passed, the result being that Beresford had his way, but I shall be surprised if Fisher does not play some trick on him, and pay him out in some way or another.[11]

It is likely that Selborne urged Fisher to give in to Beresford's threat, for his political power was considerable; credulous politicians ignorant of naval affairs were convinced by his persuasive tongue, fewer than half a dozen with knowledge of the subject. But Fisher did not give in; though he sat on no committee, Beresford hauled down his flag on the earlier date and was appointed C-in-C Mediterranean as an acting admiral. Sturdee became his Chief of Staff and recorded that Fisher had sent for him before his departure and told him to 'keep an eye on Charlie', as he was inclined to be rather rash and wild in Service matters and 'asked me to write to him privately about my Chief. This request I never complied with; such a disloyal act was so obvious it did not require a second thought.'[12] As Sturdee heartily detested Fisher, his record of the interview may be misleading. Fisher was well aware of Sturdee's enmity, which was cordially returned, and it is unlikely he would have fallen into such a trap. He well knew Beresford was not up to this command, but the politicians wanted him out of harm's way.

Fisher's concentration of ships in home waters (the new Channel fleet, formerly the Home Fleet) was placed under Wilson, whom he described as 'a born strategist and tactician . . . The Admiralty could not have had an officer better fitted for the command of this force.'[13] His praise of Wilson was overdone; he was an acknowledged tactician, but his strategic views were unrealistic.

The growing friendship with France and the humbling of the Russians justified a reduction in the Mediterranean Fleet, which now included only eight battleships, four armoured cruisers and three small cruisers. Germany's concentration in the North Sea demanded strengthening home waters and the arguments that applied when Fisher was C-in-C were no longer valid, yet Beresford protested that his fleet was inadequate – not for strategic reasons, but he claimed eight battleships was the smallest number for tactical exercises, making no allowance for those under refit, repeating Noel's arguments; it was his pride that was hurt.

The retirement age for Admirals was 65 and Fisher would have to go on 25 January 1906. The list of Admirals of the Fleet was full and Beresford, five years younger, felt secure that he would succeed Fisher, having ensured the idea was much discussed in the Press. Selborne left the Admiralty in April 1905 and was succeeded by Lord Cawdor, who fully supported Fisher's reforms and was concerned to retain him to complete them. Accordingly he arranged a special Order in Council promoting Fisher to Admiral of the Fleet, ensuring his retention to the age of 70. Beresford assumed that on promotion Fisher would retire, though both his antecedents had remained in office in the higher rank, and when it became known that Fisher was staying on, Beresford's resentment knew no bounds. He openly and publicly attacked everything Fisher stood for.

Beresford had written a letter to the *Standard* advocating closer relations with the United States, suggesting the two countries' fleets should work together. For a serving officer to write such a letter offended the King and Knollys wrote that the latter was 'surprised and sorry' that he should write on 'so vastly important and political a question'. Beresford again tried to escape responsibility by throwing the blame on others with the unlikely story that a private letter to the secretary of the Pilgrims was altered by substituting the words 'To the Editor of the *Standard*' for 'My dear secretary'.

But he again tried to ingratiate himself with the King when the Prince and Princess of Wales passed through the Straits of Messina on their way to India in HMS *Renown*:

> The fleet charged at her in line abreast, our two admirals in the centre, until shortly before reaching her our two divisions altered course outward sixteen points [180°] finishing up a little abaft her beam, still in line abreast. Our destroyers then passed down either side of her in two columns, all ships fired salutes of 21 guns and escorted the *Renown* all day. At about 7 pm we burned red and white searchlights, and fired salvos of green and red Very lights. The last ship in each column fired a bouquet of rockets, and as the *Renown* continued on her way to India, the *Queen* showed 'Good', *Bulwark* 'Bye', *Venerable* 'Good' and *Implacable* 'Luck' on our foreyards with electric lamps – a pretty and successful ceremony.[14]

In April 1906 the fleet went to Corfu to meet *Renown* on her return. The King and Queen of Greece were present and King Edward arrived in *Victoria and Albert*. Beresford was pleased that he was received by the King, who returned his call, raising his hopes that he could restore Royal favour; but the King could hardly ignore the C-in-C and took exception to his failure to meet the precise protocol in receiving the King of Greece. Beresford failed to don full dress uniform, which is quite inexplicable, and on the Greek King's departure the Royal salute was fired only by the flagship, not the whole fleet. No offence was given to the Greek King, but it gave Edward an opportunity to avoid a rapprochement.

But the visit to Corfu had more important repercussions. Fisher had selected Bacon to command *Dreadnought* and the latter wanted experience of commanding a capital ship first. The command of *Irresistible* became available, so Bacon, then naval assistant to Fisher, asked to be released. 'Sir John was not best pleased. Firstly he did not wish to change his naval assistant; secondly, he did not much relish my going to the Mediterranean and falling under the fascination of Lord Charles Beresford's seductive personality. . . . With reasonably good grace Sir John consented; but when I said good-bye to him he never wished me luck, and I could see that he still resented my apparent defection.'[15]

Bacon was met by Beresford with suspicion, having come straight from Fisher, but they were soon on friendly terms and he found the C-in-C a man of charm, popular, but easily influenced. Sturdee's dislike of Fisher amounted to paranoia and did much harm. Naturally, Beresford and his second-in-command, Rear-Admiral the Hon. Hedworth Lambton, another passionate opponent of reform, discussed the developments with Bacon, newly arrived from the centre of affairs, who was soon in possession of all their views. Equally naturally Bacon would convey to his old chief how he was getting on in his new command, and it was unlikely that he would refrain from mentioning the views expressed by the senior officers on the station, but he remained adamant that at no time did he criticize Beresford or Lambton, merely relaying their views to Fisher in an informal manner. Lambton wrote his views to the Admiralty and showed his letters to Bacon. 'So far as I remember,' wrote Bacon, 'during the six months I was on that Station, I wrote six or seven letters; not one of these contained a word of criticism of any senior or junior officer on the Station; nor, with one exception . . . did I mention any of their names.'[16]

Fisher had a habit of having private letters printed and circulated within the Admiralty when they contained important information or views, sometimes without the consent of their authors. He was himself an extremely indiscreet and prolific letter writer, many scribbled hastily and giving offence. This carelessness in private correspondence was in marked contrast to his official papers which were meticulously thought out and carefully reasoned.

Beresford searched for every means of attacking Fisher and one of the most sensitive issues was the Selborne-Fisher scheme. Specialization, it will be remembered, was to be 'definite and final'; officers specializing in engineering would be denied command and volunteers were inadequate. The alternative was compulsion and many young officers indicated their intention of withdrawing from the Service if this happened. Fisher reverted to his original scheme and, in a Memorandum issued on 30 November 1905,[17] it was stated that all officers 'will specialize for the different duties without separating into permanent and distinct branches'.[18] On promotion to commander, officers could choose whether to revert to deck duties or remain in engineering.

Hedworth Lambton was a brother of the Earl of Durham; when promoted he was the youngest captain in the Navy, having been flag lieutenant to Sir Beauchamp Seymour at the bombardment of Alexandria and specially promoted to commander. He was promoted captain at the age of 30 for service in the Royal Yacht, even though he had obtained only a third-class certificate in seamanship as a sub-lieutenant. According to Chatfield, he knew little seamanship at any time.[19] He had served at sea with the Prince of Wales and had become a close personal friend, opposing Fisher's reforms. He wrote to the Prince from the Mediterranean, who wrote in turn to Fisher: 'Yesterday I received the enclosed from our friend Hedworth. I must say I agree with him . . . I consider that this question is much more than a naval one . . . and that the Colonial Secretary and Prime Minister should both be consulted, and also the Foreign Secretary.'[20]

The Prince arrived at Corfu and Bacon found him deeply concerned at garbled accounts of Fisher's reforms. He wrote to Fisher:

Dear Sir John, – The Prince of Wales arrived here on Monday and, of course, we went on board to be received. He seized on me at once and was full of the opposition he had heard in some quarters of the Navy to the new schemes of reform and that the Navy was becoming full of cliques, which was bad, &c., &c.; that the senior officers might perhaps be more consulted and more carried with the reforms – more diplomacy &c., &c. Evidently from what he said, Admiral Moore [C-in-C, China], Admiral Poe [C-in-C East Indies], and probably the two admirals here (Lord Charles Beresford and Admiral Lambton) had been wailing and bemoaning the schemes and their exclusion from consultation. He asked if I wrote to you and whether I did not represent to you the Service feeling &c., and although he still professed adherence to the reforms he evidently has been 'got at' by the opposition, and they have had a full chance of airing their grievance. Well, he talked so much and, I must say so fluently and so well, that I could with difficulty get in a word. But I told him . . . that he need have little fear that the whole of the opposite side of the case was not put before the public by Admirals Bridge, Custance and Fitzgerald, or that the agitators in the active service were at all shy in providing them with every argument against the scheme. . . .

Well, I went away and wrote a paper on the subject and sent a copy to Commodore Tyrwhitt [Hon. Hugh Tyrwhitt, in command of *Renown*] and asked him to get the Prince of Wales to read it, also to get me an interview with His Royal Highness. . . .

Well this time was not wasted, as last night I dined on board the Royal Yacht, and after dinner the King sent for me and after talking about submarine boats, His Majesty hinted that he had heard that there was considerable opposition and asked whether the schemes could not have perhaps been launched with less friction, saying that of course he knew the Navy was ultra-conservative and hated reforms. Well I simply gave him my paper in a condensed form, . . . and told His Majesty straight out that what the Navy was suffering from was want of loyalty to the Admiralty among the admirals afloat; . . . some (of course not all) thought they were justified in throwing discipline to the winds and agitating privately against their governing body, the Admiralty. I think the King agreed to this; at all events His Majesty seemed interested and acquiesced. I think both the King and the Prince of Wales cordially approve the reforms, but the opposition admirals have been shaking their heads and grieving, and naturally the Prince of Wales has been impressed and mentioned this to the King. The question of loyalty is of the greatest importance and quite turns the enemy's flank . . . but the best policy is to become friends and corre-spond with Bridge, Custance, Fitzgerald, Bellairs and Co.; but when the fiat has gone forth from the Admiralty they must . . . accept the superior ruling!

R H Bacon[21]

On the whole this private letter between two men who knew each other well, though perhaps slightly lacking in probity to his C-in-C, seems temperate and accurate. The Prince had expected Bacon to keep Fisher informed of the feelings of the fleet and it would have been reasonable in any case.

Bacon had his further interview with the Prince and reassured him, but the discussion took place just before sailing and, with only half an hour before mails closed, he again wrote hurriedly to Fisher. In his autobiography he says that he began, 'Lord Charles and Admiral Lambton have been getting at the King.'[22] In the printed version this phrase does not appear. The first sentence makes it quite clear that this was the letter to which he was referring; moreover it is dated 15 April, which was the Sunday the fleet sailed. Either Bacon's memory was failing (he appears to have kept no copy of the letter) or it was edited before printing, to eliminate this phrase. The printed version reads:

Private and Secret
Dear Sir John,

I have just had an hour with the Prince of Wales, immediately before we sailed with the fleet. We discussed the whole vexed question of naval training under the new scheme, and I told him all that I have told you and a good deal more.

I think it will give great satisfaction all round if a complete descrip-tion of the whole scheme is issued. I should even go further and include all the schemes, and trace how they have been turned out, putting it on the plea that much misconception has arisen as to the scope &c., of all the reforms. . . .

What is upsetting the King and Prince of Wales so much is what they call a feeling of 'unrest' in the Service. Now personally I am sure this is exaggerated, but certain others do not think so.

I have tackled every single objector I can think of, and the only complaints I have been able to gather against the Admiralty are:-

(1) *Want of Information.*

This is specially felt by the senior officers, who say that the Admiralty never gave them any more information than they do the Paymaster of the ship.

If every Admiral and Captain had been supplied with a detailed account of the scheme, it would have smoothed matters considerably.

(2) *Not being consulted more by the Admiralty.*

This is of course entirely at the option of the Admiralty. As I pointed out, the Admiralty run the Navy, not the Admirals who command the Fleets and Squadrons. The Navy is not a Republic. . . .

(3) *Captains being treated with little consideration.*

Insufficient notice of appointment, and the old custom of being offered ships instead of merely being sent, being disregarded. . . .

(4) *Notion spread by your detractors that you override everyone else.*

In fact that the Admiralty is run by one man. . . . I always emphasise the Captains who have assisted in arranging the details of all the schemes of reform, and always quote the several cases where you have given up some idea you were keen on the moment a committee you trusted reported it to be impracticable or undesirable. . . .

The objectors can only repeat half truths, or statements that started by being half truths, but from which subsequent repetition has tended completely to eradicate all remnants of fact.

(5) *A total misconception of the education scheme, especially as regards interchangeability* . . .

I pressed most strongly on the Prince of Wales that the Service agitators were weakening the authority of the Admiralty. . . . The prestige of the Admiralty must be kept up and strengthened rather than diminished. I think, on the whole, the visit of the King and the Prince of Wales to Corfu has been most useful in this matter, since they have heard every objection to the reforms confuted, and also this has been the effect on their immediate entourage. The King and the Prince of Wales were always most loyal (if such a term may be used) to you personally and to the whole of the scheme of reform, but very much disturbed at the Service agitation headed by Lord Charles Beresford and Admiral Lambton.

Yours very sincerely,

R H Bacon[23]

The Prince's injunction in mind, it seemed reasonable to warn Fisher, and, though Bacon was familiar with Fisher's habit of circulating prints within the Admiralty, it appears not to have occurred to him, having marked his letters '*Secret*', that this would happen. He later claimed that, had he realized this, he would have begun the letter in a more circumspect manner.

Fisher printed and circulated these letters, but did not know that an officer serving in the Admiralty was disloyally collecting copies of all printed letters to make use of them later and a storm was to break over the 'Bacon Letters'.

Dissension over the Selborne-Fisher scheme was not confined to deck officers; the old-style engineer officers were still left out of account, without

151

executive position, while their juniors the lieutenants (E) appeared before them in the *Navy List* among the deck officers. They even continued to wear a different uniform retaining the purple cloth between their stripes, wore a plain gold band instead of oak-leaves on their cap peaks and did not wear the 'executive curl' (the curl on the uppermost stripe on an officer's sleeve). Yet they had the burden of training the young (E) officers in their duties and held all the senior engineering posts. Small wonder they opposed the scheme, for its presentation gave the impression that the profession would be studied only as a sideline.

Evidently Fisher told Bacon he intended to amalgamate the old engineers with the deck officers and Bacon vigorously opposed such a move in view of the bitterness he believed it would create.[24]

To consider this Fisher formed a committee under Admiral Sir Archibald Douglas, a former Second Naval Lord. Bacon wrote from the Mediterranean a letter of twenty pages. 'I pulled these proposals to pieces in a very rough way.'[25] He asked Fisher to delay the assembly of the committee until his return, and appoint him a member. 'He most broadmindedly did both of these things, although he knew full well that I was opposed to his proposals.'[26] The majority report agreed with Fisher's views. However, the three captains on the committee wrote a minority report stating that uniforms were intended to 'distinguish the ranks and services of officers and not to confuse such differences. In fact we interpreted in plain English, using somewhat forcible arguments, what had been the gist of the evidence of the executive officers who had come before us as eye-witnesses.' The majority report was quashed. 'Sir John was very angry. He had made certain promises to the existing engineer officers in order to smooth the way for them to agree to the new system of common entry, which by our report he was no longer able to fulfil.'[27]

Bacon's 1929 biography of Fisher quotes the minority report, but fails to mention that he was its main author. Fisher regarded Bacon's opposition as treachery, 'If I were back at the Admiralty,' he later wrote, 'three post captains would be on half-pay tomorrow.' This certainly did not include Bacon, who, though disagreeing with Fisher and demonstrating his independence of mind, remained his loyal supporter. But when he returned to the Admiralty in 1914 Fisher achieved his object.

Beresford saw his opportunity. He wrote, in contradiction of his laudatory remarks of 1902 and 1903: 'The position today is that, if the new officers are competent executives, they will not take charge of the engine-room; if they are competent engineers, they will remain below.'[28] There was some justice in this. The training Fisher proposed for engineers was inadequate and longer training would have left insufficient time for them to learn ship-handling, tactics and strategy to command ships, though many deck officers paid scant attention to such affairs.

Lord Tweedmouth took over as First Lord in December 1905 and the exasperated Fisher wrote to him in April:

> It is with extreme reluctance that I feel compelled in the interest of the Navy and the maintenance of its hitherto unquestioned discipline and loyalty to bring before the Board the unprecedented conduct of the Commander-in-Chief of the Mediterranean Fleet in publicly reflecting on the conduct of the Admiralty and in discrediting the policy of the Board and inciting those under his command to ridicule the decisions of the Board. I need not . . . dwell on the extraordinary conduct of a Commander-in-Chief canvassing the captains under his command as to whether or no they approved the policy of the Admiralty, but I take one specific case, which is the culmination of all that has gone before.[29]

The system of 'Continuous Service' had been supplemented by one of 'Non-Continuous Service', enabling men to sign on for an initial period of seven years, facilitating reduction in numbers when needed. Such men received shorter training than their contemporaries, effecting further economy.

Fisher then quoted a letter from 'a guest at the official dinner':

> ' "He (Lord Charles Beresford) held forth to the assembled company in unmeasured terms of scorn on the class of short-service bluejackets, proposing to hold a review on shore for the benefit of his guests to show the 'rotters' (as he termed them) their Lordships expected him to work with, etc. I alone of the entire company did not join in the general laughter and applause. When it had subsided, he turned to me across the table and asked whether I had any of these men in my squadron. I said yes, and I found them as good as the men raised in the training ships from boys. After this (to which the whole company had listened) there was a 'frost' and the conversation was changed by our host. He is aware of my letter to Lord Knollys on his (Lord C. Beresford's) improper letter to the King on the subject of naval training . . ."
>
> 'The above needs no comment. I don't suggest any action at present, but I think it is desirable that the Board should be aware of what is going on.'[30]

The letter was written by Rear Admiral Frederick Inglefield, in command of the escorting 4th Cruiser squadron, and exemplifies Beresford's ridicule of Fisher and all he stood for, which was wholly disloyal and subversive.

11

NOT SINGLE SPIES

Fisher's problems were not confined to Beresford's intrigues. Few holders of the office have been plagued by so many armchair experts; politicians, academics, journalists and soldiers, who joined ranks with the naval pseudo-intellectuals, assuming patronizing infallibility.

Fisher's establishment of the Staff College demonstrated his desire for a naval staff, but there were good reasons for caution. Security was almost non-existent; defence matters were openly discussed in the drawing rooms of the great houses and over dinner, even in the presence of foreigners. There was a shortage of competent officers, too many having achieved rank through patronage, few yet trained in staff work, and some in the Admiralty were agents of the Beresford clique; it was difficult to know who to trust.

Fisher had pressed joint service planning in the Esher Committee but he approached the formation of the Committee of Imperial Defence with caution. The Defence Committee of the Cabinet was established by Salisbury in 1895, but was not a very active body until 1902 when Brodrick, Secretary of State for War, and Selborne prepared a joint memorandum, when it was renamed the Committee of Imperial Defence, but with no permanent staff. Balfour as Prime Minister attended regularly, and in 1903 assumed the chair. The first report of the Esher Committee had said: 'There are . . . no means of coordinating defence problems, for dealing with them as a whole, for defining the functions of the various elements, and for ensuring that . . . in times of emergency, a definite war policy based upon solid data can be formulated.'[1]

They contended that the Prime Minister should always preside, with 'absolute discretion in the selection and variation of its members'. More important, a permanent secretariat should be established, with no executive authority. Balfour and his successors almost always included the Chancellor of the Exchequer, the Foreign Secretary, the First Lord of the Admiralty, the First Sea Lord, Director of Naval Intelligence, Secretary of State for War and the Director of Military Operations. Sydenham Clarke was appointed the first secretary and his assistant was the young Royal Marine captain, Maurice Hankey, who had served in Beresford's flagship under Fisher in the Mediterranean.

Balfour's Government fell in December 1905 and in the ensuing election Campbell-Bannerman pledged himself to reduce expenditure on the Services. Lord Tweedmouth, Winston Churchill's uncle, became First Lord, and fully supported Fisher's reforms. Subject to achieving his promised economies, so did Campbell-Bannerman. Balfour, one of Fisher's most influential adherents, maintained his support, together with Cawdor and Selborne. The opposition front bench was united with the Government in support of Fisher, though among back benchers were vociferous associates of Beresford who claimed both that his reforms emasculated the Navy and that he was a warmonger. His remarks at the Hague Conference were repeated again and again and he recognized their unwisdom.

Alarmed by the Entente Cordiale and hoping to gain from the defeat of Russia by Japan, Germany put pressure on France. After the Fashoda incident, Britain acknowledged France's interest in Morocco, whose government was near collapse. The Sultan invited Britain to establish a protectorate, but, to demonstrate goodwill to France, Britain refused and the Sultan approached Germany, who threatened France, hoping Britain would not stand by her new partner. On the advice of Von Bülow, because of the need for German coaling stations on the African coast, the Kaiser visited Tangier and made a belligerent speech, referring to Germany's 'great and growing interests in Morocco'. The next day at Gibraltar he informed Battenberg of his determination to prevent France from dominating Morocco. Battenberg provided King Edward, who was also cruising the Mediterranean, with notes of the meeting. Europe was on the brink of war, Wilson as C-in-C Channel Fleet, was ordered to be ready to attack the German coast, and Fisher was more than ever convinced of Germany's aggressive intentions. He saw war as an ultimate certainty and it was better to go to war while Britain was ready and Germany was not than to wait for her to build up her naval strength. He wrote to Lansdowne on 22 April 1905:

> Without any question whatever the Germans would like a port on the coast of Morocco and without doubt whatever such a port possessed by them would be vitally detrimental to us. . . .
>
> This seems a golden opportunity for fighting the Germans in alliance with the French, so I earnestly hope you may be able to bring this about. Of course I don't pretend to be a diplomat, but it strikes me that the German Emperor will greatly injure the splendid and

increasing Anglo-French Entente if he is allowed to score now in any way – even if it is only getting rid of M. Delcassé. . . .

All I hope is that you will send a telegram to Paris that the English and French fleets are one. We could have the German fleet, the Kiel Canal and Schleswig-Holstein within a fortnight.[2]

Delcassé, the French Foreign Minister, was indeed forced to resign at German demand, yet Grey failed to grasp the significance of a German coaling base. In 1906 Germany demanded the right to establish one at Madeira. Portugal called for British assistance, the fleet was ordered to sail and Germany backed down. Yet that same year the Liberal Government had questioned the need for the Cawdor programme approved by the Unionist Government, which had provided for four capital ships to be laid down annually and under which three dreadnoughts had been started that year, arguing that by 1909 there would be four British dreadnought battleships and three battlecruisers in commission, while Germany, from the information known, would have only one. On these figures the Admiralty had no case, but all the Sea Lords presented Tweedmouth a memorandum dated 3 December 1907, drawing attention to the accelerated German building programme:

We therefore consider it of the utmost importance that power should be taken to lay down two more armoured ships in 1909–10, making eight in all, as unless there is an unexpected modification in Germany's anticipated shipbuilding programme, resulting in her not completing seventeen ships by the spring of 1912, it will be necessary to provide eight new British ships to be completed by this date, the last two being laid down at the end of March, 1910.[3]

British naval power at that juncture was so much greater than that of Germany that German defeat in a short war would have been likely. Fisher's view was pragmatic; by rejecting attempts at appeasement, by facing Germany with a united front, the Allies could have forced her either to risk a war she was bound to lose or concede a diplomatic defeat, saving millions of lives later. Lloyd George was to echo Fisher's sentiments six years later, at the time of the Agadir Crisis, when, Churchill recorded, he 'electrified their Majesties by observing that he thought it would be a great pity if war did not come now'.[4] There was a parallel in Hitler's re-occupation of the Rhineland. Fisher believed the least misery was caused by a short war. He was one of the few men of his era who saw that agreements entered into in peacetime would be disregarded in war. He was to be proved right in two world wars.

Fisher had other problems. The National Service League, formed in 1901, pressed for compulsory military training, largely led by the ageing Lord Roberts, who, after his retirement in 1904, devoted himself to a campaign to awaken the country to what he saw as a danger of invasion, resigning in November 1905 from the Committee of Imperial Defence to devote himself exclusively to his obsession. He spoke at public meetings and in the House of Lords on the need for a large Home Army, necessitating conscription. A memorandum by Balfour on 11 November 1903 said that, with a strong Navy, 'invasion of these island is not an eventuality which we need seriously to consider'.[5] As Professor Marder says, this implied that the Army was not required for home defence but only for use abroad, which agreed with Fisher's views on amphibious warfare. 'I really think it's the most masterly document I ever perused,' he wrote to Esher, with characteristic hyperbole.[6] It did little to placate the advocates of a strong defensive Army. In 1904, while still at Portsmouth, Fisher had written to Esher:

> I was with the Prime Minister from 12:30 to 4 p.m. . . . [He] evidently didn't see his way to making the reduction in the Army Vote which is imperative. . . . I gave him figures to show the Army had been increased 60,000 men in 10 years. If he would reduce them at once he would get nearly threepence off the income tax and get rid of his recruiting difficulties. The Auxiliary Forces, 4½ millions – absurd – the Volunteers, 2 Millions – still more absurd![7]

Roberts stirred up alarm everywhere. He started rifle clubs, which in the event proved useful on the Western Front, though this was not his object. His supporters based their belief on the 'bolt from the blue'. Lieut-Col. Repington, who had been dismissed the Army and, though supported by Roberts, at the King's insistence twice refused reinstatement, was now the myopic *Times* military correspondent and suggested it would not be difficult to put 60,000 men into ships, rush them across the North Sea, especially in bad visibility or when the fleet was away on manoeuvres, and throw them ashore. This ignored the enormous preparations necessary, the logistic support and artillery, necessarily embarked simultaneously, rendering secrecy impossible. The largest navy in the world could hardly have failed to prevent a landing. 'The whole case of Roberts rests on an absolute naval surprise, which is really a sheer impossibility in view of our organised information,' wrote Fisher.[8] There were few rudimentary landing craft and the troops huddled in transports would have been slaughtered. Had they miraculously reached the coast, they would have been rowed ashore in open boats. Embarkation would take several days, giving ample warning. A hundred years earlier, Napoleon had said; 'To carry out a descent on England without being masters of the sea is the most dangerous and difficult operation that could be undertaken.'[9]

'A first-line army for home defence we do not want,' Haldane wrote, 'The first line here is composed of the divisions of the fleet in Home Waters and the flotilla of destroyers and submarines which guard our coastline. These we have to keep at such strength that they can afford adequate protection against the advent of hostile transports.'[10]

The importance lay in the reluctance of Government to allocate funds for specific defence needs, preferring to opt for a global figure, so the more spent on the Army, the less available for the Navy, hampering Fisher in his modernization programme.

In September 1905 Esher suggested to Balfour the formation of two permanent sub-committees of the CID one to consider large questions of reorganization of Imperial Defence and the other to study invasion.[11] The first, he said, 'will fulfil the highest functions of a General Staff, the only sort of General Staff suited to our requirements, i.e., a joint naval and military staff.'[12] It might therefore have been thought that Fisher's view that the two services should be coupled had been achieved. But it yielded little, the War Office continuing to regard the Admiralty in a subordinate position.

In 1907 Roberts' speeches were published under the title *A Nation in Arms* and later that year he assisted William Le Queux in preparing his novel *The Invasion of 1910*. Roberts' supporter, Lord Lovat, asked the First Lord on 18 February 1908 about the disposition of the Home Fleet and whether a large force could gain a foothold on British shores, to which Tweedmouth foolishly replied that about sixty ships of the Home Fleet were on manoeuvres off Lagos, some three days steaming away, and that only twenty ships with nucleus crews were available in home waters. As half the Regular Army was on home station he considered invasion impossible. He failed to mention how Germany could transport the 60,000 troops the League saw invading Britain with all their impedimenta.

Newspapers were mobilized and an increase in the Army vote was proposed at the expense of the Navy. Julian Corbett supported Fisher, pointing out the impossibility of invasion of Britain as long as she maintained a strong navy. It had led her enemies to disaster in 1588, 1759 and 1805 and the Navy had never lost sight of the need to destroy the transports on their way to the British coasts.

The invasion lobby suggested the fleet might be lured away as Napoleon had tried; it might be absent on manoeuvres or the crossing might take place in poor visibility. With modern communications, telegraphs and developing wireless, such was virtually impossible, but Fisher, unwisely, conceded that perhaps 12,000 men could be landed before their communications were cut, and it might be necessary to maintain two divisions in Britain, but increases in the Army should not be allowed to interfere with the development of naval power. Britain had no need to fight a continental war; if Germany engaged Britain as a primary enemy there was no place for them to fight except on the sea. The only use for the Army would be on the continent, and the War Office adopted more and more rigidly the view that the British Army should fight alongside the French, even though the two armies bore no comparison in size. The attitude of the War Office was encapsulated by the breathtaking statement of Liddell Hart when he wrote:

> The reason for the curious contrast between Britain's determination to maintain a supreme Navy and her consistent neglect, indeed starvation of the army lay partly in her insular position which caused her to regard the sea as her essential life-line and main defence. . . . Small as to size, [the army] enjoyed a practical and varied experience of war without parallel among the continental armies.[13]

Since Waterloo the only major wars the Army had fought were the mishandled Crimean and Boer wars. Germany and France had at least fought a continental war in 1870 and, though 37 years had passed, had some experience of such warfare; and what is 'curious' about regarding the sea as Britain's lifeline? She is still surrounded by it.

Fisher saw the Army employed in a different fashion. It was a 'projectile to be fired by the Navy', to create diversions along the littoral, to outflank the enemy. He saw the British part in a European war as amphibious operations, of harrying the enemy by raids, keeping huge numbers of men occupied defending the coastline where potential attacks might be expected, forcing the enemy to do exactly what the invasion lobby wanted Britain to do. But such operations demanded sea supremacy, which Britain had and Germany had not. These views were fully supported by Hankey and Haldane. Beaverbrook records contemporary correspondence indicating that Haldane had argued 'that if the Expeditionary Force were retained [in Britain] it might form the nucleus of a far more formidable force to be dispatched at some future date; that its present accession to the French strength would be trifling; that its extinction would hamper us in the struggle later on. Such a stronger force might be used subsequently to cut across the German communications behind.'[14]

In July 1905, at Fisher's suggestion, Balfour appointed a committee to study combined operations, but attention was diverted by the Morocco crisis and conversations were held by the British and French Naval and Military staffs, unfortunately separately. In the case of the Admiralty they consisted of talks between Fisher and the French Naval Attaché, resulting in an understanding that in the event of war the French Navy would be responsible for the Mediterranean, with the use of Malta, while Britain operated in the North Sea, the Channel and French Channel coast This made sense in view of the extent of the French Mediterranean coast and bases, the strong British bases in the Channel and her proximity to German North Sea ports. But for some reason unclear, the military conversations were held through the intermediary of Repington. They were not discussed in Cabinet, nor, until later, in the CID. When the change of government took place early in the new year the same blind eye was turned and Grey wrote to Sir Francis Bertie,

Ambassador in Paris, informing him of a discussion he had had with Paul Cambon, French Foreign Minister: 'He thought it advisable that unofficial communication between our Admiralty and War Office and the French Naval and Military Attachés should take place as to what action might advantageously be taken in case the two countries found themselves in alliance in such a war.' Some communications, had, he believed, already passed and might, he thought, be continued. They did not pledge either Government. 'I did not dissent from this view.'[15]

Grey continued that Campbell-Bannerman 'was apprehensive lest the military conversations should create an obligation or at least an "honourable understanding",' and it was not until the Agadir Crisis in 1911 that they were revealed to Cabinet ministers other than members of the CID.

The result was that the sub-committee on amphibious warfare never really started, though in December 1905 'a small group of naval and military officers began to meet informally at 2, Whitehall Gardens to study the proper utilization of the forces of the United Kingdom in the event of our becoming involved, alongside the French, in a war with Germany'.[16] Ottley was the Admiralty representative and it quickly became clear that the conversations between the War Office and the French had crystallized a plan for the British Army to fight on the French left flank, to which the General Staff had immutably committed the country. It was more than an 'honourable understanding' and in effect was an obligation to which the Government was inextricably committed, whether they liked it or not. Fisher was furious and withdrew Ottley in a forlorn attempt to arrest the agreement, or at least demonstrate the Admiralty's opposition. He was highly suspicious of the manner in which Clarke was manoeuvring the CID into a position of authority over the Admiralty. He described it as an 'Aulic Council' (the supreme court of the Holy Roman Empire, from which there was no appeal). In October 1906 he sent to Esher for comment an insensitive paper he had written about the arguments advanced by the Beresfordites against his various policies. Esher was appalled:

Many thanks for the paper. I am glad you sent it to me. As you know I am a Fisherite, and do not require converting. . . . Your argument disposes of Mahan, and of Custance and Co.

But, I deprecate . . . your method of dealing with these opponents. Mahan may be passé, but from his writing this does not appear. Therefore he should be answered and argued with. . . .

In a country like ours, governed by discussion, a great man is never hanged. He hangs himself. Therefore pray be Machiavellian, and play upon the delicate instrument of public opinion with your fingers and not with your feet – however tempting the latter may be . . . .

The best way of preventing [the Defence Committee] from

meddling in things which do not concern it is to give it plenty to do!
. . . read up the work of your 'Aulic Council'!

In war, it played the devil, because in war you want a Man!

In peace, you want a party behind the Man. . . .

No Englishman ought to be Sir John Fisher's 'enemy'. Every Englishman should be his Lieutenant. It depends on the First Sea Lord himself.[17]

No better advice was ever offered to Fisher. He could, like many another man, have achieved much more if he had learned the art of persuasion, but he was not built that way; he was impatient, and there was so much to do; he was fighting on many fronts and could not waste time on persuasion. Esher wrote to his son, Maurice Brett, in March 1907: 'Fisher has been in stormy waters during the past week, owing to the pointed attack by C.Beresford and the flank attacks from his various enemies on the redistribution of the fleet.'[18]

He complained,

You are always chaffing me about the excellent 'advice' which I now and then diffidently give you. You never take it! . . . My advice always was – Take the Committee of Defence into your counsels, and force them to register your decrees.

Then it is not Fisher Contra Mundum, but the Defence Committee which has to be pilloried.

Haldane referred his whole scheme to a sub-committee of the Defence Committee. In spite of Clarke . . . he has carried his whole scheme, one of the most controversial on record, right through the Cabinet. He will carry it through Parliament as well. . . .

In my humble judgment you have made a mistake. During the past week or so, the forces ranged against each other have been Fisher versus Beresford. They should have been Fisher plus Defence Committee plus Cabinet versus Beresford, and the odds would have been overwhelming.[19]

Knollys wrote of this, 'Your letter to Jacky has terrified him',[20] But Fisher soon showed his indelicate touch again. When in August Balfour prepared another paper on invasion, Haldane complained that the Admiralty was opposing its reference to a sub-committee of the CID 'on the silly ground that the question is one for the Navy alone',[21] and Esher expressed himself as 'furious with the Admiralty. . . . I am writing to Fisher on the subject and giving him a bit of my mind'.[22] He certainly did, for his letter was blunt to the point of rudeness, something quite out of Esher's character, and obviously he had concluded that only the sledgehammer would have any effect on the ingenuous admiral:

What on earth do you mean by maintaining that a paper written by Mr. Balfour for the Defence Committee is 'purely an Admiralty business'? and talking of an 'irresponsible sub-committee'? . . .

The Committee for Imperial Defence, of which the Prime Minister is the Chief, and its sub-committees, if appointed by the Prime Minister, are every bit as 'responsible' as the Board of Admiralty, of which the First Sea Lord is the chief. . . .

The Admiralty will have to recognise, as the War Office has recognised, that the Defence Committee is a new factor in our administrative system, having its origin in the proved weakness from 1899–1901 of the older system, now superseded.

The Prime Minister has now got, in the Defence Committee, a department of his own, working under him and the Cabinet and it is pure anachronism to speak of the Committee for Imperial Defence or its sub-committees as 'irresponsible'. There are my views for you.[23]

To this Fisher replied, like a contrite schoolboy, 'I quite expected to get "slated" by you and I've got it. Also I fully expected you would have your wicked way and you've got it!'[24] Esher was perhaps a little unfair, for the 'proved weakness' of 1899–1901 was that of the Army, though clearly the Navy had many weaknesses which Fisher was trying, against so many obstructionists, to correct.

The next month Repington wrote an article in *The Times* again raising the invasion bogey and repeating all the well-worn 'Bolt-from-the-Blue' arguments. Fisher wrote to Clarke, reminding him of the several letters he (Clarke) had written in support of the naval or 'Blue-Water-School' and encouraging him to write again: 'Repington calmly and with cool insistence dictates to the Admiralty what the naval arrangements should be to render the problem of invasion impossible and has the audacity to make absolutely unfounded statements implying that the responsibility of directing the naval force of this country is distributed "amongst several semi-independent Sea Wardens round the coast" and the Naval Force permanently stationed in Home Waters is inadequate to cope with the German Fleet. Why, the whole business of the Admiralty for the last three years has been to concentrate our Sea Force in such a preponderating mass in Home Waters as absolutely to preclude the faintest possibility of invasion or even a raid!'[25] He continued by praising a paper by Clarke criticizing a statement by Roberts, Lovat, Samuel Scott and Repington on invasion, which he thought had been 'laid aside forever':

No one outside the secret offices of the Board of Admiralty can possess the elements of a judgment on the momentous problems involved in the naval defence of the Eastern littoral of these islands against an oversea invasion. For a military officer, however able, to pronounce a categorical opinion upon this maritime question is therefore no less absurd than it would be for the First Sea Lord to write for Mr. Balfour's perusal a note criticising in a similar strain the adequacy of British Military dispositions against invasion on the North West Frontier of India. . . . It is the Admiralty's business to decide and keep its own counsel on such matters.[26]

Fisher's opponents were coalescing – the invasion lobby and the Beresfordites and in December he wrote to Corbett, 'Repington's object is especially to call Beresford to give evidence against the Admiralty. A scandal impossible to tolerate, but a splendid platform for Beresford to resign on!'[27]

Mistrust grew between Fisher and Clarke, whose view was that the CID should direct the War Office and Admiralty, with which Esher agreed, but Clarke's intrigues with malcontent admirals came to light when Campbell-Bannerman inadvertently sent one of his letters to the Admiralty and the whole sordid campaign was revealed. Esher used his influence with the King and Clarke was appointed Governor of Bombay, Ottley, a talented naval officer, succeeding him. No longer fit for sea service, he had been nursing a constituency with a view to retiring and entering Parliament, but Fisher, wrote Hankey, 'with his unerring instinct for picking the right man for the right job, had by this appointment given him a new lease of official life. . . . Ottley left little to be desired. He was always open to consider new ideas and displayed a discriminating judgment.'[28]

But so pressing were Roberts and his associates that the Sub-Committee on invasion was formed, with far-reaching consequences. It included Grey, Tweedmouth (later McKenna), Haldane, Esher, Fisher, Slade, Neville Lyttelton (CIGS), Nicholson, French and Ewart, with Asquith in the chair and Ottley as secretary.

Said Esher: 'Fisher refused absolutely to hear any evidence . . . prior to Lord Roberts. . . . Lord Roberts came to see me this morning with his list of witnesses; a very long and rather absurd list including the Prince of Wales!'[29]

Fisher had some military allies. Haldane made a speech re-stating the plans for the Army, containing nothing to justify Roberts' expectations. Sir John French, one of the more enlightened generals, supported Fisher. Esher recorded on 24 November 1907: 'The General came to tea. He met C.Beresford at dinner this week and heard the whole case against Fisher. Beresford is anxious to be called before the Committee of Imperial Defence. Whether Jacky will cross-examine him is the problem. He may refuse to do so. The General agreed that the hypothesis – the Bolt out of the Blue – upon which Lord Roberts' case is founded, is absurd.'[30]

The inquiry opened on 27 November and Esher commented, 'Lord Roberts' peroration, delivered with rhetorical emotion, was very well done.

Repington put his case and the mass of information and carefully compiled detail was impressive. Fisher was full of wrath. I said to him that he was fond of quoting Mahan's famous passage about Nelson's storm-tossed ships, upon which the Grand Army never looked, which stood between it and the dominion of the world and it should remind him that the Defence Committee, upon which he wished he had never looked, stood between him and a Royal Commission to inquire into the state of the Navy.'[31] And the next day, 'Fisher tried hard to burke any further inquiry. . . . He made a great point of the impossibility of divulging a naval plan of campaign. Everyone agrees to that, but there is no necessity for anything of the kind.'[32]

The inquiry went on for eleven months, when the report stated:

1. That so long as our naval supremacy is assured against any reasonable probable combination of Powers, invasion is impracticable.

2. That if we permanently lose command of the sea, whatever may be the strength and organisation of the home force, the subjection of the country to the enemy is inevitable.

3. That our army for home defence ought to be sufficient in number and organisation, not only to repel small raids, but to compel an enemy to cope with so substantial a force as will make it impossible for him to evade our fleets.

4. That to ensure an ample margin of safety such a force may, for purposes of calculation, be assumed to be 70,000 men. . . .

6. That on the assumption that the Territorial Force is embodied on the outbreak of war, there will always be, after the expiration of six months, a sufficient number of regulars and trained Territorials to make it practically certain that no enemy will attempt the operation with a smaller force than that assumed above.[33]

It might be thought that the first two paragraphs established that a defensive army in Britain was pointless. With a Navy invasion was impossible; without it, defence was impossible. As long ago as 1888 the Report of the Three Admirals had made the point clearly:

Under the conditions in which it would be possible for a great power to successfully invade England, nothing could avail her, as, the command of the sea once being lost, it would not require the landing of a single man upon her shores to bring her to ignominious capitulation, for by her Navy she must stand or fall.[34]

But Roberts initiated a debate in the House of Lords on 23 November 1908, before which the King wrote to him: 'As your Sovereign, and with the full concurrence of my Ministers and the Leader of the Opposition, I must ask you, as a patriot, not to raise the question of Germany or to refer to the decision of the Committee of Defence.'[35] To the King's displeasure, this deterred the old soldier little; he made his point of view very plain and won his motion by 74 votes to 32.

The report was an Asquithian compromise between the obvious naval adequacy and the Army's determination to maintain forces at home. 'The figure of 70,000 men,' wrote Roberts to Churchill in 1913, 'is purely hypothetical. I believe it arose from my saying in answer to a question put to me at a meeting of the Committee of Imperial Defence that I considered 70,000 the smallest number with which the Germans would dream of invading this country.'[36] In fact the figure was first postulated by Roberts in 1903 and referred to invasion by France, not Germany, and he wrote in 1913, 'In any case 70,000 men could not conquer Britain'.[37] Repington illogically recorded in his diary in November 1915, 'There is no fresh standard against invasion since Lord Roberts and I got it raised from 10,000 to 70,000 after our fights with the Defence Committee.'[38] A serious attempt at invasion would have required a far greater force, and mere raids, such as those at Scarborough and Hartlepool, a far smaller one, and no troops were ever landed. The raids were purely naval operations to persuade Britain, which they successfully did, to maintain a large home army, which otherwise would have been available for operations elsewhere. The invasion scare was whipped into hysterical proportions; a play by Du Maurier entitled *An Englishman's Home* provoked Esher to form an association called 'The Islanders', to convince the public that Britain 'floated on the British Navy'; but it was not until 1915 that Balfour 'completed the process of reassurance' by asking Kitchener to put himself in the enemy's place and say how he would like to have to land 70,000 men in face of opposition with all communications cut, without many heavy guns or much ammunition and being attacked from the sea as well as from the land within 24 hours of his arrival.[39]

12

BLAST AND COUNTERBLAST

As his time in the Mediterranean approached its close Beresford was again a thorn in the flesh of the Admiralty and Government. Unless given a new appointment he would re-enter Parliament where his facile tongue would destroy Fisher. To prevent his re-election a new command was essential. He had already refused an appointment as Commander-in-Chief of one of the Home Ports, usually a last command before retiring. Having been C-in-C Mediterranean he would be satisfied with nothing less prestigious. On paper the Channel Fleet (the old Home Fleet) was the main fleet in home waters and on 9 July 1906 he was offered command. 'My life ambition is now realised,' he said.[1] Fisher's plans for home waters rested on the new Home Fleet. The nucleus crew ships were to be placed under one admiral based at the Nore, where six of the thirteen battleships were fully manned; the remainder, at Portsmouth and Plymouth, were now manned with three-fifths complement, with which they could carry out all the exercises required. The new fleet was capable of mobilization in hours.

But the Government was anxious not to attract the attention of Germany; the deployment of the fleet in the North sea had to be done unobtrusively. As new dreadnoughts and battlecruisers completed trials they were un-ostentatiously sent to the Nore, on the pretext that they could not be fully manned, thus building up a powerful modern fleet. All destroyers and submarines in home waters were to be formed into separate commands, which would exercise periodically with the Channel and Home Fleets.

Beresford got wind of Fisher's plans, for he later told McKenna, Tweedmouth's successor, that his acceptance was on condition that he would 'have control of the protection of the whole of Home Waters' and that 'the organisation and training for war of all torpedo craft . . . would rest with me'.[2]

Some Unionist backbenchers argued that the Home Fleet should be

166

combined with the Channel Fleet, under Beresford. Fisher's reorganization seemed inexplicable and a destruction of British naval power, exemplified in a letter from Lord Hardinge to Knollys:

> It is perfectly childish to expect sane people to believe that ships with nucleus crews, lying in home ports, can be regarded as efficient items in a fleet, and he has failed to prove that the reductions in our fleets in commission have not reduced our fighting strength. Also, it can hardly be denied that the ships available for police duties abroad will be considerably reduced and British interests and policy will suffer for the sake of concentration in the Channel against a possible attack by Germany, which even Fisher regards as a very remote eventuality. The only explanation of the scheme is economy and Fisher's desire to truckle to the Liberal Party.[3]

Certainly the Liberal Party would have emasculated the Navy rather than give up social reform. Hardinge was mistaken, for Fisher believed an attack by Germany was not remote, but a certainty. He wrote to the Prince of Wales in October:

> Our only probable enemy is Germany. Germany keeps her *whole* fleet always concentrated within a few hours of England. We must therefore keep a fleet twice as powerful concentrated within a few hours of Germany. If we kept the Channel and Atlantic Fleet *always* in the Channel (say in the vicinity of the Nore) this would meet the case, but this is neither feasible nor expedient, and if, when relations with foreign powers are strained, the Admiralty attempt to take the proper fighting precautions and move our Channel and Atlantic fleets to their proper fighting positions, then *at once* the Foreign Office and Government veto it, and say such a step will precipitate war![4]

The formation of the new Home Fleet under Sir Francis Bridgeman was announced on 23 October 1906, to be effective from the date of Beresford's appointment. He exploded with frustrated rage. He had expected to command the most important fleet, and now an admiral five years junior to him was to have that distinction. Furthermore, two battleships and two armoured cruisers were to be transferred from the Channel Fleet to the Home Fleet.

Fisher was tactless, or even, as some said, determined to humiliate Beresford, but Beresford was far from competent to command the embryo Grand Fleet. If Fisher had had his way he would have been retired. Beresford wrote: 'The Channel Fleet was reduced from sixty-two fighting vessels to twenty-one . . . the balance being transferred to the Home Fleet. An order was issued under which ships taken from the Channel, Atlantic and Mediterranean Fleets for purposes of refitting, were to be replaced during their absence by ships from the Home Fleet.'[5] The first sentence is misleading, for it includes destroyers, submarines and other small craft. Beresford said the changes were made without reference to him 'as future Commander-in-Chief in war', and that it was 'altogether different from what I had been led to expect'.[6] Had Fisher taken him into his confidence it would certainly have precipitated a violent row, which Beresford would have made as public as possible, and he now wrote a long letter of protest to Tweedmouth, who referred it to Fisher. Early in January 1907 members of the Board went to Malta to see Beresford to sort things out. He 'declined verbally to take command of the Channel Fleet under such changed conditions.'[7] On 20 January Fisher met Beresford at the Admiralty and subsequently wrote to George Lambert, civil Lord: 'I had three hours with Beresford yesterday, and all is settled, and the Admiralty don't give in one inch to his demands. But I had as a preliminary to agree to three things:- (i) Lord C.Beresford is a greater man than Nelson. (ii) No one knows anything about the art of naval war except Lord C.Beresford. (iii) The Admiralty haven't done a single damned thing right!'[8]

But all was not settled. Two days later Beresford again declined his appointment. He gave as his reason that 'a fleet composed of fourteen battleships, four armoured and three unarmoured cruisers, without such necessary adjuncts as scouts [light cruisers] and destroyers would be seriously incomplete and could not be properly trained for war'.[9] Fisher was angry. The First Sea Lord was solely responsible for the disposition of ships and their employment. Beresford wished to establish himself as the Admiralissimo. Yet only a few days earlier, having had a month's leave, he had asked for another month to go abroad for the benefit of his health. 'The "one man on whom all depends",' wrote Fisher, 'would surely ask that some other admiral should take his place (and that he resign), to be ready for the German invasion, which is to come without warning like the last trump!'[10]

Beresford raised support in Parliament and demands were made for an inquiry into the policies of the Admiralty. On 24 January, Fisher wrote: 'It means that the Board of Admiralty will abdicate its functions and take its instructions from an irresponsible subordinate, who is totally unacquainted with the world requirements of the British Navy, and is only thinking of magnifying his own command, which is far stronger under the new conditions than when it was first commanded by his distinguished predecessor, Sir A Wilson.'[11] Three days later he wrote to Knollys, 'I followed your advice and wrote a most cordial letter to Beresford and enclose you his reply. It will not be my fault if he resigns, as Tweedmouth says he will. . . . Anyhow, as explained in enclosed print, it is simply impossible to submit to Beresford's dictation. *The position would be intolerable ever after!*'[12]

That many admirals still believed their importance and grandeur was proclaimed by the size of their fleet was demonstrated by Battenberg, who, in 1909, wrote to King-Hall that the scheme would have been accepted had Fisher not been determined that Beresford should 'not have so big and honourable a command. I think CB has been badly treated. . . . You know how much I admire JF; he is a truly great man and almost all his schemes have benefited the Navy. But he has started this pernicious partisanship . . . there is no denying it. Anyone who opposed JF went under. His hatred of CB has led him to maintain for the past two years an organisation of our home forces which is indefensible.'[13] That Battenberg, with his experience, should be so wide of the mark demonstrates current attitudes and the need for discretion, which Beresford would have ignored. Against a report by Pakenham Fisher wrote, 'Impossible to tell Lord C.Beresford anything as he talks at random about the most secret matters to any or every listener.'[14] The notorious leakiness of the Services at that time explains his reluctance to take officers into his confidence; the matter would have been in every paper the next day. That Battenberg should blame Fisher for the rift Beresford had so energetically engineered is surprising.

Fisher began to suspect Beresford was attempting to escape the Channel command. 'My conviction is that Beresford funks the Channel and wants to clear out! Fog and short days and difficult navigation very different to Mediterranean white trousers!!! Wilson also hard to follow.'[15] Truly, Beresford's love of glitter and glory could hardly be satisfied in the cold, bleak North Sea, and his limited ability would be compared with the outstanding Wilson.

Tweedmouth and the Cabinet gave signs of giving in to Beresford's threats; his friends in Parliament were pressing for an enquiry into Admiralty policy. Tweedmouth's ill-health was not yet apparent, but he was quite unable to make up his mind whether to support Fisher or capitulate to Beresford, so the Sea Lords jointly prepared a memorandum to him threatening resignation in a body if he gave in, which was presented by Drury. Almost certainly Beresford's spies informed him, for the very next day he agreed to compromise conditions. The Home Fleet would be put under his orders from time to time for war training, a number of scouts and forty-eight destroyers allocated to his fleet for such exercises, an arrangement which impeded Fisher's plans, but provided a compensating advantage; the scouts and destroyers would be better exercised in company with the Channel Fleet than separately. A paper embodying these arrangements was signed by Tweedmouth, Fisher and Beresford.

Balfour told Fisher that he 'would resist any inquiry into Admiralty policy to the utmost of his power. Lord Goschen is apparently the only formidable malcontent'.[16] Arthur Lee (later Lord Lee of Fareham) was also 'dead against' an enquiry. 'I am all for crucifying the Board if they deserve it, but who is there competent to "enquire" into them? The worst of it is your "Committee of 3" on the War Office was a bad precedent, but I am always in favour of damning precedents.'[17] Fisher was not convinced. 'It is only putting off the evil day!' he wrote to Tweedmouth, 'but having adopted a policy of endeavouring to keep him, and in view of the action that has been taken, there seems no other course than to go on as now arranged. The way it has been arranged by Beresford (Bellairs being his tool) extorts one's admiration. . . . The whole affair is about the worst on record, *especially when one knows the secret part of it*.'[18] Balfour, with an intelligent interest in naval strategy, which he discussed with Fisher, remained one of his keenest supporters.[19]

Beresford hoisted his flag as C-in-C, Channel Fleet, on 16 April 1907 in *King Edward VII*, with Custance, now a vice-admiral, as his second-in-command; he had held the appointment under Wilson. Beresford exhibited his hypocrisy by writing in his memoirs in 1914 that Custance was a 'most distinguished strategist and tactician, one of the most learned officers in his profession',[20] yet writing to Admiral Sir John de Robeck in 1917, 'He did not have much idea as to what was necessary in winning an action at sea'.[21]

Commander W.H.D.Boyle, (later Earl of Cork and Orrery), a fellow Irishman and admirer of Beresford, executive officer of Custance's flagship, *Hibernia*, described him as a 'writer and thinker, ahead of his time . . . of a shy and retiring nature . . . [who] laid the foundations of modern fleet tactics and the deployment of a fleet for battle'.[22]

The brilliant young Royal Marine Officer, Maurice Hankey, found him less cordial as Director of Naval Intelligence: 'Personally I did not find him a very inspiring chief. His nature was rather suspicious.'[23]

Custance had never been second-in-command of any ship, but had commanded the battleship *Barfleur* on the China station. When Chatfield joined his flagship, Custance was unhappy about the ship, which was in poor order and Chatfield found him 'exacting' and said he showed neither captain nor flagship any mercy, having fads and showing total lack of consideration for the ship's company. He installed a wearisome routine, without understanding the problems he was creating for officers and men. His flag captain was unwilling to confront him in these matters and Chatfield, with his permission, had it out with the admiral. '"Dear me, Chatfield," the little man said, "I did not appreciate this at all".'[24]

Beresford's Chief of Staff was again Sturdee for whom he attempted to persuade Fisher to bend the rules to enable him to count this as sea time for promotion, though such a thing was not at all the same as command of his own ship. Fisher refused and Sturdee was relieved by Captain Montague Browning.

Beresford's vainglory was vividly described by Captain the Hon. V. Wyndham-Quin:

He was venerable in appearance, looking all his sixty-one years. He lived in great style, his stewards and his galley's and barge's crew being all Irish. Mostly they had little to do except be on hand looking smart – and smart they were; but one was required to attend on Kora, the Admiral's bulldog, his duty being to follow this fat, overfed bitch about the upper deck equipped with dustpan, brush and cloth to clear up the messes she was always making .

Though there was a bathroom in his quarters, Charlie B always bathed in a round tin bath. . . . His motor car, for which he had a marine driver, was stowed in the booms amidships, being hoisted in and out with special slings by the main derrick and taken ashore in the launch. Wherever we went he used it, means of getting it out of the launch being devised in the most remote places.

The C-in-C's yacht *Surprise* went nearly everywhere with the fleet, and Lady Charles was often in her. . . .

When we were in Irish waters the Old Man often went fishing, usually accompanied by a lieutenant, myself and sometimes another midshipman, our job being to get flies out of weeds or bushes and disentangle knots. The coxswain and two of the galley's crew followed with lunch-baskets, landing nets, rugs and other gear – and the inevitable Kora. We midshipmen had our reward in the evening; the admiral's steward used to come to the gunroom with half a case of champagne. On Sunday two midshipmen were always asked to break-fast; we had to appear in the fore-cabin at two minutes to eight and sit on each side of him, whilst he told a string of Irish stories, which it was best to greet with loud laughter. Like King Edward VII, he had his uniform trousers pressed down the sides.[25]

Beresford, as Fisher had done, had an extra topmast fitted to fly his flag higher than usual, but with unhappy results, for it was knocked off when the ship passed under the Forth Bridge. Captain Lionel Dawson, then a lieutenant, gives other glimpses of Beresford:

All the old expressions remained in his vocabulary. 'Let the catchers have a chance, Roper,' he would remark to his signal lieutenant; by which he would intend the destroyers to be sent to attack some one. 'Catchers' was a relic of the early days of torpedo-boats, when torpedo-gunboats were sent to 'catch' them. . . .

The line led by his second-in-command was, to him, the 'lee-line', a relic of sailing ship days when the Commander in Chief led the 'weather-line' and the next senior admiral the 'lee-line'.

The midshipmen were, of course the 'young gentlemen'.[26]

I am bound to record my conviction that by 1907 the peak of his curve of service had passed; at sixty-two little but his famous

171

personality remained to recall the Charlie B of past days. . . . He had not moved forward mentally with the instruments he wielded and his attitude was reactionary, and inclined to dwell upon past days. Never have I known such a 'flagshippy' flagship. Everything centred around the person of the Admiral, with whom ceremonial had become an obsession. Every time he showed his head above the coaming of his hatch, the officer of the watch was required to call the quarterdeck to attention, everyone remaining stricken into immobility until the well-known and slightly nasal voice graciously commanded: 'Carry on, Mr. Officer of the Watch'.[27]

These affectations may have been silly, but apart from the cost to the tax-payer, they were at least harmless. Such posturing and conceit, the number of men employed in waiting on the Great Man, the pomp and ceremony, the fawning obsequiousness he demanded, in contrast to Fisher's dislike of protocol and passion for fighting efficiency, have to be measured in the context of the time. In matters of vanity, personal ambition and mendacity he was far from unique; many admirals of the day shared these traits, combined with a humourless rigidity to their subordinates, whom they treated with patronizing condescension. Where Beresford differed was in his charm, that endeared him to many of his subordinates, especially less competent officers, enabling them to forgive his faults. He hungered for popularity no less than for personal advancement, exhibiting bon-homie and sybaritic tastes calculated to advance it. When he visited *Hibernia* after her success in a regatta, he asked who was coxswain of the ship's gig:

'Tis me, Sorr,' said a small man stepping forward. 'And what is your name?' 'Tis Michael O'Holigan, Sorr,' 'And where do you come from?' 'County Cark.' 'And how many Irishmen have you got in your boat?' 'Tis four I have, Sorr.' 'Put it there,' said the C-in-C and the two Irishmen shook hands. Lord Charles could do that sort of thing, always a happy remark at the right time. And it endeared him to everyone.[28]

Beresford always stressed his Irishness, trading on the English affection for that troublesome race.

Despite his boasting, his solemn warnings of the unreadiness of the fleet, he made little effort to prepare the Channel Fleet for war. In 1907 it proceeded at a leisurely pace round the United Kingdom, when the ships were opened to the public, Beresford all the while receiving deputations, addressing meetings held in his honour and receiving the freedom of in-numerable ports and cities, 'varied by a few hackneyed steam tactics. Exercises . . . took place from time to time with the "catchers" . . . performing set piece attacks by day and night, but I do not recollect that any very serious problems of war were either attempted or solved.'[29]

The Times on 30 July wrote of the 1907 prize firings: 'The flagships of the Channel Fleet are very low in the list, their places being respectively 35 and 41 out of 60. . . . It must be very difficult for an admiral to find fault with the other ships of his fleet if the vessel in which his own flag is flying is low down the list.' This incensed Beresford, for Ponsonby wrote:

> In September 1907 I heard the other side of the controversy from Charlie Beresford . . . presumably hoping that I would pass on to the King what he said. He always began by saying, 'I wish to keep all arguments impersonal', but after a short time he forgot and went on, 'If it were not for that damned fellow Fisher'. The whole of his conversation was impregnated with hatred of Fisher, whom he accused of having poisoned him with the King.
>
> The chief points he made with the present administration were:
>
> (1) That the firing which had attracted so much attention was really a farce. Fisher and Prince Louis of Battenberg had been duped by the Flag Captain, Mark Kerr, who had produced wonderful results under unfair conditions.
>
> (2) The firing on the *Dreadnought* had been a farce and was laughed at by the Navy.
>
> (3) The Home fleet was a fraud and a deception. The ships were really a lot of lame ducks produced for effect.
>
> (4) The nucleus crew system, although sound in theory, was really unworkable in practice and had really broken down owing to the details not being properly worked out.
>
> (5) The whole Navy was dissatisfied, and until we had a real Board of Admiralty we should never advance on sound principle. At present it was packed by Fisher.
>
> Whenever I tried to bring him to the point by asking what he would do if he were to be appointed First Lord, he never seemed to have any satisfactory answer.[30]

Though Beresford had paid lip-service to satisfaction with the concessions he had wrung from Fisher and Tweedmouth, his cynicism was betrayed less than a week after he hoisted his flag. On 22 April 1907 Fisher wrote: 'I had a letter of yours planted in my hand five minutes after I arrived, with the proposed answer, which I suppose had better go to you; but I was hoping that hereafter all such questions could be arranged without these official State Papers; nor is it conducive to the harmonious working which is essential, if your staff are always preparing ammunition for you to fire off at the Admiralty. . . .'

'All I wish to assure you is that so far as I am concerned I am most anxious that we should avoid friction and undesirable correspondence – so I think in all ways that we should discuss things personally.'[31] To this he received the smug reply: 'There is not the slightest chance of friction between me and you, or between me and anyone else. When the friction begins I am off. If a senior and a junior have a row, the junior is wrong under any conceivable condition, or discipline could not go on. As long as I am here I will do my best to make the Admiralty policy a success.'[32]

But three weeks later a stormy meeting of the Navy League showed it bitterly split. Among the most influential of Beresford's supporters was Leslie Cope-Cornford, naval correspondent of the *Standard*, and his editor, H.A.Gwynne. The next day the *Standard* wrote:

> How can the League rest content, when appropriations are reduced by millions and ships are manned by nucleus crews? . . . Sir John Fisher is a public servant for whom we have great respect, but the supremacy of the Navy is something which cannot be taken on trust, and when it is in question, no consideration should impede free discussion, or, if necessary, a fresh campaign. As it would be perfectly idle to contend that the Navy is safe under the present administration, we fear that the Navy League must look forward to more acute crises in its career, unless it is prepared as a body to take an active and uncompromising course.

At the meeting two energetic supporters of Beresford and opponents of Fisher, with no obvious claim to naval knowledge, H.F.Wyatt of Exeter College, Oxford, and L.G.H.Horton-Smith, a barrister and Fellow of St. John's College, Cambridge, demanded a protest on 'seven specified points of naval administration'. Against this, another member, Seymour Trower, pointed out that if Beresford and Custance continued to hold commands under the current administration, 'they must be satisfied with it'. The *Standard* said, 'It is, we believe, the duty of every citizen who regards the security of his country as worth a thought, to protest against the present naval policy of the Government'. Every day, throughout May, June and July, the *Standard* published pro-Beresford and anti-Fisher comments, the source of which was obvious, for on 9 June figures published of the strength of the Channel Fleet compared with that in Wilson's time coincided precisely with those earlier quoted by Beresford. Leo Maxse of the *National Review* and even the Liberal *Observer* joined the hunt. On 30 June the latter remarked in an editorial: 'At this moment we cannot afford to surrender the smallest advantage. Our fleet is reduced below the proper standard of efficiency, with no better motive than to save money to win votes. The Navy League, the proper guardian of our interests, is lulled to sleep by the siren, Sir John Fisher, and economy seems a weightier argument than patriotism.'

174

Arguments were becoming hysterical. An MP, Rowland Hunt, interviewed by the *Standard*, said:

> I am more directly concerned about the weakness of our Channel Squadron [fleet] which is to be ready for immediate service – to meet a sudden attack. If it is not strong enough to deal with the German Fleet – which would appear to be the case at the present moment – we are literally in danger of invasion on the sudden outbreak of a quarrel. That is the fact, however people may try to minimise it or dress it up. Germany, by a *grand coup*, might throw an army into London, and once in possession of our capital could dictate her own terms of peace. ... I certainly do not think that the Channel Fleet under the command of Lord Charles Beresford is anything like strong enough. More than 40 warships have been taken from the immediate command of that able and energetic officer.

On 19 July the *Standard* wrote that 'The Home Fleet was formed by reducing the sea-going squadrons and placing them in the Reserve. Therefore it does not "increase" the immediate striking strength of the Navy'. On the same day Wyatt and Horton-Smith proposed a resolution 'That this meeting further expresses its profound concern in view of the reduction of the Channel Fleet from sixty-seven units under its late Commander-in-Chief, Admiral Sir A.K.Wilson, to twenty-one units under its present Commander-in-Chief, Admiral Lord Charles Beresford, and in view also of the relegation of units withdrawn from this fleet to conditions of far inferior efficiency either in the Home Fleet (too largely manned with second-class stokers and immature boys) or in ships in reserve with nucleus crews.'[33] In August Beresford made a statement to the Press on board his flagship: 'This is not a fleet. A fleet under modern conditions consists of battleships, armoured cruisers, scouts and torpedo-boats. This is merely a squadron of battleships.'[34]

Beresford well knew that Wilson kept his war plans to himself and never committed them to paper, distrusting the notorious 'leakiness' of Government departments, so he 'innocently' asked for copies, following this up with an official letter artfully stating that he had been unable to find any plans of campaign for the Channel Fleet. 'I submit that I may be supplied with the plans of my predecessors.' Such plans would now be out of date and the Admiralty replied that Wilson was engaged in bringing them up to date, which touched a raw nerve in Beresford. 'I never asked for any war plans ... for present conditions. I am well able to make out such plans myself.'[35] This might provoke the question why he wanted out-of-date plans, for when he wrote he had already received Admiralty's war plans, which were for obvious reasons in broad terms. He returned them accompanied by a virulent attack on them. Again he attempted to drag the King in, writing to Knollys:

175

I am most distressed and alarmed at the complete absence of organisation and preparation for war in the Fleet. It is a danger to the State
and if Germany attacked us suddenly she would inflict terrible disasters on us and she might win. My predecessor had sixty-seven ships
though I can find no plan as to what they had to do; I have only twenty-
one – at this moment thirteen. The Home Fleet is the greatest fraud
ever perpetrated on the public, and every single admiral who knows
anything about war is of the same opinion. I am very much perturbed
in my mind whether I ought to remain here, struggling to get some sort
of plan effected, or go straight out and tell the people the facts as I did
before. . . . I am doing the best I can to help authority to get things
right, but it will be absolutely impossible under the present allocation
of ships and fleets.[36]

Less than a week later he wrote to Knollys: 'There is no fleet ready at a
moment's notice; neither the Home nor the Channel Fleet could successfully tackle the German Fleet in a sudden emergency as they are at present
constituted. . . . As the man who will have to do the work, I have represented
all these things to Authority, but not until I have *proved* our unreadiness and
complete want of preparation for war in the coming manoeuvres, of which
I am in charge, will I write my final letter. . . . If my statements are untrue I
ought to be cashiered.'[37]

His statements *were* untrue. At that time either fleet was more powerful
than the whole German Navy and no one at Admiralty intended that he
should command in war, but his constant repetition of the claim established
it. Denial would have created a political row, while silence implied acquies-
cence. Fisher prepared a memorandum dealing with the matter which he
marked 'Most Secret'.

> This memorandum has become necessary for the information and
> consideration of the Admiralty in view of the fact that the present
> Commander-in-Chief of the Channel Fleet (Lord Charles Beresford)
> who assumed his command last month (April) . . . has taken up a
> position of antagonism both to the policy and the administrative
> arrangements of the Board of Admiralty. He infers also, quite wrongly,
> that his distinguished predecessor (Sir A. Wilson) was totally un-
> provided with schemes of war. He has forwarded his own plan of
> campaign against Germany which involves . . . more battleships,
> cruisers &c., &c., than the British Navy possesses. . . .
>
> Further, in official conversation, Lord C. Beresford has spoken of
> our naval position being such that 'the Empire is in jeopardy', and his
> Chief of Staff (Captain Sturdee) has stated his opinion that we are
> 'living over a live mine', but it is fully admitted by them that the whole
> fleet can now be mobilised for war within a few hours. . . .

The truth is that such language on the part of Lord Charles Beresford and Captain Sturdee, besides being insubordinate, is perfectly preposterous. . . . It is certainly a great blow to discipline that such disloyalty should be overlooked. . . .

[Beresford claims that] Sir A.Wilson 'had turned over the Channel Fleet absolutely unprepared for war'. (These are words actually used by Lord Charles Beresford).

What seems necessary is a carefully worded letter to Lord C.Beresford, summing up the political and strategical situation. . . . It is desirable to avoid sensational communications to the Press. . . . It seems advisable that a revised set of war orders should be issued to Lord C.Beresford . . . disabusing him of the idea that now possesses him that his is the sole responsibility for the conduct of the naval war, 'because the country relied on him . . . for its protection by sea'. . . .

Admiralty must make it plain to Lord C.Beresford . . . as to the fixed determination of the Admiralty not to delegate any of its power or its responsibility for the full conduct of war.[38]

This brought a cautious politician's response from Tweedmouth. He would regret that Fisher's paper should be circulated to the Board in its present form. 'No one is more alive to the objections that can be taken to Lord Charles Beresford and his methods of action. I know him to be ambitious, self-advertising and gassy in his talk, but we all know these bad qualities of his, and no one better than you, when you very wisely recommended his and Sir Reginald Custance's appointments. You and we then considered that some serious disadvantages were outweighed by the advantages which were to be gained by their good qualities and their record of services in the past.' He went on to praise what he saw as Beresford's good qualities. He was cheerful, active, zealous in the Service and attracted the affection of officers and men under him, and if Fisher's memorandum were acted on it 'must forbid his continued employment. . . . I am the last person in the world to abrogate one iota of the supremacy of the Board of Admiralty, but I do think we sometimes are inclined to consider our own views to be infallible and are not ready enough to give consideration to the views of others.'[39]

The dig at Fisher in the last paragraph was most unjust and ignored the enormous damage done by Beresford, though it is charitable to attribute Tweedmouth's political cowardice to the onset of his sickness and Beresford was merely told to submit revised war plans, whereupon he answered on 27 June:

It is manifestly impossible for me to submit 'detailed plans for the carrying out of operations under the several contingencies of an outbreak of war with the powers indicated' unless I know what ships

177

are available to carry these plans out and where such ships are to be found. . . . At present I have not the faintest idea of the number of torpedo craft and submarines in Home Waters that are actually ready or where they are stationed, neither do I know what torpedo boats and submarines are at the disposal of the Commanders-in-Chief of the Home Ports for local defence.[40]

This further attempt to establish his responsibility for the conduct of a European war was illogical. Strategic plans had to be flexible and capable of responding to enemy reaction; they could only be made by the Admiralty with knowledge of the facilities available and intelligence of enemy intentions. Beresford's purpose was to pillory the Admiralty and enhance his own position. Fisher wanted to remove him, but the politician Tweedmouth suggested he should see Beresford again to see if the matter could be patched up 'without further irritating correspondence'.

Accordingly, on 5 July a meeting was held between Tweedmouth, Fisher and Beresford. To his credit, Tweedmouth put four questions challenging Beresford: (1) The number and types of ships he should have under his command? (2) The further information he needed? (3) Why did he not try to cultivate good and cordial relations with the Admiralty, who were most anxious to achieve this end? (4) Would he explain to them his reasons for saying that 'the Home Fleet was a fraud and danger to the Empire'?

Verbatim minutes of the meeting were kept.[41] Beresford, without the support of his staff, felt cornered, and hedged. Tweedmouth stressed the question of relations with the Admiralty. Beresford sneered: 'Then this thing – question number 3 – you will allow me to smile for at least ten minutes over question number 3 . . . there is not any question of want of cordial relations with the Admiralty. Not privately or publicly have I ever said anything against the Admiralty.'

Beresford had used the words 'a fraud and danger to the Empire' repeatedly in private and official correspondence and in interviews with the Press. Tweedmouth continued: 'To tell the First Lord of the Admiralty that what is a very important part of the Board's policy is absolutely useless and is a fraud and danger to the Empire, I do not think that is very friendly to the Admiralty.'

Beresford began to panic:

It is a private letter. . . . It was only a 'term'. If we went to war suddenly you would find it is true. If I had said officially that the Admiralty had created that, or if I had pitched into the Admiralty about it, it would be different. . . . That I had any notion of insubordination I absolutely deny. That letter of mine to the First Lord has no right to go before the Board, a private letter like that.

'It is not marked private. Other letters have been marked private.'

'I ought to have put "private" and "confidential" on it.'

'I cannot look on that as simply a private communication to me. I think it is a very important letter.'

Fisher tried to take the heat out of the argument: 'What you want to say to us now is, "You must not take my letter in that way. I was only doing it as giving you a friendly criticism and not meaning you to take it as anything insubordinate"? . . . I am quite sure you understand that we are all equally interested, as you are, in having friendly and cordial relations but it is absolutely impossible if the Chief Executive Officer of the Admiralty afloat is going to be "crabbing" the Admiralty in everything the Admiralty is doing, and writing such letters to the First Lord.'

'I think,' said Tweedmouth, 'so serious a charge against the Home Fleet ought to be substantiated; you ought to say how it is a fraud, and how it is a danger to the State.'

'It is a "term". I can write it all out for you in detail. The public think it is ready for instant action. What is your own term? – Without an hour's delay; well it is not. . . . I do not dictate to the Board of Admiralty. The Board has the right – it is the constituted authority, it is responsible, and nobody else. It may do things wrong, but it is the responsible authority – I have never written to you, officially or privately, except in the most respectful manner.'

Fisher pointed out that the composition and disposition of the Fleet were not matters for a Commander-in-Chief afloat, nor even the Admiralty, but the Government. On the question of training ships and crews, if the C-in-C's views were reasonable the Admiralty had acceded to them and would continue to do so. The discussion turned to war plans and Beresford collapsed: 'I have no right to put myself up against the constitutional authority of the Admiralty.'

The interview ended inconclusively. 'The answers to the questions put to the Commander-in-Chief are a series of clumsy fencings, evasions and dodgings, and are often contradictory,' recorded the minutes.

Even after this Fisher tried to maintain peace and made concessions to Beresford's self-esteem by agreeing that the Channel Fleet should be further reinforced in September, (which was immediately leaked to the Press) writing the next day to Beresford, 'I am most anxious to be as cordial in my relations with you as in the warmest days of our friendship'.[42] Beresford replied amicably, saying that he had been given all he asked for, but he had hardly returned to his fleet when Custance, an Iago to his Othello, who had in May 1905 contributed an anonymous article to *Blackwood's Magazine* entitled *A Retrograde Admiralty*, began to stir things up again. Sturdee spurred both and before the month was out Beresford again complained bitterly of having two fleets in Home Waters and argued both should be under his command. On 30 July Admiralty wrote officially that 'My Lords

179

. . . cannot enter into a controversy with an officer acting under their authority,'[43] and three weeks later regretted 'that you should have pressed your own opinion on the value of the Fleet in your report on the recent exercises'. Beresford had carried out the threat in his letter to Knollys to 'prove' the Home Fleet's unreadiness. The *Standard* carried a report that the manoeuvres 'upon the evidence of those officially recognised exponents of Admiralty policy who were privileged to witness them, furnished a last convincing demonstration of its unreadiness for instant emergency'. Beresford wrote again to Admiralty, with heavy sarcasm, once more attempting to establish his claim to command all home forces in wartime. Fisher commented to the First Lord:

> I think we shall have after all to issue the suspended minute of the Board, as Beresford returns to the charge . . . in what I call a *very impertinent* remark to the Board of Admiralty in paragraph 4 of his letter of August 28th, number 1023/5098:- 'I note that Their Lordships consider that the Admiral who in wartime is responsible for the fleet in Home Waters, should not press his opinion as to its efficiency in time of peace'. To my mind this sort of official language is intolerable. The military correspondent of *The Times* is in obvious collusion with him.[44]

That Repington as a soldier should express views on this thorny naval problem was the more curious since his colleague, the *Times* naval correspondent, Thursfield, was a keen supporter of Fisher, who wrote to the King on 4 October:

> I got this letter last night. . . . The writer says to me à propos of the virulent and persistent attacks of the *Standard* and the *Daily Express* (they belong to one and the same owner) . . . Mr. Gwynne, the editor of the *Standard*, told me that the Home Fleet Review had knocked the bottom out of their case and also that he was bitterly disgusted with Beresford for having accepted his two armoured cruisers and twenty-four destroyers and not resigned his command of the Channel Fleet as he had led his journalistic friends to believe he would do. . . . The position is becoming intolerable and . . . I intend to bring the matter to a direct issue at a meeting of the Board and Flatten out Beresford once and for all. Lambton said to me the other day, *'Seize Beresford by the scruff of the neck and he will collapse – he is a blusterer'.*[45]

But Beresford was no easy man to flatten. He intended the matter should be made as public as possible and fed information to the retired admirals who swore the Service was going to the dogs. 'The naval clubs rang with the outraged sentiments of half-pay officers, and ancient admirals . . . fired broadsides at the iconoclast through the portholes of *The Times*.'[46]

Newspaper correspondents surrounded Beresford demanding his views. 'I have come to the conclusion,' thundered Wemyss, a future First Sea Lord, but then only a junior captain, 'that Sir John Fisher and his Board are playing the very deuce with the Service . . . with his dispositions, appointments and his way of ignoring all precedents and valuable experience. The state of unrest all through the Service is very serious. . . . Nothing seems able to stop him in his mad career of perfectly unnecessary reforms.'[47]

That Wemyss, a prime example of the reactionaries, could not see that the unrest was due to resistance to change and destruction of the seagoing gentlemen's club, that he should regard Fisher's reforms as 'perfectly un-necessary', was hardly surprising considering his inexperience. One of the midshipmen selected by Beresford ('an old family friend') to accompany the Princes in *Bacchante*, he had served with Prince George in HMS *Canada*, as Flag Lieutenant to Rear Admiral R.E.Tracey and in the Prince of Wales' yacht *Osborne*. He had been promoted commander for service in the Royal Yacht, in which, he said, the duties 'were not very onerous', and to Captain for service with the Duke of York in the cruise of the *Ophir*. Under the Buggins' turn system his future was assured.

On 19 October an anonymous letter was published in the *Standard:*

> Sir,
>
> Since the present First Sea Lord has been at the Admiralty a system of espionage has grown up in the British Navy. Officers are reported upon, privately and unofficially, to Whitehall. Any criticism among ourselves of Admiralty policy is whispered and not openly discussed as in the old days. A feeling of suspicion is growing in consequence; officers look askance at their neighbours, and keep their mouths shut for prudence sake, for it is pretty obvious that no man who has a bad secret record can hope for promotion or employment. It is easy to imagine what the effect of this feeling must be on the *esprit de corps* of the commissioned ranks. Good men want to get out of the Service as quickly as possible, and soon, if his dictatorship last long enough, the First Sea Lord will be able to surround himself with an impenetrable ring of his own supporters. . . .
>
> All the wealth of England cannot remedy the destruction of a corps of officers which centuries of splendid tradition have built up. I believe that the methods of Sir John Fisher are ruining the tone and moral [*Sic*] of that corps. . . .
>
> I understand that an inquiry into the policy and actions of the Board of Admiralty has been refused by the Prime Minister on the ground that if it were granted Sir John Fisher would resign. Surely if he has done nothing worthy of reproach he ought to welcome investigation.
>
> I am, Sir, Your obedient servant, NAVAL OFFICER.

The editor described his correspondent as 'a distinguished naval officer'; *on that same day* Bellairs announced that the Prime Minister had refused to initiate an inquiry requested by him into the administration of the Admiralty. The next month Fisher spoke at the Lord Mayor's banquet:

> Recently, in the equinoctial season in the North Sea we have had twenty-six of the finest battleships in the world and twenty-five of the finest cruisers, some of them equal to foreign battleships, and over fifty other vessels . . . and I look in vain to see any equal to that large fleet anywhere. That is only a fraction of our power. . . . The gunnery efficiency of the fleet has surpassed all record. . . . My friend over there talked about a two-power standard – a million power standard is no use unless you can hit. You must hit first, you must hit hard and you must go on hitting. . . . So I turn to all of you and I turn to my countrymen and I say – Sleep quietly in your beds, . . . I do not know what league is working this one. . . . This afternoon I read the effusions of a magazine editor . . . that an army of 100,000 German soldiers had been practising embarking in the German fleet. . . . You might as well talk of embarking St. Paul's Cathedral in a penny steamer. I have no doubt equally silly stories are current in Germany. But he said, 'in respect of the number of fighting ships, their armament, and general capacity, the British Navy was never in so satisfactory a condition as it floats today'. So we let him off that yarn about 100,000 German troops.[48]

Fisher's speech was met with resounding cheers and applause by an enthusiastic audience. But Wyatt and Horton-Smith wrote to the *Standard*:

> Hitherto even those who realised the deadly harm which was being wrought in the Navy, in ways that you have again and again pointed out, have generally abstained from open, public and direct censure of Sir John Fisher. But now that, to the violation of all constitutional usage, he has chosen to take upon himself the function of a Cabinet Minister, he has ceased to have any right to his cloak of sacrosanct security, and all who love their country and know her peril are now entitled to make Sir John Fisher the mark for public scorn as they recall those written words of his which you quote today: 'Favouritism is the secret of efficiency.'[49]

This distorted statement exemplified the malice directed at Fisher by those seduced by Beresford's clique. Later they described the speech as 'bragging utterances'. On the day after its delivery, at a meeting of the London Chamber of Commerce, whose secretary had attempted to recruit Sir Frederick Richards, the latter answered leading questions in moderate terms, describing the Selborne-Fisher Scheme as a 'hazardous experiment' and, though he preferred 'not to express my opinion on these matters in detail', he agreed that a commission of Enquiry would 'clear the air', and should be appointed 'while there is yet time'. His letter was read at the meeting and Sir Richard Vesey Hamilton expressed the view that an enquiry was 'most necessary'. Spenser Wilkinson, the opinionated defence correspondent of the *Morning Post*, deprecated the idea that the Home Fleet was ready for war and declared that it was 'necessary that advice as to preparations for war should be given by a great expert in strategy. The present state of the Navy conclusively proved that the advice . . . did not emanate from a man who was such an expert.'[50] He told Grey that the separation of the Home Fleet was a strategical blunder of the greatest moment and 'has lost the present Admiralty the confidence of strategists',[51] in which category he presumably placed himself. Wilkinson said that the management of the Navy was in 'dangerous hands', a view held by 'the greater part of the officers of the Navy. . . . The Board of Admiralty is dominated by one man whose strength – *consensu omnium* – consists in his determination to have his own way and to crush out of the Navy those who disagree with him or will not be his tools, and whose weakness – *consensu omnium* – is that his subject is not war.'[52] Wyatt followed, describing Fisher as an 'autocratic personality'. A public meeting was held in Wandsworth 'to protest against naval reductions', when a resolution proposed by Wyatt and seconded by Horton-Smith was passed which endorsed the 'recommendation of Sir Frederick Richards that a public inquiry should be held into the state of the Navy'. Thus, with classic distortion, it was suggested Richards had initiated the idea.

Staunch resistance by Dr Ginsburg, Secretary of the Navy League, frustrated attempts by the rebels to take it over. They formed a breakaway organization which they named the Imperial Maritime League, whose avowed aims were to remove Fisher and form a 'Department of Strategy' at the Admiralty. By now Fisher was getting heartily sick of the whole business, discouraged, frustrated and depressed. He wrote to Cawdor:

I had a very long visit from Pretyman [formerly Civil Lord of the Admiralty and later Parliamentary and Financial Secretary], who had been much perturbed by a visit to the Channel Fleet and I am not surprised, as I regret to say we have Beresford in a state of almost open mutiny, which of course reflects on all under him (I enclose you a note from Drury as a specimen of Beresford's wild talk). . . . My own firm belief is that Beresford would fizzle out in a week if he resigned as he threatened to do the other day. He told the Prime Minister *(who told me this himself)* that he (Beresford) if he resigned, would join the radical party and get a seat in Parliament as the most effective way of damaging the Admiralty! (I think the Prime Minister fancied him a bit off his head). Beresford and all the malcontents are now coalescing to have a Parliamentary inquiry or Royal Commission on Admiralty policy and administration.[53]

Drury's note was a further copy of the letter from Inglefield about Beresford's claim to be waiting to 'crumble up' the Admiralty, which Fisher had sent to Tweedmouth. Fisher continued, 'Personally I am getting rather sick of being vilified and calumniated daily.' All his efforts to placate Beresford and restore harmony had failed and it required little to bring the matter to a head. This was not long in coming.

13

PAINTWORK AND POMP

The support Fisher had given Percy Scott in his obsession and remarkable ability in gunnery had never persuaded him to take sides in the Fisher-Beresford quarrel. He remained aloof, concerned only with the efficiency of the fleet, and in July 1907, when appointed Rear-Admiral Commanding, First Cruiser Squadron under Beresford, refused to join in denigrating Fisher, which persuaded Beresford that he had been planted by Fisher to report on him, as he believed Bacon had been in the Mediterranean. Scott wrote:

> Lord Charles appeared to be of opinion that he could either enforce his views on the Admiralty, or procure the retirement of the Sea Lords; that the Admiralty were not to remain in control of the Navy unless they accepted him as a dictator of what they should do. . . .
>
> I listened to all this. Very politely, I refused to join in a campaign against the Board of Admiralty. In so doing I fully appreciated that my Commander-in-Chief would be very much annoyed. I remained firm in my determination to do my duty to the country and to the Admiralty as I saw it.[1]
>
> I ought to have realised the conditions and to have been on my guard. But wrapped up in my own work, and thinking more about naval efficiency than personal squabbles, I neglected to take precautions.[2]

Scott disliked the prevailing 'paintwork and polish' fetish and despised slavish compliance by captains with admirals' whims. In China, under Cyprian Bridge, who enjoyed petty fads, the latter, noticing *Terrible*'s picket boat was not alongside, signalled: 'Why is your picket boat away in the dinner hour?', to which he received the tart reply, 'Because she didn't get back early enough.'

The German Emperor was due to pay a visit to the Channel Fleet on 8 November 1907. Beresford was delighted; he could publicly enjoy the hobnobbing with Royalty he adored. On 14 October the fleet sailed from the Forth, the cruisers to sail ahead of the main body. They became separated in fog and Scott's flagship *Good Hope* was delayed by machinery defects. On reaching Portland the rest of the squadron had already arrived and *Roxburgh* was carrying out gunnery exercises outside the breakwater. *Good Hope* proceeded into the harbour and anchored. A memorandum from Beresford arrived by mail, instructing the cruisers to paint ship for the visit of the Kaiser. *Roxburgh*, however, asked Scott if she could complete her gunnery exercises, to which he saw no objection. Scott's Flag Captain pointed out that if *Roxburgh* failed to take advantage of fine weather she might not complete her paintwork in time. Scott's secretary, adapting a well-known maxim of Scott's – 'Gunnery is more important than paintwork', made the facetious remark, 'This appears to be a case where paintwork is more important than gunnery!' Scott then dashed off a signal to *Roxburgh*: 'Paintwork appears to be more in demand than gunnery, so you had better come in in time to make yourself look pretty by 8th'. Informal perhaps, but there could be little objection to this signal between an admiral and one of his captains.

Later, Beresford arrived with the remainder of the fleet and made a signal for all ships to be 'out of routine' to paint ship. Nothing more would have been heard of the matter had not a lieutenant from Beresford's flagship, Lionel Dawson, happened to visit *Good Hope* and in social chatter heard of Scott's signal. 'My gorge rose at the gratuitous insult offered to Lord Charles.'[3] Dawson returned to the Flagship and, bent on mischief, told the flag lieutenant, who rushed off to the admiral, and Beresford sent for *Good Hope*'s signal log. His magnificence had been slighted and an opportunity was presented to degrade in public a man admired by Fisher. He called for all flag officers to repair on board, excluding Scott. Dawson describes the scene:

> I was officer of the watch when, with flags flying and much saluting, bugling and parading of guards, Vice-Admiral Sir Reginald Custance, Rear-Admiral Lowry and other flag officers in the port with the exception of Sir Percy Scott, arrived on board *King Edward VII* to be received by the Chief of Staff. . . . Lord Charles appeared and engaged them in conversation. Sir Percy had meantime been signalled to 'repair on board'. . . . He came up the ladder with a confident and almost jaunty bearing, but when he saw the group aft his face fell, and a puzzled look spread over it. Everyone was now ordered off the quarterdeck with the exception of myself placed as a sort of sentry to allow no one aft. . . . I heard enough to know that Lord Charles, white with suppressed

anger, was sparing his subordinate nothing. When he had finished he went below, followed by the admirals. But Sir Percy remained on deck, while his barge was called alongside. Silent and white-faced, he looked like a man stunned.[4]

Such a theatrically contrived insult to a distinguished admiral by a commander-in-chief is probably without precedent. But, not content, Beresford made a signal to his fleet:

> The Lords Commissioners of the Admiralty having directed me to prepare the Channel Fleet to do honour to HIM the German Emperor an order was given to all vessels under my command to be out of routine and paint ship after the manoeuvres. . . .
>
> The Rear Admiral commanding the first Cruiser Squadron, a squadron forming part of the Channel Fleet, made the following signal to the Captain of *Roxburgh*: [There followed the text of the signal in full].
>
> In regard to my order to the Fleet to paint ship, this signal made by the Rear Admiral commanding the First Cruiser Squadron is contemptuous in tone and insubordinate in character.
>
> The Rear Admiral is to issue orders to the *Good Hope* and *Roxburgh* to expunge the signal from their signal logs and report to me by signal when my orders have been obeyed.[5]

Beresford made the matter public to every officer and man. But his spite was not vented; the same day he wrote officially to the Admiralty: 'I sent for Rear Admiral Sir Percy Scott, and . . . informed him that I considered his signal was pitiably vulgar, contemptuous in tone, insubordinate in character, and wanting in dignity. . . . in this case there could be no explanation. . . . It is impossible that the matter rest where it is. . . . I submit that Rear Admiral Sir Percy Scott should be superseded from the command of the First Cruiser Squadron.'[6]

The only rational explanation of Beresford's histrionic display is that it was a device to rid himself of Scott. There were some 25,000 men in the fleet and when it arrived at Portsmouth the port was full of reporters covering the Kaiser's visit. The headlines in the next morning's papers were sensational. Following normal custom the Press did not wait to hear the full facts, but jumped to the conclusion that Beresford was in the right. The next day they discovered that Scott's signal had been made before Beresford's arrival and later that it had been made before Beresford's 'out of routine' order. One wonders what Gilbert and Sullivan would have made of an admiral systematically conspiring to bring down the Board of Admiralty and complaining of insubordination by another admiral when no indiscipline had taken place. However, the damage was done. The *Morning*

Post said 'the state of weakness and unreadiness for war [had been] made worse by the accompanying decline in discipline. . . . Statements are circulated intended to justify or palliate the recent insubordination of an admiral.'[7]

The story was not confined to the British Press, but was taken up by the French and German newspapers. Some speculated that Scott would have to resign, though *Vanity Fair* said they would 'have expected Lord Charles to smile on hearing the signal' but in fact he had acted 'like Englishmen are perpetually acting in Ireland; taking seriously what should be treated with sympathetic humour, and now everybody expects Sir Percy Scott to resign. We can only hope he will do nothing of the sort.'[8]

Scott had no such intention and Admiralty replied to Beresford's letter that 'the case will be sufficiently further dealt with by the conveyance to Admiral Scott of Their Lordships' grave disapprobation'.[9] But Beresford retorted that he was far from satisfied as the 'act of insubordination to my command was of a public character.' However, he forwarded the letter to Scott who went on board *King Edward VII* and attempted to heal the rift: 'I should like to take the opportunity to apologise to you for the incident . . .' Beresford cut him off, saying no private apology would suffice and ordered him back to his ship, telling Scott that any future communication between them was to be made on paper or by signal.

Scott should have insisted on a trial by Court Martial which would have made Beresford look so ridiculous as to enforce his resignation, not Scott's. Later Scott summarized the matter: 'He acted in a hasty, high-handed and intemperate manner, he condemned without investigation, he wrote without knowing the facts . . . he talked without knowing what he was saying, he signalled without knowing what he was signalling about.'[10]

The Press divided along Party lines, but *The Navy* got close to the nub of the matter: 'Lord Charles's subsequent action was a mystery which could only be explained by some deeper controversy behind the scenes.'[11] *The Naval and Military Record* commented that 'up to the present Admiral Sir Percy Scott has very wisely preserved strict silence on the reprimand which he received from Lord Charles Beresford and has not taken any notice of inaccuracies which have been published with regard to the incident'.[12]

Press speculation grew; wardroom ditties appeared in the papers and the music halls. *The Manchester Guardian*, despite Liberal sympathies, suggested the signal showed an insubordinate spirit and an inquiry seemed likely, which would 're-establish respect for discipline'. The Admiralty, having difficulty in finding an impartial Board, resisted an inquiry. Fisher wrote to Corbett: 'We have already had to tell him in an official letter a fortnight ago that his official language is "without parallel from a subordinate to the Board of Admiralty" and have censured him accordingly. He is dying to stump the country but wants to go off in fireworks! He "demanded" Percy Scott's supersession and meant to go on that; but Percy Scott is as much a "lime-light" man as Beresford, so that fell through, as we declined any further action.'[13] Beresford confirmed Fisher's view when he wrote to Balfour in March 1908 that, had he gone at that time, 'it would have been construed as a personal matter'.

Public discussion faded while Scott's squadron was at Berehaven, but on his return to Portsmouth was again emblazoned in the Press. Beresford tried to blame Fisher for the resurrection of the affair, though some historians have suggested it was inspired by Scott, and this is possible; no modest man, he knew the value of publicity. It was probably neither and in December it was revealed that Beresford's signal placing his ships 'out of routine' was made *after* Scott's signal to *Roxburgh*. Beresford's case had been based on disrespect for his order and it collapsed. Indeed it was further evidence of his incompetence, for he only had to look at the times of origin of the two signals to see this. Overnight the Press, except for the *Daily Express* and *Standard*, rallied to Scott's support, That month he was invited to speak to the Worshipful Company of Makers of Playing Cards, when he praised Fisher's reforms and said gunnery was recognized as more important than 'other matters to which attention had been bestowed'. He stressed the advantage of speed and supported the *Dreadnought* policy, pointing out that if she were located in the middle of Epsom Downs, with Mont Blanc between her and his hearers, they would not be immune from shell fire. He was cheered to the echo and the next morning his speech was prominently reported.

Scott's remarks were directly contrary to the notions of Custance, who advocated light, quick-firing armament, heavy armour and slow speed, like choosing a tortoise to fight an adder. Then an article appeared in the scurrilous journal *John Bull*, giving a detailed history of the affair, for once getting the facts right, taking a hostile attitude to Beresford. 'It has been an open secret for some time past, not only that Lord Charles Beresford does not see eye to eye with Sir John Fisher – of whose school Sir Percy Scott is the most eminent disciple – but that he wishes to succeed him as First Sea Lord, and would go far to please the Government if he could secure the reversion of Sir John Fisher's post.'[14] A copy of the article, accompanied by a *John Bull* poster which read *Grave indictment of Lord Charles Beresford*, was sent to every officer in the Channel Fleet. Who was responsible remains a mystery, but Beresford's reaction was violent; he wrote again to the Admiralty and to Sir Edward Carson, the outstanding Irish lawyer and politician, to whom he said:

> The thing evidently emanates from Fisher, as the concluding sentence
> . . . says that I would be prepared to please the Government to get into

189

Sir John Fisher's position. This must have reference to the conversation I had when I met casually the Prime Minister, Harcourt and Haldane. There is no doubt that it is one of the most determined, audacious, treacherous and cowardly attacks upon me inspired by the gentleman from Ceylon.[15]

Casually? Beresford had sought the interview and feigned illness to attract Cabinet Ministers to his bedside. He took 'sick' leave and temporary residence at Claridge's, where he engaged in a campaign of intrigue with the 'Syndicate of Discontent'. It was, wrote Esher to Knollys, 'worthy of the seventeenth century and Mr Pepys. Imagine interviewing Beresford in a night-cap, with Lady Charles holding his hand on the far side of the bed. What a picture of naval efficiency and domestic bliss.'[16] Lady Charles, embittered by her failure to achieve the social status of the First Sea Lord's wife, had joined battle on her husband's behalf and spread venom about Fisher.

Many questions were asked in the House, most denigrating Scott and Fisher, yet, despite the latter's protests, the ailing Tweedmouth and the dying Campbell-Bannerman refused to take any action. Tweedmouth even consented to Beresford circulating to the captains of the Channel Fleet some of the correspondence between himself and the Admiralty. The air was thick with rumours, including the claim that Scott drank heavily. In fact he drank no more and probably rather less than most naval officers of the day.

Support was building up for Beresford to succeed Fisher as First Sea Lord and the latter was concerned. Esher wrote in his journal: 'Called on Arthur Balfour and was with him ¾ of an hour. . . . We talked almost exclusively of Defence matters. He is strongly in favour of Fisher and against C. Beresford.'[17] But Esher was over-optimistic; only three days later Fisher received a message from Harcourt asking him to come to his room at the House of Commons. There was evidently need for secrecy. 'Please come by the Lady's entrance,' he wrote.[18] Harcourt explained that a motion by J.A.Murray Macdonald to reduce the estimates was expected to be supported by many radical Liberals. Balfour had asked his party to support the Government, but had been refused, so the motion would be carried. The Cabinet had decided to cut the estimates by £1.34m to bring them below those of the previous year. 'Fisher remarked that the Navy Estimates had already been approved by the Cabinet and signed. It was a mere accident that they were not laid now on the table of the House. He added that the Board of Admiralty had gone into them with the greatest care, that they had been reduced by £750,000 and were at their irreducible minimum.'[19]

On his return Fisher found a letter from Winston Churchill inviting him to dinner that night to discuss matters with Lloyd George, who repeated Harcourt's arguments in a more conciliatory way, asking Fisher to help them by agreeing to a reduction in the estimates, 'or some change would be inevitable at the Admiralty or in the Ministry'.

> Fisher said, 'Well, there is a way. Reduce the estimates by deducting the sum you name, and present them to Parliament with a note to the effect that the Board of Admiralty declared the Navy to require the larger sum, but they consented to accept the smaller on the understanding that the efficiency of the Fleets should be maintained and that any deficit would be met by supplementary estimates.' Churchill laughed at this, evidently enjoying the quandary of his colleague. Lloyd George then said, corroborating Harcourt, that Beresford was ready to accept the post of [First] Sea Lord, and was prepared to reduce the estimates by £2,000,000.
>
> Fisher replied that they had better appoint him, but that he would 'sell' them in three months, and again asserted that the irreducible minimum had been reached.[20]

Noticeably, the Cabinet dealt directly with Fisher; Tweedmouth was not consulted, but at 9 am the next day he announced that there would be a special Board at midday. At 10 Fisher received a message from Lloyd George that he wished to see him privately and did not wish to come to the Admiralty. Refusing the furtive implication Fisher walked boldly into the Board of Trade where Lloyd George offered him an untrustworthy compromise, urging him to agree to a reduction *this* year, adding that he might have any sum he pleased *next* year. Fisher was not fooled and invited Lloyd George to explain to the Board, to which he agreed. Fisher then told Tweedmouth and his colleagues and, determined not to resign, opening the way for Beresford, said it would be improper to force the hand of the Government with a threat of resignation and suggested they should intimate that if the estimates were reduced it would be contrary to the advice of the Board. Having supported him loyally already in cutting the estimates by £¾m, he would abide by their decision. When Lloyd George appeared he was firmly informed of the Board's resolution not to yield.

Fisher believed no consultation had taken place between the various Cabinet Ministers and asked Edmund Robertson, Parliamentary and Financial Secretary, a friend of Campbell-Bannerman and 'little Navy man', to take the estimates to the Prime Minister and go through every figure to show that they could not be reduced. This he did, Campbell-Bannerman sent for Asquith, Chancellor of the Exchequer, informing him that he had decided that the Navy Estimates must stand and the Army Estimates would be reduced by £300,000.

The Navy League gave Fisher strong support. 'We back Sir John Fisher', affirmed its secretary,[21] while the Imperial Maritime League poured out a torrent of abuse. Bellairs published an article entitled *The Proposed Naval Inquiry*[22] in which he claimed that 220 MPs had asked for one and had been refused by the Prime Minister, again quoting Sir Frederick Richards and Sir Richard Vesey Hamilton and claiming the support of Sir William White, former Director of Naval Construction, who had suffered two nervous breakdowns, leading to his retirement, and was approached by Beresford to contact friends to join the dissension,[23] White entered a long correspondence with Custance, rather naïvely supporting the latter's vicious attacks on Fisher. Sir John Biles, a former pupil of White's, attributed his attitude to jealousy of his successor.

Beresford demanded that Admiralty should sue *John Bull* for libel, which was manifestly absurd since he could not expect Admiralty to fight his case for him. The Imperial Maritime League kept up its pressure and significantly declined to publish the names of those attending its meetings, until it was fortuitously revealed that Waterford, Beresford's brother, had attended one. The Board again tried to get rid of Beresford, but the ineffectual Tweedmouth failed to persuade the Cabinet, who feared the political consequences. Many of Fisher's friends were approached to join the League, including Esher, who damned the organizers, pointing out that Fisher was the most feared man in Germany, right up to the Emperor. A copy of the letter was sent to the Kaiser (Beresford was on Christian name terms with the Kaiser) and a storm broke. Disregarding protocol, the Kaiser wrote directly to Tweedmouth, stating that he could not understand the fears in England at the growth of the German Navy, which was not aimed at Britain and did not challenge her. That a foreign monarch should write to a Cabinet Minister was startling and the King was indignant. But Tweedmouth, flattered, bragged to anyone who would listen and replied to the Kaiser enclosing a copy of the new Navy Estimates before they had even been submitted to Parliament, to which, astonishingly, he had the agreement of Grey. Repington soon heard of the matter and published it, but so out of touch with events was Asquith, who was acting Prime Minister during Campbell-Bannerman's illness, that the first he knew of it was when he read about it in *The Times*.

In March *The Times* again commented on the gunnery of the Channel Fleet, observing that Beresford's flagship was below the bottom of the ships of the China Station. The following June *Good Hope* achieved top place in the Navy and, though Beresford grudgingly congratulated her, he subjected Scott to a studied insult when he gave a dinner to Custance, who was leaving the fleet, and invited all the admirals and captains, omitting Scott.

When Asquith formed his Government on the death of Campbell-Bannerman in April 1908 McKenna became First Lord, Lloyd George

Chancellor of the Exchequer, and Winston Churchill entered the Cabinet as President of the Board of Trade, whereupon the last two became leaders of the social reform group in the Cabinet, campaigning for reductions in naval estimates to pay for them. McKenna and Fisher immediately established a rapport, the former being guided in naval affairs by his advisers.

Then at King Edward's Levée on 11 May Beresford deliberately affronted Fisher who extended his hand, when, in full view of the King and all others, including officers of his own fleet, he deliberately ignored it and turned his back on the First Sea Lord. The story spread rapidly throughout the Navy and the King privately called the Government 'a pack of cowards' for not ordering the C-in-C to haul down his flag.

Soon afterwards the Channel Fleet visited Christiana (Oslo) where the harbour could not accommodate all the ships, so the cruisers anchored in the adjacent Bydgö Bay. King Haakon inspected the fleet in *Surprise*, and on his arrival in Bydgö Bay was impressed to find sailors dressed in white on staging on *Good Hope*'s grey side, forming the words *Leve Kongen* (long live the King). Beresford was greatly angered at Scott stealing his thunder but was compelled to swallow his gall when the King expressed his pleasure. The story reached home and *The Naval and Military Record* publishing an article headed '*Wanted, an Olive Branch*'. which made a 'respectful appeal to Lord Charles Beresford to put an end to the scandal which menaces the efficiency of the Navy. . . . Sir Percy Scott has been placed in a very delicate position. It is not within his power to heal the breach. . . . The interruption of all personal intercourse between the two responsible officers may, at any moment, become a danger to the country, and it is already a potential menace.'[24]

Scott's dignified silence, contrasting with Beresford's public brawling, had paid off, but was too late, for, the day before, the fleet had been manoeuvring. In *échelon* formation, the cruisers led by Scott in *Good Hope* were in the starboard column ahead, Beresford in *King Edward VII* leading the centre column about 3,200 yards apart. Beresford wished to take up cruising formation, leading the centre column in arrowhead formation, the other columns eight cables (1,600 yards) from him. He signalled Scott accordingly, who started to turn 16 points to port, leading his ships round in succession to drop astern of Beresford, when the C-in-C took direct charge of Scott's ships and ordered them to turn 16 points *together*. Had they turned to port, when *Good Hope*, expecting them to follow her, had started her turn, there was danger of a collision between *Good Hope* and *Argyle*, the second ship in the column, turning in her path. They therefore all wisely turned to starboard. *Good Hope*, having already started her turn to port, would have lost so much distance had she changed the direction of her turn that she continued turning to port. The result was that *Argyle* and *Good Hope* were almost abeam, about 1.300 yards apart, heading in the opposite direction from that of the remainder of the fleet and it was at this moment that Beresford signalled: 'Third Division turn together, 16 points to starboard' and 'Good *Hope* turn 16 points to port.' He was ordering a turn inwards, towards each other.

Signalling practice was to acknowledge sighting of a signal with an 'answering pendant' hoisted 'at the dip' (half mast). When the signal had been understood, the pendant was hoisted 'close up' to the yard, which indicated that the ship concerned was ready to obey. When the senior officer was satisfied all concerned were ready, he would haul down the signal, which was the order to execute its purport.

Scott's flag captain, Grafton, hoisted his answering pendant at the dip and kept it there while his officers checked the distance between *Good Hope* and *Argyle* which they found to be too close to execute the turn inwards. Without waiting for *Good Hope* to haul her answering pendant close up, Beresford's flagship hauled down the signal, ordering its execution. A collision identical to Tryon's was inevitable and Scott's flag captain, standing beside him, said he intended to turn to starboard, as the remainder of the division had been ordered. Scott approved and *Good Hope* turned in the same direction as *Argyle* so a collision was averted.

On completion of the manoeuvre, Beresford signalled: 'Did *Good Hope* take in the signal to turn to port?' Grafton replied, '*Good Hope* did not go close up before the signal was hauled down'. Ignoring this, Beresford repeated his question and then, without waiting for an answer, signalled: 'If *Good Hope* took in the signal to turn to port and the Rear Admiral thought *Good Hope* was too close to *Argyle*, the Rear Admiral was right in turning to starboard'. Scott might have been wise merely to acknowledge this last signal, perhaps adding 'Thank you', but he replied, reasonably enough, '*Good Hope* took in signal to turn to port but did not go close up as there was danger in such a turn. As the signal to turn to port was hauled down before *Good Hope* had answered it, I concluded that the danger had been realised and *Good Hope* therefore acted on the signal to the Third Division to turn to starboard.'

Strictly speaking neither admiral was right. Beresford should not have made the executive order until *Good Hope*'s answering pendant was close up; but Scott's assumption that it had been cancelled was also incorrect. The proper procedure would have been for Beresford to hoist a 'negative' to cancel the order. But Grafton and Scott had averted a collision and Beresford should have been grateful. Perhaps he was, even if he did not admit it, for little more was said at the time. But someone, probably an officer in the pay of the Press, was passing information and the matter was quickly discussed in *The Times* under the heading *A strange Occurrence in the Channel Fleet*.[25] Once again the differences between Beresford and Scott were discussed in detail in the newspapers. *The Evening Standard* described the report as a 'vindictive indiscretion of *The Times*', and a letter from Wyatt was published in the *Morning Post:*

> Here we have one of our greatest admirals, our Commander-in-Chief at sea, engaged in work calculated to strain all the powers of body and mind, and yet exposed to the most deadly imputation of professional incompetence, which imputation is published in the London newspapers at a moment when explanation or reply from himself is obviously impossible. Moreover . . . this imputation can only have been communicated to the Press by one of three kinds of betrayal. Either an officer of the fleet must have made that communication himself, directly, in defiance of all decency and all regulations, or a private letter or telegram has been so communicated, or else – which would be the worst of the three treacheries – a communication made officially or otherwise from someone in high command under Lord Charles Beresford to the Admiralty has been sent by the Admiralty on to the Press . . . and therefore for the honour of the Navy it is clearly necessary that an immediate *investigation* by independent investigators should be demanded. . . . The choice of time and method of attack seem, under all the circumstances, to be Asiatic rather than European, and they are certainly the very last to have been expected by any English gentleman. [26]

On the same day an anonymous letter appeared signed 'Admiral':

> Many of the senior officers of the Navy were astonished that Sir Percy Scott was not either tried by a Court Martial, a Court of Inquiry or ordered to haul his flag down. As neither of these courses took place it gave the public, and . . . the Naval Service in general, an impression that the Admiralty did not take a serious view of the matter. Such a course as this cannot be conducive to discipline, and gives the very worst impression throughout the Service.[27]

Arthur Lee demanded to know what steps the Admiralty or Cabinet were taking to end 'a gross scandal which is not only sapping the foundations of discipline and good feeling throughout the Service, but constitutes a serious menace to our national security'.[28] Sir John Colomb, the ex-Royal Marine naval historian brother of Philip Colomb, insinuated that the seeds of discord had been sown by Fisher, who, of course, had nothing whatever to do with the matter. The conflict in the Navy again became the main story of the day. Lee pointed out that Beresford was not on speaking terms with either Fisher or Scott and *The Times* commented: 'We say frankly that if, as is alleged, Lord Charles Beresford is at loggerheads with the Board of Admiralty or with any individual member of it, he is, in our judgment, *Ipso facto*, in the wrong. . . . If, as is also alleged, he is not on speaking terms with one of his Flag officers he is equally in the wrong.'

Dissension in the Navy was again the subject of questions in the House, Bellairs dragging Fisher into the affair. But another member, getting to the core of the matter, asked whether 'the rules and regulations for discipline apply only to humbler rank, stokers for instance, while Lord Charles Beresford is allowed to break them with impunity?' Fisher was hurt and bewildered at the manner in which the opportunity had been taken to attack him again.

> With extreme adroitness Custance and others cloud the issue between Beresford and myself by importing Scott into the case, and what is really clever, they have avoided the fact of whether the signal to Scott was deadly or not by the red herring of improper communications to the Press by Scott! . . . The danger is that a big agitation is being worked up that if Beresford goes, I should also. *But what have I done wrong?*[29]

Beresford demanded a Court Martial of Scott, writing to McKenna, who passed the letter to Fisher, who commented:

> The falsehood gains increasing credence that I communicated the signal incident to *The Times*. As a matter of fact I had no knowledge of it whatsoever till I saw it in *The Times*. It is also untrue that I had any conversations with or in any way inspired Thursfield as to the leading article in *The Times* This adroit lie (or lies) has clouded the main issue as between Beresford and myself, and he has again reiterated (confirming the Levée incident) that he will not shake hands with me. That being the case, how is cordial cooperation possible? A false charge is therefore widely promulgated against me, and what the Cabinet or some members of it thought an inadvertence at the Levée is confirmed as a premeditated insult. Is it possible that this state of affairs can be allowed to continue? Every trivial action has to be studied and even who one talks to considered as perhaps being indictable![30]

In view of Fisher's close friendship with Thursfield it is not impossible that he briefed the journalist and there is no proof either way. But he would have done better to have insisted on a Court Martial, which would have cleared Scott and demonstrated Beresford's dangerous incompetence. A good barrister could have concentrated on this aspect. When the Channel Fleet returned home McKenna sent for Scott and heard his side of the story, telling him that he intended making a statement in the House exonerating him and asked him to remain silent. 'It's dangerous to get mixed up with the Press, Admiral, they'll suck you dry. And when you can't feed them any more – they'll eat *you*.'[31]

But his statement in the House was less than satisfactory. Beresford was a political opponent and with a politician's calculation McKenna tried to pacify everyone. The Board was 'satisfied the manoeuvre was not dangerous. At the same time the Rear Admiral, as he thought there was a risk in carrying out the order was justified in turning the other way, and the Commander-in-Chief so informed him at the time.'[32] McKenna, who was no moral coward, may have been influenced by the calculating Asquith, the master of compromise, but a Board of Inquiry of unbiased naval officers would certainly have concluded otherwise. An opportunity to get rid of Beresford was missed and Fisher should have forced the issue. The political admiral was right, however; he could get away with anything. An anonymous correspondent of the *Globe* wrote the next day:

> The answer given by Mr. McKenna . . . emphasises . . . the unfairness of *The Times* in publishing the signal . . . without taking the trouble to ascertain the facts of the case beforehand. . . . The paper had thus been guilty of a wretched piece of sensation-mongering utterly unworthy of the leading journal, and it is monstrous that the professional reputation of any officer, especially one of the most distinguished in the Fleet [Beresford] should be reflected upon in such a manner. Would to heaven the name of *The Times* correspondent could be discovered![33]

The *Daily Express* carried the headline: 'Navy Scandal Exposed: Full Story of the Anti-Beresford Intrigue', and the *Morning Post* in a leading article commented: .

> The statement . . . made insinuations which were entirely unfounded against the professional skill of the Commander-in-Chief. . . . it is now proved that the communication from the Fleet . . . was contrary to discipline, besides being a dastardly attack on the Commander-in-Chief. . . . The public wants to know . . . who sent the communication, and to punish him. . . . The public wants the cur dragged to light and whipped.

That Beresford and Scott must be separated was certain. Fortunately the new Union of South Africa was about to celebrate its formation. Scott, so well known there, and his aptly named ship would take a squadron to visit that country. Beresford, more confident than ever, continued to plot Fisher's downfall and the latter, hearing of Beresford's plans to create 'a great upheaval', wrote to McKenna, 'What really amounts to incipient mutiny is being arranged in the fleet. Beresford evidently thinks you will what is vulgarly called "funk" his leaving and his stumping the country, but, as Mr. Balfour told me, he would "fizzle out" in a week!'[34]

Beresford's campaign of denigration continued in the hope of ousting Fisher. In November Gwynne, Editor of *The Standard*, arranged for an eight-page letter to be presented to Asquith indicating, so Fisher said, 'why

I should be hung'.[35] Almost daily there were meetings of the energetic Imperial Maritime League in private houses, and at a meeting in the City of London on 19 November John Colomb proposed a motion for an inquiry 'into the scope and effect of the recent changes in the Navy', again quoting Richards and Vesey Hamilton in support, though his speech was almost entirely hyperbolic. Significantly, the first annual banquet of the league on 30 November was 'held privately, in order to allow of full and unhampered expression of opinion on naval questions by recognized authorities. No reporters were allowed to be present; and the names of those present will not be published.'[36]

The Channel Fleet was to be absorbed into the Home Fleet early in 1909 and in July McKenna had tried to remove Beresford, but was thwarted by Asquith's pusillanimity. As the argument, the vilification and invective continued through the latter half of the year, McKenna told Fisher he had reluctantly concluded Beresford was incompetent and a liar.

Then another international crisis occurred, known as the Casablanca Conference. Three German deserters from the French Foreign Legion were assisted in their escape by the German consul in Casablanca, but the French arrested them. Germany demanded an apology and the French refused, proposing arbitration. But Germany insisted an apology must come first, and the crisis dragged on until the middle of November, when arbitration was agreed. Esher noted that war looked extremely likely and, though France had not asked for British assistance, Asquith, Grey and Haldane had decided to join in. After two sleepless nights during which he lay awake pondering Beresford's unfitness for command, McKenna was reminded by Fisher that the Channel had formerly been a two-year and not a three-year commission. Armed with this information, he went to the Prime Minister. At last on 16 December Beresford was informed he would strike his flag the following March. He determined to have his revenge, as indeed the King now foresaw. 'Knollys explained to McKenna that the King was "afraid that he will now make a disturbance and give trouble and annoyance".'[37] The King was right. Beresford was convinced that the Liberal Government would fall, due to the developing Navy scare, which he had done so much to inflame, and a month before hauling down his flag he asked Balfour what the latter would do when he became Prime Minister, telling him that if made First Lord he would say nothing about the state of the Navy, but if not, he would 'stump the country and agitate'. Balfour disabused his mind. The Liberal Government would probably remain in power for another two years and he had given no consideration to a new cabinet or a new Board of Admiralty.

But such was the esteem in which Beresford was held by a gullible public that, when he finally hauled down his flag, on 24 March 1909, never to serve again, he was met at Portsmouth by huge crowds who cheered him to the echo, singing *He's a Jolly Good Fellow*, and in London, whither he went by train, cheering patriots broke through police cordons carrying him shoulder high through the streets. 'The unparalleled enthusiasm and emotion displayed by the crowds at Portsmouth and later in the day in London suggested that a national hero had returned home from a great naval victory.'[38]

14

THE MUTTER OF DISTANT THUNDER

German warlike intentions created a spy hysteria. Spy stories and war novels like Erskine Childers' *Riddle of the Sands* were turned out in dozens and rumours of German spies spread. A CID sub-committee considered 'the nature and extent of foreign espionage' and the invasion lobby claimed there were 350,000 German reservists resident in Britain. A routine training notification to German reservists in Canada created a rumour that they had been ordered back to Germany. Fisher called it 'moonshine'.

'Aerial navigation' or 'aeronautics' were occupying attention. In 1906 Colonel J.D.Fullerton proposed that a committee of military and naval officers, 'aeronautics' and engineers should investigate 'the whole question of aeronautics'. Germany had already started work on dirigible (powered and navigable) airships and it was estimated that she would soon have twenty, with an endurance of 600 miles carrying 3 tons of explosives. In 1908 the Admiralty considered the possibility of enemy aircraft attacking ships with 'high explosive grenades' and, though it was not yet feasible, the matter was 'one to be watched'. In July that year Bacon, as Director of Naval Ordnance and Torpedoes, prepared a paper for Fisher in which he suggested a rigid airship should be built, based on the Zeppelin design, and Haldane supported Fullerton. Asquith asked Lord Rayleigh, President of the Royal Society, to preside over an 'Advisory Committee on Aeronautics'. In October 1908 he appointed another committee of the CID, with Esher as chairman. Bacon represented the Admiralty. They concluded that 'the full potentialities of airships, and the danger to which we might be exposed by their use can only be ascertained definitely by building them ourselves'. The principle naval use was in scouting and it was pointed out that from a height of 1,000 feet the horizon is 40 miles, and from 2,200 feet 60 miles, compared with 12 miles from the surface. The cost of such an aircraft was estimated at £35,000.

It is not clear that under existing conditions the Aeroplane would be of much value in naval operations. Until complete reliability and independence of meteorological conditions has been demonstrated, it would be very dangerous to utilise them for scouting purposes in the open sea. Their offensive powers must in any case be limited for some time to come by their small carrying capacity. . . . There appears to be no necessity for the Government to continue experiments in aeroplanes, provided that advantage is taken of private enterprise in this form of aviation.[1]

The die was cast in favour of the airship, the necessary £35,000 included in the Naval Estimates for 1909–10 and an order placed with Vickers. The airship, unhappily named *Mayfly*, never flew and was wrecked in 1911 while being taken out of her shed in gusty weather.

Mining too was uncertain; though Fisher had been a pioneer, in February 1895, when he was controller, the Admiralty, 'after careful consideration of the subject, . . . *decided not to adopt blockade mines* as a form of naval warfare',[2] allowing Germany to overtake Britain; by 1914 the German mine was considerably more efficient than the British. 'What justification can we advance for our apparent supineness?' asked Fisher.[3] This was more than a rhetorical question; in 1902, when Second Naval Lord, he had urged the adoption of mining, the provision of mines and minelayers. There were two types, the moored mine which could be laid to form a minefield, to close areas to enemy ships or to close their harbours, and the floating mine which could be dropped by a retreating fleet in the path of its enemy.

'If we do not adopt them,' wrote Fisher 'we shall lack one weapon possessed by our enemies, which will be used against us and we shall not be able to retaliate in the same manner. . . . We cannot afford to leave anything to be a matter of opinion which affects, in the slightest degree, the fighting efficiency of the Fleet.'[4]

Experience in the Russo-Japanese war strengthened his views:

Automatic mining will inevitably form part of the operations of any future naval war and [we] are therefore preparing for this contingency. The Estimates for 1905 make provision for 300 blockade mines of modern type. This, however is a very small beginning, . . .At Port Arthur alone, the Russians laid 5,000 mines. . . . It is clear therefore that preparations on a much larger scale will be necessary.[5]

In 1905 Fisher formed a committee, chaired by Ottley, to examine 'The supply of automatic submarine mines to the Fleet', who concluded they should be laid 'in large numbers in definite and prearranged lines at some considerable distance from the enemy's coast, but in waters through which the enemy would have to pass if leaving the port for sea'.[6] They recommended that a total of 10,000 mines should be provided over a period of several years, which would enable the estuaries of the Jade, the Elbe and the Weser to be mined, and leave about 2,000 as floating mines.

But Fisher was not impressed with the practicability of blockade by mines. He saw their use as a barrier to prevent the entry of enemy ships to British waters or as a temporary means of blockade, when ships were unavailable, stressing that sweeping was not difficult unless the minefield was protected by guns.[7]

He was far from satisfied with the British mine.

> The bedrock principle of all mines . . . is the power they possess of automatically taking their depth. . . . But the form of mine case to which we (from motives of economy) decided to adapt [the mine sinker] 20 years ago, and to which it has ever since been affixed [is] . . . almost valueless for automatic mining on a large scale. . . . We have only now . . . begun to make provision for the introduction . . . of a more rational type of automatic mine.[8]

In his War Plans Fisher proposed the protection of the Home Ports by mines and warned that Germany might mine the Thames estuary, advocating the provision of minesweepers, though these were to be hired or purchased 'before the stage of "strained relations"', and crews 'told off'. He does not seem to have envisaged peacetime exercises.

In Fisher's term as First Sea Lord mines were included in the estimates every year. This continued until, persuaded that mines were the weapons of the weak, Churchill, as First Lord, discontinued their stockpiling. Marder wrote: 'British naval officers did not hold mines in high regard; they were the weapons of a weak power on the defensive. There was provision for sweeping up enemy mines, but little interest in providing the Navy with effective mines for its own use.'[9] The Press and public opinion were more in harmony with Fisher's views and another exaggerated scare led to conjectures that German merchant ships would drop mines in the Solent and Thames estuary before the outbreak of war. Balfour took this seriously, but Fisher said, 'I am too busy to waste my time on this cock and bull story'.

Yet another sub-committee of the CID, 'to consider the military needs of the Empire', exposed the lack of coordination between the War Office and the Admiralty. Since 1905 the General Staff had been working on their plan for an expeditionary force in France. Even though in 1906 the plan had been communicated to Major Huguet, the French Military Attaché, no discussions were held with the Admiralty, no consideration given to naval operations, combined operations or the need for naval cooperation in embarking and escorting an army to France. The scheme was not officially binding on the Government, but four divisions and a cavalry division were to fight on the French left flank and this was now recommended by Asquith's subcommittee. 'They want *our* troops to be placed under the French Generalissimo,' commented Esher, who was a member of the Sub-Committee, 'They would form part of the reserve. The idea that an English contingent is wanted for its "moral effect", which is an idea prevalent here, is scouted by the French. They want the additional force at the decisive point. I am confident that great difficulties would arise if this proposal was known in certain quarters. The placing of the whole of our Army under French generals is such a wholly new departure. There is no precedent for it at all. Certainly alternative plans will have to be prepared.'[10]

In March 1909 Fisher wrote to Esher:

> I have just finished in these early hours a careful study of your paper E.5. (which I love) and the criticisms thereon by French and the General Staff. I dismiss French's criticisms as being that of a pure correct cavalry expert and not dealing with the big question. The General Staff criticism is, on the other hand, the thin edge of the insidious wedge of our taking a part in continental wars apart absolutely from coastal military expeditions in pure concert with the Navy. . . . I don't desire to mention these expeditions and never will, as our military organisation is so damnably leaky! But it so happens that for two solid hours this morning I have been studying one of them, of inestimable value, only involving five thousand men and some guns and horses, about 500, – a mere fleabite! but a collection of these fleabites would make Wilhelm scratch himself with fury! However, the point of my letter is this – ain't we d——d fools to go on wasting our very precious moments in these abstruse dispositions on the Grebb line or the passage of the Dutch-German frontier river and whether the bloody fight is to be at Rheims or Amiens, until the Cabinet have decided the the great big question raised in your E.5. Are we, or are we not, going to send a British Army to fight on the Continent as quite distinct and apart from coastal raids and seizures of islands, etc., which the Navy dominates?[11]

He might have gone further, for army intentions assumed that the enemy would comply with their forecasts, which was poor staff work. Fisher believed in amphibious attacks rather than tying the Army down to the bloody scrum on the Western Front and that command of the sea would enable the Navy to bring such economic pressure against Germany as to achieve her defeat, (though he was no exception to the under-estimation of her ability to obtain supplies from countries she overran). This was set out in a memorandum of which Fisher was the main author, but the committee came to unanimous conclusions:

(a) In the event of an attack on France by Germany, the expediency of sending a military force abroad, or of relying on naval means only, is a matter of policy which can only be determined, when the occasion arises, by the Government of the Day.
(b) In view, however, of the possibility of a decision by the Cabinet to use military force, the committee have examined the plans of the General Staff, and are of the opinion that in the initial stages of a war between France and Germany, in which the British Government decided to assist France, the plan to which preference is given is a valuable one, and the General staff should accordingly work out all the necessary details.[12]

Once again a political compromise evaded the issue. It was never Fisher's idea to 'rely on naval means only', but for the two services to cooperate. The decision was to be left until the occasion arose, so no cooperation would take place in preparing such plans. No alternatives were to be studied, no consideration given to amphibious operations, like landing forces behind German lines in the Baltic or Schleswig-Holstein, or a joint operation to take one of the Frisian Islands. The only plan ignored Britain's overwhelming naval power. Consequently, no thought was given to peacetime preparations, like the design and provision of monitors and landing craft, combined training or studies of equipment needed. Within a few months, it was suggested, the two divisions remaining in the United Kingdom could be replaced by newly-trained Territorials, bringing the British strength in France to 160,000. Yet they endorsed the Admiralty's plans for economic pressure, inviting them to work out detailed schemes. The report was a superb example of political indecision, of agreeing that everyone was right. The politicians refused to make a decision; both services were to go their own way. Strangely, Fisher, perhaps influenced by security, signed the unanimous report, though he cannot have agreed with it.

But worse even than the War Office failure to consult the Admiralty, they had never even obtained Cabinet approval before committing Britain to an irrevocable course of action. In October 1911 Esher was to write:

The Prime Minister came into my room this morning. . . . We talked about the General Staff scheme for landing an army in France. The Prime Minister is opposed to this plan. He will not hear of the dispatch of more than four divisions. He has told Haldane so.

But I reminded him that the mere fact of the War Office plan having been worked out in detail with the French General Staff (which is the case) has certainly committed us to fight whether the Cabinet likes it or not, and that the combined plan of the two general staffs holds the field. It is certainly an extraordinary thing that our officers should have been permitted to arrange all the details, trains, landing, concentration etc., when the Cabinet have never been consulted.[13]

Fisher was one of the first men in the United Kingdom to recognize the German naval challenge. Using the wide influence and support of Esher, he subtly and quietly created a political and strategic revolution. Nothing if not a realist, he did much to create the Triple Entente and would have liked to have included Turkey. Russia was essential for an attack on the German coast in the Baltic, and Turkey to keep communications open with Russia through the Dardanelles. He wrote to King Edward:

> *Russia and Turkey are the two powers, and the only two powers that matter to us against Germany, and that we have eventually to fight Germany is just as sure as anything can be, solely because she can't expand commercially without it. . . .* If we fight we want Russia and Turkey on our side against Germany.[14]

Esher's statement at the time of the Tweedmouth letter, that Fisher was 'the most feared man in Germany' was accurate. Esher had been sent by the King to sound out the Kaiser, who had said England wanted war.

> Not the King, nor perhaps the Government; but influential men like Sir John Fisher! . . . He thinks it is the hour for attack and I am not blaming him. I quite understand his point of view; but we too are prepared. . . . Fisher can no doubt land 100,000 men in Schleswig-Holstein – it would not be difficult – and the British Navy has reconnoitred the coast of Denmark with this object during the cruise of the fleet. But Fisher forgets that it will be for me to deal with the 100,000 men when they are landed!
>
> I admire Fisher, I say nothing against him. If I were in his place I should do all that he has done and I should do all that I know he has in his mind to do.[15]

In the same year Tirpitz, through a mutual friend, made an approach to Fisher, asking if he would agree to limiting the size of guns and ships, as this was vital to Germany, who could not build bigger than *Dreadnought* because of the limitations of the Kiel Canal, depth of the Baltic Harbours and docking facilities. 'I wrote back to him by return of post yesterday morning, "Tell him I'll see him damned first!" (Them's the very words). I wonder what Wilhelm will say to that if Tirpitz shows him the letter.'[16]

Fisher's knack of forecasting events was never better demonstrated than when, in 1908, he said Germany would go to war in September or October 1914, basing this on German shipbuilding capacity, the date when the enlargement of the Kiel Canal would be completed and the German harvest in. 'I shall never rest,' said the Kaiser, 'until I have raised my Navy to a position similar to that occupied by my Army. German colonial aims can only be gained when Germany has become master of the ocean.'[17]

The Kaiser's remark about the 'hour for attack' referred to Fisher's desire to emulate Nelson at Copenhagen by attacking the German Fleet at Kiel. The difference was that Britain was at peace with Germany, while Denmark was a hostile nation. He twice mentioned the idea to the King, in 1904 and 1908. On the first occasion the King said, 'Fisher, you must be mad!' There is little evidence, however, that he expected to be taken seriously, but the view today of the iniquity of the comparable Japanese attacks on Port Arthur and Pearl Harbor are not sustained by historical fact; there had been only eleven declarations of war between advanced states since 1700, the war with Spain in 1762 being the last occasion when Britain had made such a declaration and in the nineteenth century over sixty acts had been made without notice. There is no record of Fisher putting the idea forward to the Board and it was never discussed. He later wrote:

> It seemed to me simply a sagacious act . . . to seize the German Fleet when it was so easy of accomplishment. . . . Alas! even the very whisper of it excited exasperation against the First Sea Lord, and the project was damned. . . . And consequently came those terrible years of war, with millions massacred and maimed.[18]

Tirpitz's 'risk theory' gained him approval for the two Navy Laws, shrewdly using the build-up of the Navy to change the alignment between nations. The German Navy, concentrated in the North Sea, both threatened Britain and defended the vulnerable German North Sea Ports, but, by maintaining her fleet in the North Sea, Germany opened it to the danger of destruction before it was large or experienced enough to act as a real threat to Britain. She provoked the very danger of a 'Copenhagen' that she most feared. The risk to Britain enhanced the risk to herself. Latterly, irritated by the men-dacious opposition to his schemes, Fisher was less inclined to prepare the ground, more inclined to try to force his way by exaggeration. His Copenhagen theory added ammunition to his enemies' arsenal and it is interesting to speculate how the idea came to the ears of the Kaiser and how he became possessed of Fisher's plan for an attack on Schleswig-Holstein, which was certainly a serious proposition.[19]

So close was the immediate accord between Fisher and McKenna that within six weeks the latter had agreed to a programme for 1909 of four dreadnoughts and if necessary six. Fisher had adopted Stead's 'two keels to one' policy in dreadnoughts. For every one Germany built, Britain would build two; Germany would never overtake the British Navy. Grey was prepared to resign to support McKenna and Fisher, but Lloyd George and Churchill insisted that four capital ships were more than enough and Churchill, returning from a visit to Germany convinced of the peaceful intentions of the Kaiser, was even more determined to reduce defence estimates. In a speech at Swansea on 17 August 1908 he said:

> I think it is greatly to be deprecated that persons should try to spread the belief in this country that war between Great Britain and Germany is inevitable. It is all nonsense. In the first place the alarmists have no ground whatever for their panic or fear. . . . There is no collision of primary interest – big, important interests – between Great Britain and Germany in any quarter of the globe.[20]

On entering Parliament, Churchill had tabled an amendment to Brodrick's Army Reform resolution, 'That this House . . . cannot view without grave apprehension the continual growth of purely military expenditure, which diverts the energies of the country from their natural commercial and naval development'.[21] Now he had crossed the floor.

Churchill was not alone. Harcourt told his constituents that nothing but 'the diseased imagination of inferior minds could see an overt menace to the Peace of the world from Germany', and the Liberal Press, with absurd naïvety, continued to urge social security legislation at the expense of defence; instead of enjoying social security, men died in misery in the trenches. In that year the Kaiser was writing:

> I do *not* wish for a good understanding with England at the expense of the extension of the German fleet. If England only intends graciously to hold out her hand to us with the indication that we should curtail our fleet, then this is excessive impudence, which contains a great insult for the German people and its Kaiser and which should be refused *à limine* by the ambassador! . . . The Navy law has remained unchanged for eleven years! This law is being carried out to the very last tittle; whether the British like it or not does not worry us. If they want war *they* may *start* it, we are not afraid of it![22]

Public opinion was strengthened in favour of the two-keels-to-one policy by the indiscretions of the Emperor, who gave an interview to Major Stuart-Wortley (later Major General) in which he claimed that the German navy was being built to protect Germany's overseas interests, which was transparently untrue, for her dreadnoughts were built with an endurance fitting them only for the North Sea. He added that the whole of the German people were hostile to Britain.

Some newspapers said six dreadnoughts were an irreducible minimum and others began to demand seven to provide the ten per cent margin of the old two-power standard. The Navy League demanded eight, and the naval Press complained of Government lip-service to naval supremacy. Asquith attempted to placate public opinion by re-drafting the two-power standard as ten per cent above the combined strengths of the next two strongest powers, and this statement was cheered on both sides of the House, but the radical Liberals were appalled, especially when they learned that the Naval Estimates would be increased by £6m if the eight went ahead.

Throughout 1908 the Government refused to disclose its hand and the Admiralty expressed no alarm, for Fisher was convinced that no war would come until completion of the reconstruction of the Kiel Canal. British naval forces were twice as strong in home waters as German, who only had two harbours in the North Sea suitable for her battle fleet, Wilhelmshaven and Brunsbüttel, the latter open to torpedo attack and the former only capable of accommodating twelve ships. Moreover, Germany was dissatisfied with her coast defences.

On surrendering his post in July 1908, however, Captain Philip Dumas (later Admiral Sir Philip), British Naval Attaché in Germany, said that the new Navy Law would give Germany thirty-seven 'sound' battleships by the spring of 1915, and by then the German public would be looking for an excuse to attack Britain. Some 'Temporary trouble abroad would be used as a pretext. At the bottom of every German heart today is rising a faint and wildly exhilarating hope that a glorious day is approaching when by a brave breaking through of the lines which he feels are encircling him, he might even wrest the command of the seas from England and thus become a member of the greatest power by land or sea that the world has ever seen.'[23]

In October Austria annexed Bosnia-Hertzegovina and Germany accelerated her naval programme. McKenna recommended to the Cabinet a programme for the following year of six dreadnoughts (though Fisher pressed for eight), instead of the planned four. Churchill, Lloyd George and other radicals vehemently opposed him, but the Cabinet decided on the proposed programme unless the German programme was reduced. Metternich, the German Ambassador, was informed accordingly.

By 1912 Germany was expected to have thirteen new capital ships in commission and Britain would have eighteen. This was neither a two-to-one nor a two-power standard and information was received that German ship-building capacity had been significantly increased, while Krupps had vastly improved their production capacity for heavy gunmountings, which now exceeded that of Britain. Then came the 'nickel crisis'. Krupps had secretly accumulated, in excess of their allowances under international treaty, large quantities of nickel, whose only use could be in the manufacture of armour plate and gunmountings. The Admiralty was convinced that German warship building capacity was now equal to that of Britain. The first two instalments of the 1908–09 German Navy Estimates showed a 50% increase in expenditure, which must mean either, as Jellicoe, the new Controller, believed, vastly more powerful ships, or, as the Board concluded, the building rate had been speeded up. Jellicoe was right, but the Admiralty were informed that materials for capital ships had been stocked in advance, so that, once laid down, rapid production could go ahead. In January 1909 the Sea Lords concluded that Germany would have seventeen dreadnoughts and battlecruisers by 1912, only one short of the British programme, and there was a possibility that she would have twenty-one. They therefore proposed that two additional armoured cruisers should be laid down in 1909–10, making eight in all, the maximum possible within British building capacity. Churchill, fed with technical arguments by Custance and White, the former DNC, warned that Liberal support in the House would decline if this £6m programme was conceded. Churchill and Lloyd George challenged McKenna, refusing to accept that the outlook for 1912 was as bleak as he warned. They insisted that four dreadnoughts would be adequate, refusing to believe Germany was building in greater numbers than authorized in the 1900 Navy Law, Lloyd George suggesting that all Germany was doing was to relieve unemployment.

Churchill attempted to subvert Fisher and, on 21 December 1908, the latter wrote to McKenna:

> In reply to my inability to lunch with him, Winston wants now to know if there is *any time* I could see him to-day, and I've replied (what is the truth) that I am engaged all the afternoon with Ottley on a strategic discussion about the Baltic and Denmark and the Belts which I cannot defer; but he is evidently very bent on seeing me (for some evil purpose, I fear!). I shall of course be sure to keep you informed and, as you advise, I shall maintain an impenetrable reserve as to our inner life at the Admiralty.'[24]

He wrote again:

> After writing to you last night I went to the Athenaeum to read the *Nation*. Presently Winston Churchill came in. I nodded and went on reading. When I went out he followed me out. I told him I could n⟨⟩ discuss the naval situation with him. He was extremely cordial ⟨⟩ expressed his anxiety as to my future. I told him as a great secre⟨⟩ my future was 20 dreadnoughts before April 1912! This rath⟨⟩ him and we parted. This morning I have a huge letter from⟨⟩ marked 'Personal, secret and private', so I can't send it t⟨⟩ send my reply. He indicates an inquiry into the Admiralt⟨⟩ tion, etc. He knows that would imply want of confide⟨⟩

enforce resignation. I trace White and Custance there! My idea is we shall come out on top! *It is not his!*.[25]

The same day he wrote to Churchill:

> I am sure you won't expect me to enter into any discussion with you, as there can be only one exponent of the Admiralty case – the First Lord. As to want of foresight on the part of the Admiralty, the Sea Lords expressed their grave anxiety in a memorandum presented to the First Lord in December 1907. The Cabinet ignored that anxiety and cut down the estimates. You want to do the same again! We can take no risks this year – last year we did. We felt then there would be time to pull up – the margin now is exhausted.[26]

Asquith was in a predicament. Lloyd George and Churchill, together with Morley, Loreburn, Burns and Harcourt, would all resign if more than four dreadnoughts were put into the programme. McKenna and Grey, with Crewe, Runciman and Haldane, were equally determined on six dreadnoughts as a minimum. McKenna and Fisher were quietly working for a total of eight, though they were prepared to compromise on six. The arguments became heated, including personal abuse. Knollys wrote to Esher in February 1909, 'What are Winston's reasons for acting as he does in this matter? Of course it cannot be from conviction or principle. The very idea of his having either is enough to make anyone laugh,'[27] and claimed Churchill was motivated only by personal ambition.

McKenna disliked Lloyd George for his lack of integrity. At a meeting with Grey, McKenna, certain other Cabinet Ministers and the Sea Lords, to discuss the supply of gunmountings, Lloyd George remarked, 'I think it shows extraordinary neglect on the part of the Admiralty that all this should not have been found out before. I don't think much of you admirals, and I should like to see Lord Charles Beresford at the Admiralty and the sooner the better.' McKenna retorted vehemently, 'You know perfectly well that these facts were communicated to the Cabinet at the time we knew of them and your remark was, "It's all contractors' gossip", or words to that effect.'[28] Jellicoe recorded the slight in a memorandum for McKenna, in which he said, 'With regard to the remarks of the Chancellor of the Exchequer, your attention is drawn to the enclosed extracts from the memorandum signed by the four Sea Lords and handed to the First Lord on Jan. 15th/09.'[29] One extract read: 'A memorandum prepared for the information of the First Lord and signed by the four Sea Lords on Dec. 3rd 1907 clearly shows that they were at that time very anxious about the possibility of accelerated German shipbuilding, and that anxiety is now fully justified.'[30] Lloyd George's distasteful remark demonstrated a politician's ignorance of naval affairs and the character of the men he was dealing with.

With stalemate in the Cabinet, Fisher awaited developments. He had assured Austen Chamberlain that he had the whip hand, as the Government did not want to be defeated, and Asquith, losing patience, threatened to dismiss both Churchill and Lloyd George, while the Conservative Press agitated vigorously for at least six ships. Chamberlain urged the Sea Lords to stand firm.

At length McKenna tendered his resignation, but Fisher informed him that, if he resigned, the whole Board would resign with him. On 20 February 1909 McKenna told Fisher a compromise had been proposed by Churchill. Six ships were to be included in the estimates, with the proviso that only four would be built if in November the Cabinet so decided. Fisher wrote to Jellicoe, 'The Cabinet could do in November, when Parliament is not sitting, what they dare not do now'. When Grey saw the strength of Board opinion he re-examined the Admiralty case and persuaded the Prime Minister to call another Cabinet meeting when Asquith proposed that four dreadnoughts should be laid down in the coming year and, if necessary, a further four on 1 April 1910. This united the Cabinet but enraged the Conservatives. Chamberlain said that if the Sea Lords accepted, 'they deserved to be shot, and unless the whole story is false, Asquith deserves to be hung'.[31] The Sea Lords urged McKenna to clarify the compromise which they thought a bluff, insisting that he should demand a clear statement in the estimates that materials and equipment for the second group of four should be stockpiled so that they could be laid down as planned and completed without delay. At last a footnote appeared in the estimates:

> His Majesty's Government may, in the course of the Financial Year 1909–10, find it necessary to make preparations for the rapid construction of further ships commencing on 1 April of the following financial year. They therefore ask Parliament to entrust them with powers to do this effectively. Such powers that would enable them to arrange in the financial year 1909–10 for the ordering, collection and supply of material for guns, gunmountings, armour, machinery and ship-building, thus making possible the laying down at the date above indicated of four more ships to be completed by March 1912.

Churchill and Lloyd George, recognizing the inevitability of the second batch, expressed the view that six would be acceptable, rather than four. But they were too late. The Board would not hear of it and McKenna supported them loyally.

The day before, Fisher attempted to bury the hatchet with Churchill:

> 'It's too sad and most deplorable. Let us write the word 'finis'. The Apostle is right! The tongue is the very devil! (NB – yours is slung amidships and wags at both ends).
> Yours till the Angels smile on us.'[32]

211

An Argentine naval mission had visited Krupps works and claimed they had seen 100 12-inch and 11-inch guns nearly complete, and in the shipyards twelve capital ships in progress, with a thirteenth about to be started. 'We ought to build as fast as ever we can,' Fisher wrote to McKenna, 'the Germans could certainly have 21 dreadnoughts in April 1912, if they wish it.'[33]

Metternich made reassuring noises to Grey who revived a plan for mutual inspection of shipbuilding. Fisher disbelieved Metternich's honeyed words. ('We've got to have a margin against lying!') To Metternich himself he said, 'How all this scare would vanish ambassador, if you would let our naval attaché go and count them!' Metternich replied, 'That is impossible. Other governments would also want to. Besides, something would be seen which we wish to keep secret.'[34]

'This evening I spent two hours with Jacky,' wrote Esher, 'and I read all Grey's memoranda and Jacky's on the long naval controversy. Certainly no one could have made a more gallant fight and it reflects the greatest credit on him. It was pleasant reading as I was doubtful as to the reality of the fight he had made. Now it only remains for Arthur Balfour to *force* the Government tonight to say that all ships are to be commenced this year.'[35]

The debate on the Estimates opened in a state of feverish excitement, with a crowded House. The Prince of Wales was present and so was Fisher. McKenna opened the debate while Churchill, attempting to ride two horses at once, shouted 'Here-heres' whenever McKenna mentioned the need for British maritime strength. Characteristically, McKenna's speech was clear, frank and sincere. Then Asquith echoed his words; the House sat stunned at the revelations. The two-power standard had gone out of the window; so had the two-keels-to-one policy and it was doubtful if Britain was even maintaining parity with Germany. At best she would have twenty capital ships to Germany's seventeen, and at worst sixteen to her twenty-one. The defeated radicals remained mute; the motion to reduce the estimates was forgotten and the Liberal Press accepted the dreadnought programme, though insisting that the second batch of four should not be laid down until April 1910. 'I feel, however,' wrote Esher, 'that unless the B of Admiralty get their eight ships ordered *at once* they ought to be hanged. I'm going to try and put the fear of God into Jacky this morning.'[36]

Having defeated the 'little Navy men', Asquith had played into the hands of the Conservatives, who demanded all eight should be laid down at once. 'We want eight and we won't wait!' became their battle cry. The *Daily News* referred to 'panic spreading like the plague'; the *Saturday Review* regarded McKenna's speech as 'miserable, humiliating news', while *The Observer* called on the public to 'insist on the eight, the whole eight and nothing but the eight, with more to follow and break any man or faction that now stands in the way', and the *Pall Mall Gazette* said that, as in France in 1792 and

1870 'the cry is beginning to echo through the land, *"Citoyens, La Patrie est en danger!"'* *The Daily Telegraph* referred to the 'most shameful national surrender accorded in the whole pages of history' and *The National Review* took the opportunity to blame the transfer of naval supremacy to Germany on Fisher, whom it described as the re-incarnation of Marshal Le Boeuf, the War Minister of France, who had said on the eve of Sedan that the French Army was 'ready to the last gaiter button'.

Esher lunched at the Mansion House and sat next to McKenna, who, he said, 'is very bitter against Lloyd George and Winston Churchill. He spoke of Asquith's "weakness"'.[37] The Government did not yield until, on 10 March, Balfour gave notice of a motion of censure. 'Since Nero fiddled, there has never been a spectacle more strange, more lamentable than the imperilling of the whole priceless heritage of centuries, to balance a party budget.'[38] Grey again pleaded for mutual inspection and proclaimed that if the armaments race went on, 'sooner or later I believe it will submerge civil-isation', disregarding the now obvious fact that if Britain did not keep up the armaments race it would submerge Britain, France and probably Russia as well. The censure vote was lost but the argument continued, everyone producing his own figures culled from the naval journals of the time. Churchill, when later First Lord, said, 'In the technical discussion of naval details there is such a wealth of facts that the point of the argument turns upon their selection rather than their substance'.[39] In 1909 he attempted to include the two 'Lord Nelsons' as dreadnoughts, though they had been designed before *Dreadnought* and completed after her, with a mixed armament.

Lloyd George's social service budget of April distracted attention. The radicals' case came out of hiding and Churchill, Lloyd George and their supporters recognized no definite commitment for the extra four dread-noughts, while the Admiralty worked on the basis that the material would be stocked and the keels laid on 1 April 1910. Churchill and his friends argued that they should be regarded as an advance instalment of the 1910–11 programme, though the Admiralty anticipated four more ships that year, a total of twelve. McKenna and Grey threatened resignation and Asquith attempted hopelessly to compromise, suggesting the unwisdom of laying down eight battleships that year because 'a better type might be discovered thereafter'!

In December 1908 Fisher had warned that the Austrian naval programme included dreadnoughts. Now intelligence reports indicated Germany was building three or four for Austria. These must have been among those seen by the Argentinians, but so concerned was Asquith that he sent for Fisher at 11 pm one Sunday night for immediate information.

Italy, alarmed at Austrian plans, followed suit, and though none knew on whose side she would fight, if at all, her union with the Central powers would stack the odds against the Entente. The news resolved the argument and in July McKenna announced that the four extra dreadnoughts would be laid down in April 1910 and completed by March 1912, forming part of the 1909–10 programme, without prejudice to succeeding years.

Germany now tried to placate Britain, Von Bülow, Tirpitz and the Kaiser differing on the way this should be achieved. Tirpitz summed up the process desired as: 'first "detente" and then "entente" in the political field, then an agreement for disarmament, but not in the reverse order, first military weakening and then vague promises for better treatment'.[40]

Through German eyes this was sound reasoning, and she attempted a neutrality and non-aggression pact, received coldly by Britain who regarded it as an attempt to divide her from France. So Germany attempted an unconvincing offer of relaxation of the tempo of naval building, which merely deferred the evil day and then hinted that a reduction of the total programme was a possibility, suggesting an agreement similar to the Baltic agreement signed by Russia, Sweden and Denmark, which guaranteed the *status quo* in the Baltic. The Foreign Office was unconvinced; any agreement would leave France at the mercy of Germany, who sought British neutrality. She would never consent to naval reductions unless an alliance between Britain, Russia and France could be eliminated, which was unacceptable to Britain. There was no possibility of compromise between the radical desire for naval reductions and the German aim of British neutrality.

In the event there was no acceleration of German naval building, which, years later, McKenna said was discontinued due to its exposure in the House of Commons, though Marder finds some evidence in German archives that it never existed. The 1908–09 and 1909–10 plans were not advanced, and the 1910 programme delayed by eight months by British progress to 13.5-inch guns, so that in April 1912 Germany did not have twenty-one modern battleships, nor even seventeen, but only thirteen. The British programme also lagged and only fifteen modern capital ships were in commission by the end of March. However, had it not been for Fisher, the story could have been different. As Churchill later wrote: 'The greatest credit is due to the First Lord of the Admiralty, Mr. McKenna, for the resolute and courageous manner in which he fought his case and withstood his Party on this occasion.'[41] As Marder so fairly says, 'he might have included Fisher in this encomium!'

There were important results from the 1909 Navy scare. The Empire and the Dominions no longer felt it the duty of Britain alone to defend them, and in March that year New Zealand offered to provide one dreadnought, and another if necessary. The Australians followed and a few years later Malaya contributed HMS *Malaya*.

The events resulted, too, in the acceptance of the possibility, even probability, of war with Germany. Articles appeared in the Press suggesting that

Germany aimed at world hegemony. Had the eight dreadnoughts not been brought forward by McKenna and Fisher, by January 1915, after the loss of *Audacious*, with five ships under refit, Britain would have been reduced to twenty-one modern capital ships against Germany's twenty, a margin quite inadequate, considering Britain's wide interests. By 1912 the two-power standard, no longer necessary, had disappeared. The French and Russian navies had declined; the next two navies after the British were the United States and the German. There was universal agreement that 'we are not going to be dragged into a civil war with our kith and kin in the United States' and, in a memorandum to the CID, the Admiralty said an Anglo-American war was 'not merely the supreme limit of human folly, but also . . . so unlikely a contingency against which it is unnecessary to make provision'.[42]

German attempts to gain British neutrality and Tirpitz's *Memoirs* demonstrate that Germany hoped to keep Britain out of a war with France, who could be defeated on the continent; Britain could then be dealt with in detail, provided a naval lead, or at least near-parity, was achieved. But for Fisher's maintenance of Britain's naval lead, war would have broken out earlier. Yet the obloquy to which he was subjected, primarily manipulated by Beresford, Custance and Sturdee, was succeeding, and after the Navy Estimates debate of 1909 was greatly intensified. If Beresford could blame Fisher for all Britain's naval problems, he could still become First Sea Lord, and a national campaign against Fisher was mounted.

15

THE BERESFORD INQUIRY

When, in 1908, Fisher considered retirement, McKenna did not discourage him. But the view that he was driven from office by Beresford is an exaggeration; his departure would open the way for Beresford's supporters and he would have none of that. He wrote to McKenna:

> I am anxious to assure you of my sense of your kindness and to remove any impression that I wish 'to lag superfluous on the stage'. My only desire is to avoid the wreckage of the various arrangements now in progress, all of which, I am convinced, are for the good of the Navy, and the next two years will make them safe [Beresford would retire in February, 1911] and only for that reason had I any desire to wait the time of my retirement. . . . However, the real limit is the period of cordial harmony between the First Lord and the First Sea Lord.[1]

He was becoming dejected by the machinations of the Beresford clan, the perfidious politicians and uninformed attacks of the Press. He wrote to Arnold White: 'I am getting sick and meditating a sudden and unexpected departure *à la* Elijah, but I am not going to jeopardise. I shall look out to have Elisha standing right under, so that the mantle may not miss! . . . But I am getting really wearied out with all the flabby "blue funkers" all around one, that parley with mutiny.'[2] Elisha was Wilson.

Esher did not trust McKenna, but Fisher did, and on 27 November he asked Esher if he had any evidence.

> The more I think over it the more satisfied I am to do Elijah next King's birthday *(provided Elisha is ready!)*. That would forestall any such black treachery as you have in mind. Only you and dear Knollys know of my idea and I think it's best kept secret, as opposed to the view I first had of putting it in writing to McKenna and the King. *Anyhow, let's first see*

216

what happens about Beresford! He's as quiet as a mouse now. I am not going to say one word. There is now personal animosity between McKenna and Beresford, and McKenna calls him a liar!! But this doesn't count if political expediency says otherwise![3]

Fisher had long considered his successor. In the normal course he could stay in the Admiralty until his 70th birthday, 25 January 1911, but he wanted to ensure his replacement would continue his work and was a man respected in the Navy. Most of his followers were younger men he had encouraged because he believed in young men, but few of them would be considered as First Sea Lord. He therefore chose Wilson, with whom he had always been able to work, who had kept himself aloof from the Beresford-Fisher wrangle and shunned publicity, which gave him support from both sides. But he was due to retire in 1907 at the age of 65, on hauling down his flag as C-in-C Channel Fleet, so Fisher had arranged for Wilson to be promoted to Admiral of the Fleet by special Order in Council, over the heads of some of his seniors, giving him a further five years' service. Wilson was only a year younger than Fisher, so if the latter served out his full time Wilson would only hold office for a year; such a short appointment was unlikely, so Fisher planned to retire a year early, giving Wilson two years in office, barring the way for the Beresford adherents. Dispirited by the Cabinet's failure to support him, by the attacks of the Beresfordites and the virulence of the Press, by 1908 Fisher was considering even earlier retirement. Yet there remained much to do to prepare the Navy for the Armageddon he foresaw. The uncertainty of his position was evidenced by Esher, who wrote in his journal on 13 June 1908, no doubt reflecting the views of Meux [Lambton][4] and Wemyss, 'The Prince of Wales . . . talked mainly about the Navy and Jacky Fisher. He thinks the condition of the Navy is serious, partly its weakness in ships and stores, partly its discipline, so that it would be better if Jacky were to cede his place to some other'.[5] Again on 3 November, 'This evening Jacky telephoned. He was most anxious to see me. He was undecided what to do, having qualms about leaving the Admiralty next year. I urged him to write to McKenna telling him that on November 9th next year [the King's birthday] he would resign. He said that McKenna had expressed to him the strong hope that he would not lose him. "Very well. If he is sincere, you will have made a wise move!" Jacky then said he was resolved to act upon this advice. *Nous verrons!*' Six days later, 'Jacky came into the Defence Committee this evening. He thought better of his resolve to write to McKenna. . . . The fact is that he cannot bring himself to say good bye to the Admiralty, even a year hence.'[6]

Fisher's reluctance to retire has been attributed to a desire to retain power, but the opposite is the case. He desired retirement, but was concerned at the damage to the Navy if he opened the way for Beresford or his adherents.

Beresford's extraordinarily magnetic personality, his ability to pull the wool over so many eyes, brought him immense popularity with a naïve British public. His flamboyant character brought the accusation that he had been dismissed 'because he had fearlessly told the truth'. The fact was that his jealousy of Fisher amounted to paranoia. Vociferous, articulate and devious, yet giving an impression of frank honesty, his bitter frustration at Fisher's determination to remain in office after promotion inflamed his jealousy. He entertained lavishly in his house in Grosvenor Street, his title and Irish charm making him the idol of society ladies led by Lady Londonderry, who held drawing-room meetings addressed by him. Fisher contemptuously dubbed them 'the Duchesses', but they were important, for they and their husbands had great influence. Queen Alexandra sent for Fisher to warn him of what was going on.

Worse were Beresford's assemblages of discontented admirals. Bridgeman, who had just become Second Sea Lord and had served under Beresford in the Mediterranean, paying a courtesy call on him and announcing his name to the butler, was shown into a library where he found seated round a table a number of embarrassed admirals who attempted to evade recognition by burying themselves in their papers or turning to look out of the window, obviously engaged in plotting against the Board of Admiralty.

Beresford was on Christian name terms with Balfour, whom he used and consulted in his campaign against Fisher, criticizing the state of the Navy, the strategic distribution of the fleet and a shortage of cruisers and destroyers, asserting that the Admiralty had no plans. He asked Balfour if he had any objection to his raising these matters in public, though still on the active list. Balfour, with evident distaste, could see no formal objection, but advised him to consult the Prime Minister, adding that he was satisfied Admiralty had ample war plans, though he might not agree with them. Beresford saw Asquith and wrote his views to him, threatening to speak out, warning Asquith of his intention to 'turn out the Government' unless his demand for a public inquiry into the conduct of the Admiralty during Fisher's term in office was carried out. He publicly called Fisher 'our dangerous lunatic', accusing him of neglecting the safety of the country. He attacked all Fisher's policies, the scrapping policy, the economies and the *Dreadnought* ('We start at scratch with that type of ship'). He repeated that the Home Fleet was a fraud and a danger to the Empire; there was a dangerous shortage of destroyers and small craft (which in the event proved accurate) and the Admiralty lacked power to put any strategic plan immediately into action. He claimed he had never been able to obtain from Fisher any plan for the employment of the Channel Fleet in war.

Asquith tried to placate him and, with McKenna's support, appointed a sub-committee of the CID to investigate the charges, which became known

218

as the 'Beresford Inquiry'. Initially Esher and Wilson were appointed members. As members of the CID this was perfectly proper, but Beresford objected and Asquith removed them. Instead of playing the whole thing down, appointing a low-level committee and keeping its conclusions secret, Asquith exalted its status by taking the chair himself and appointing four Cabinet Ministers, Crewe, Morley, Grey and Haldane. No naval officer was a member, nor even the First Lord. Fisher saw red and wrote to Esher: 'Imagine what a state of affairs when a meeting of naval officers on the active list in a room in Grosvenor Street is able to coerce the Cabinet and force the strongest Board of Admiralty to totter to its fall! Why, "the young Turks" are not in it! The country must indeed be in a bad way if so governed!'[7]

Fisher resigned, but Esher and the King persuaded him to remain 'in spite of all' and filled him with determination. *'I am not going until I am kicked out!'* As Marder says: 'One of the humiliations which he had to endure was that, for the first time in history, a Board of Admiralty was to be put on trial to defend itself against the charges of an undisciplined subordinate.'[8]

With nice timing, the 'Bacon Letters' were now revealed, aptly summed up by the German Naval Attaché; 'After Sir George Armstrong was discharged as a young naval officer [1892] on account of imprudent remarks about Sir John Fisher, for which he had to apologise publicly, he had vowed vengeance to him. To fulfil this vow he collected material for years and now makes use of some of it (the Bacon Letters which had been slipped to him) to proceed against Fisher, according to plan.'[9]

Armstrong was crafty and sharp-witted, his venom like manna to Beresford. He revealed the Bacon Letters in a speech at the Constitutional Club on 2 April 1909, without mentioning Bacon's name. An hysterical Press and Parliamentary campaign was launched, members asking daily questions suggesting Fisher had operated a system of espionage. Bacon, recognizing certain phrases used, realized the letters were his and that they had been circulated within the Admiralty. He went at once to McKenna and asked that his name should be mentioned in Parliament, 'as there was nothing that I had written that I had the slightest desire to disown,'[10] and wrote to Beresford assuring him that nothing he had written was intended to reflect on him, to which he received 'a charming reply'.

A member (Carr-Gomm) asked McKenna 'whether his attention had been called to some extracts from a letter alleged to have been written three years ago by a captain of six years' seniority to Admiral of the Fleet Sir John Fisher; whether he is aware that a charge has been publicly made that the letter revealed a system of espionage, and that the captain who wrote it criticised his superior officers wholesale; and whether he proposes to take any steps in the matter?'[11] The most important letter has already been reproduced (page 149 ante) and clearly the claim was false. McKenna replied openly; 'The letter in question was written by Captain R H Bacon. . . . I have read the letter; it is a perfectly proper letter to have been written by Captain Bacon and I cannot find in it the smallest ground for any of the calumnious charges which have been based upon it. It contains no opinion of Captain Bacon of any officers of the Fleet.'[12]

McKenna was in a difficulty; the letter contained direct mention of the King and had been written at the suggestion of the Prince of Wales and protocol forbade them being drawn into a controversy, which Fisher's enemies knew perfectly well. 'The only complaint,' said McKenna, 'is that before these letters were printed the reference to my Honourable Friend [Bellairs] was not struck out. That is a matter for which he [Fisher] is extremely sorry, and for which I am extremely sorry. As regards anything else in the letters, it was entirely proper that they should be printed, because they were worth preserving.'[13] But a few days later he was saying, 'Is the House seriously going to be asked to condemn a great man because he has ordered to be printed a number of letters it would have been better, I would say, not to have been printed at all? . . . This sort of attack is doing a cruel injustice to the First Sea Lord, who has had the unreserved confidence of four successive First Lords . . . and I appeal to the House not to be misled by any such trumpery matters as these into censuring in the slightest degree a man who has given the very best service to the public that any man could give.'[14]

The *Westminster Gazette* was apt: 'When the worst has been said about these things, they are quite trivial compared with the interests of the Service, and to return again and again to them is to produce the impression that the object in view is not merely to vindicate the proprieties, but to conduct a campaign against a particular individual.'[15]

The virulence and vindictiveness of the campaign mounted. Even the Prince of Wales, much under the influence of Meux, was convinced, and it changed Fisher's attitude to the Prince and, after the death of his friend Edward VII, to the monarchy. Sections of the Press were vicious:

> The sole responsibility for the fact that in a few months Great Britain will be in a more vulnerable position than she has been since the Battle of Trafalgar belongs to the First Sea Lord. . . . Above all he is responsible for the starving of the Navy during the last three years. . . . If he had threatened resignation when an unsatisfactory programme was being prepared he would have forced the hands of the economaniacs. Moreover, his notorious 'sleep safely in your beds' speech was a direct justification of radical policy. We arraign Sir John Fisher at the bar of public opinion, and with the imminent possibility of national disaster before the country, we say again to him, 'Thou art the man!'[16]

Few more inaccurate paragraphs have ever appeared in the Press. Fisher was accused of having been 'caught napping' by German acceleration. Though

German naval rearmament had started with the 1900 Navy Law, some claimed the construction of *Dreadnought* had precipitated it, whereas it had delayed her programme. He was following the maxim of all times, *Si vis pacem, para bellum*. He failed to prevent war, but it was the superiority he created that won it.

The Beresford Inquiry began on 27 April 1909. At a later date Commander Thomas Crease left undated notes describing the scene, probably written after he had retired:

> At the inquiry Lord Charles Beresford was allowed to have Admiral Sir R. Custance present, to assist him in prosecuting his charges.
>
> The Admiralty was represented by the First Lord (Mr. McKenna) and the First Sea Lord (Sir John Fisher), and Commander T.E.Crease attended with them. Comm[r.] Crease was then on Sir John Fisher's staff as a personal assistant.
>
> Sir John Fisher promised faithfully that he would not open his mouth at the meetings unless directly addressed by the PM or the Committee. If he had spoken there would have been continual altercations with Lord Charles, who was in a very excited state. Consequently the First Lord did all the talking. Sir John Fisher only broke out once during the series of meetings, when there was somewhat of a scene – wh. is not recorded in the minutes! Comm[r.] Crease sat between Mr. McKenna and Sir John Fisher, and passed on the comments of the latter.[17]

The committee took oral and documentary evidence from McKenna, Beresford and Custance. Asquith said he thought Beresford presented his case with ability and moderation, but most of those present became convinced of Beresford's incompetence and inability to comprehend much less present the charges, and it was revealed that to assist him in his case, two Assistant Directors of Naval Intelligence, Captain H.H.Campbell and Captain Arthur Hulbert, had provided him with confidential documents, including a letter from Vice-Admiral George Egerton, Commander-in-Chief of the Cape of Good Hope, demanding more ships, though no reason seems to have been given for them! Campbell, another friend of the Prince of Wales, explained that he never divulged the contents of any paper to Beresford, but had suggested that he ask for certain documents that would support his case – surely a fine distinction! The King was undeceived and, through Knollys, suggested disciplinary action. [18]

Fifteen meetings were held over six weeks and the Report was issued on 12 August as a Parliamentary Paper in two volumes, 328 pages of proceedings and 245 of appendices, including 2,600 questions. Beresford claimed that since he had taken command of the Channel Fleet on 15 April 1907 until 2 April 1909, the date of his letter to the Prime Minister, the Admiralty had failed to make adequate arrangements for the safety of the country; the fleets in home waters were dispersed and should have been under his command throughout; that the Channel Fleet had not been kept at sufficient strength due to the absence of ships under repair and refit. The system of concentration adopted by Germany demanded all ships in full commission under one command.

McKenna responded that during Beresford's command the fleets were steadily being reorganized into a single command. Problems must be expected during change and great care had been taken to maintain efficiency. There was no harbour in the North Sea adequate to accommodate even two divisions of the ultimate Home Fleet. Dispersion was unavoidable, but constituted no danger even in the event of sudden attack, when losses would be lessened by dispersal. Future policy was to concentrate the fleet at sea, but base their various divisions separately. He agreed Channel Fleet ships had not always been replaced while under refit, because this had not always been possible; but the policy applied only to extensive refits and not, as Beresford implied, to periods of annual maintenance. He denied that the Home Fleet was an inefficient striking force, pointing to the frequent surprise tests that had shown it able to mobilize in five hours. He produced figures showing the gunnery of the Home Fleet to be better than that of Beresford's fleet. Bridgeman, who had been in command of the Home Fleet during almost the whole period, said he was entirely satisfied with its readiness. McKenna continued that the organization Beresford proposed could hardly be distinguished from that developing, except that for strategic reasons the Atlantic Fleet was an independent command. Wilson said that *in his time* there had been 'a great deal of force' in Beresford's arguments, but his objections had been met.

Beresford claimed the deficiency of small craft, including unarmoured cruisers and destroyers, obliged him to utilize armoured cruisers instead, making the protection of trade impossible. The Admiralty claimed the total of cruisers was sufficient both for scouting and protection of trade, and six armoured cruisers were being laid down annually, to Germany's two. Beresford's case hinged on whether German merchant ships were armed and provided with ammunition, which was not then the case. (Later, they were.)

Beresford conceded there were 198 British to 154 German torpedo craft, but claimed deductions should be made from the British figures to allow for ships refitting, which enabled Germany to choose her moment. He rightly regarded few of his destroyers suitable for the North Sea, claiming German ships were more powerfully armed. He disparaged submarines, which were 'always in a fog'; they were defensive weapons, unsuitable for an offensive fleet. He accentuated his unrealism by his opposition to the scrapping policy; he desired a 'big' navy of useless old ships.

The Admiralty said destroyers were rapidly developing and if Germany took the offensive the old ones could be used against the few German ones able to undertake offensive operations. Sixteen destroyers were included in the 1908–09 estimates and twenty in 1909–10. The older German craft were armed with one 12-pounder and five 6-pounders, while the majority of British destroyers were armed entirely with 12-pounders. Germany had introduced a 23-pounder and Britain was countering this with a 4-inch (31-pounder). For security reasons McKenna did not discuss Beresford's remarks on submarines, which sufficiently abnegated themselves, as did those on the scrapping policy.

Finally Beresford complained of the refusal to provide him with strategic schemes or plans for war. The report said that Beresford, under cross-examination, 'very considerably modified' his views and reproduced a narrative of the correspondence and meetings with him on the subject in 1907–08.

Beresford said he had not been provided with information on the readiness of the Home and Atlantic fleets, which he asserted would come under his command in war. Marder believed this was partly true and the difficulty lay with the absence of cordial relations between him and the Admiralty. Had this been true, the fault lay with Beresford, much time and effort having been devoted to his petty cavils. But it was not true. There was never any intention that Beresford should command a Grand Fleet, though he had spread the concept and it was widely believed outside the Navy and by many of his adherents inside.

On the question of war plans Wilson was clear. It was neither practical nor desirable to draw up firm plans in peace which would circumscribe action in war and tempt all concerned to assume that *that* plan, and only that plan, would be adopted, and since such plans would have to pass through so many hands secrecy would be prejudiced and surprise lost. He was 'perfectly certain that any plan drawn up in peace would not be carried out in war'. He accepted that plans should be drawn up, but must be flexible enough to cope with changed circumstances. Such plans had been provided to Beresford and were almost as a routine criticized by him and Custance, neither of whom had alternatives to offer.

The report stated that since March 1909 the whole of the naval force in Home Waters, except the Atlantic fleet, had been united under a single flag officer, which met Beresford's point. But to Fisher's understandable fury a paragraph was included 'that the Admiralty would have been better advised in adhering throughout to the principle of placing the chief command in Home waters in the hands of a single officer' – a political sop to Beresford. The Committee were satisfied that there was no deficiency of small craft in Home waters to constitute a risk; there was no foundation for Beresford's apprehension regarding provision for the protection of trade (effective submarine warfare was not yet feasible). With regard to war plans, though Beresford had not raised the matter, McKenna provided a résumé of steps taken to develop a war staff and indicated further advances in contemplation. Under the heading *General Conclusion* the committee stated:

> The investigation has shown that during the time in question no danger to the country resulted from the Admiralty's arrangements for war, whether considered from the standpoint of organisation and distribution of the fleet, the number of ships, or the preparation of war plans. . . .
>
> They feel bound to add that arrangements quite defensible in themselves, though not ideally perfect, were in practice seriously hampered through the absence of cordial relations between the Board of Admiralty and the Commander-in-Chief of the Channel Fleet. The Board of Admiralty do not appear to have taken Lord Charles Beresford sufficiently into their confidence as to the reasons for dispositions to which he took exception; and Lord Charles Beresford, on the other hand, appears to have failed to appreciate and carry out the spirit of the instructions of the Board, and to recognise their paramount authority.
>
> The Committee have been impressed with the difference of opinion amongst officers of high rank and professional attainment regarding important principles of naval strategy and tactics and they look forward with much confidence to the further development of a naval War Staff, from which the naval members of the Board and Flag Officers and their staffs at sea may be expected to derive common benefit.[19]

Beresford's arguments had generally been shown to be easily rebutted personal attacks and the vital words in the whole lengthy report were: *Lord Charles Beresford . . . failed to appreciate and carry out the spirit of the instructions of the Board and recognise their paramount authority.* This was the bedrock. Most self-respecting men would have crawled to some quiet corner to lick their wounds, but Beresford's skin was thick. In a circular a few days later he announced to the Press that he had derived 'in the main, great satisfaction from the report', which showed that the reforms advocated by him and resisted by the Admiralty were being adopted on precisely the lines he had advocated. Yet he was being supplied with information by his spies in the Admiralty (Campbell and Hulbert were not the only ones) and was always able publicly to claim credit for proposals already in hand. He quite genuinely believed himself the victor. He wrote to Balfour: 'The Committee as a matter of fact could not have found more strongly in my favour without removing the heads of the Admiralty, but by judicious legal verbiage it was inferred that I was insubordinate, which, as you would define it, is a 'frigid lie'.[20]

Beresford's insubordination was publicly exposed, yet in October he published in *The Times* his correspondence with the Prime Minister, referring to 'intimidation on the one hand and favouritism on the other for which the Admiralty have of late years been notorious',[21] and wrote again to Balfour: 'I have not been able to show up the Admiralty methods of blackmail before, as it would have looked personal, but now I have begun to fight for my brother officers, all disgusting intimidation must come out that has been practised for the last five years'.

Beresford badgered the Prime Minister in further attempts to damage Fisher, claiming Sturdee, Hulbert and Campbell were victimized because of their connection with him. Hulbert and Campbell were placed on half pay, McKenna telling Asquith that their posts had been abolished due to a reorganization, and their retention in the Intelligence Department was anyway undesirable as their disclosure of confidential documents had caused 'no small friction' with their superior, Admiral Bethell. Indeed, only political expediency saved them from Court-Martial.

On 1 November Beresford again wrote to *The Times:*

> The validity of my case still remains unaffected. . . . I say again, as I said before, that a system of espionage, favouritism and intimidation exists at the Admiralty.' To Sturdee he wrote, 'I have proved by the correspondence that blackmail was going on in order to enable the mulatto to carry out his autocratic and dangerous administration.

Fisher's supporters, including the King, hailed the report as his vindication, though he did not think so. He felt, with good reason, that his censure for not adequately consulting Beresford was unjustified. If a First Sea Lord always had to consult every C-in-C afloat before making a decision, he would never achieve anything. The committee should have censured Beresford in stronger terms, but Fisher should have recognized the perfidy of politicians. He wrote to Crease:

> I . . . am bitterly disappointed by the Committee's Report – It's a most cowardly production!! Not in the least what it was intended to be by any of the five members on the day that Asquith cross-examined Beresford on the Campbell incident *à la* an old Bailey Attorney! – It was a dirty trick to say the Admiralty had not given its confidence to Beresford when Beresford had abused that confidence within 24 hours of hoisting his flag! and again a very dirty trick to bring in the red herring about the Naval War Staff when all five members knew about the great work done in establishing the Naval War College at Portsmouth and the practical proof of great advance in strategical thought in the Navy by the concentration of our fleets instead of their previous dispersion and the getting rid of 160 vessels that could neither

fight nor run away. . . . I am very sick about it all, considering what each member of the Committee had previously said to me. Burn this letter.[22]

Beresford's indiscipline and disloyalty had done much to destroy morale in the Navy and Fisher rightly believed it purely a political report. He was supported by Knollys: 'I am not surprised myself at the colourless report, considering the composition of the Committee which I have always thought an absurd one, and that the members of it were terrified at C.Beresford, as shown by the way they all treated him when examined, especially Asquith.'[23]

Asquith might have grasped the opportunity to discredit once and for all this retroversive intriguer and political opponent, but lacked the courage and condoned his insubordination. The real problem was Beresford's dual role as naval officer and politician. His political activities nearly brought him to the top of the Navy, and he was considerably over-promoted. Fisher's distress was justified; he was subjected to ridiculous invective by the radical Press. *The National Review* said there was 'no end to the catalogue of his high crimes and misdemeanours . . . Should it come to hanging he will be entitled to the nearest lamppost.'[24]

The King supported Fisher wholeheartedly and on 20 April 1909, a week before the inquiry had opened, had written to him through Ponsonby that 'even under pressure' he was not to think of resigning. On 28 May Fisher wrote to McKenna, 'I want to stick to you now until the day you leave office, no matter when that is. . . . Please don't talk of any other First Sea Lord till January 1911.' (his 70th birthday). But alternatives to Wilson were being considered and in October he was writing :

The King concurs in all your ideas as to your humble servant, so I assume it may be all considered as settled. . . .

Now I have got a blow for you. It was a blow to me anyhow this morning! Bridgeman told me wherever I went he was going. I said you counted on his remaining with Fawkes, and so had I. But he said No, he wouldn't serve under Fawkes or May. He had a contempt for both of them, but he would gladly remain as First Sea Lord with Callaghan as Second Sea Lord. . . . I don't know why you should not have Bridgeman as First Sea Lord, especially with such an excellent man as Callaghan as Second.[25]

But all was not settled. Evidently the Second Sea Lord's refusal to serve under Fawkes, then Commander-in-Chief Plymouth, put an end to this idea, for on Friday of the same week Fisher went to Sandringham and on his return wrote to Esher, '*I honestly believe* it'd due to you and Knollys that I am safe!' And on 20th to Stead, 'I am not going until Elisha is right underneath, all expectant for the mantle dropping on him!'[26]

McKenna supported his choice and it was agreed that he would resign a year before his seventieth birthday, to give Wilson two years in office. Asquith wrote to him that on the King's birthday, 9 November, he would be elevated to the peerage. Fisher took his title as Baron Fisher of Kilverstone, from Kilverston Hall, the property left by Josiah Vavasseur to Cecil Fisher. However, he was offered only a Barony, 'like the man who makes linoleum or lends money for elections', and thought he should have been made Viscount, 'the same as a brewer'. A warm letter from the King silenced him, 'the very best letter I have ever received in my life,' and he asked Ponsonby to do nothing more.

Wilson was reluctant to accept the appointment. Bacon wrote:

> He was, without exception, the least egotistical of human beings, but at the same time a man of extraordinary tenacity and indomitable pluck. . . . He had no regard for himself or for his own comfort; he looked on his body as merely a shell to carry out the dictates of his mind. He did not seek rewards or honours, and later he refused a peerage when it was offered to him. He was undoubtedly the finest admiral of his day in command of a fleet, and he had been for five years in command of our largest fleets. He was scrupulously just and level-headed. He had no communication whatever with the Press; but unfortunately he was not himself an adept at argument, and therefore he was always at a disadvantage when dealing with politicians.[27]

Fisher was anxious, and asked the King to see Wilson, 'and get him *fixed* to be First Sea Lord, so that McKenna's communication to Wilson hereafter will be purely formal. The reason for urgency is that, as 3 or 4 persons now know about Wilson, it will probably leak out and Wilson would be got at and persuaded he was keeping the bread out of someone else's mouth, etc . . . and the Beresford object is to get Sir Arthur Moore as my successor as embodying hostility to all that has been done.'[28] Moore would not be 65 until July 1912, so was certainly a contender. Wilson's succession was announced on 2 December, giving him over two years in office, eliminating Moore, Custance and all Beresford's adherents (though his time was to be cut short). He fully supported all Fisher's reforms and the eight super-dreadnoughts of the 1909–10 programme.

Fisher said he left the Admiralty 'in the nick of time'. As he foresaw, Wilson's appointment had leaked and within two days of the announcement of his peerage Beresford disclosed that he was certain of his election as MP for Portsmouth and a change of government; he was to become First Lord, 'to keep Wilson right'! His grounds were dubious in the extreme.

Despite the odium to which he had been subjected, Fisher's retirement was greeted with dismay by many men-in-the-street, to whom he was a hero in his own time, regarded with something of the adulation bestowed on

227

Nelson, exemplified by the flower seller from whom he bought a button-hole. She had never met him before, but refused payment from her hero. He had never commanded a great fleet in wartime and in this respect had never been tested, but few of his contemporaries, least of all himself, had any doubt that he would have discharged the task admirably. 'Oh my! That I was born too soon!' he wrote. But if he had not been born when he was, if he had not been First Sea Lord at the critical time, it would have been disastrous for Britain.

His opponents blamed him for the break-up of the Band of Brothers spirit that had characterized the Navy. The unity that Marder describes as 'Nelson's principle legacy to the Navy, had been replaced by disharmony and embittered recrimination, of which he was the centre.' But the Band of Brothers spirit was not Nelson's legacy to the Navy; it did not long survive his death. It was replaced by a spirit of esotericism, nepotism, Buggins' turn, an inner wheel. 'Interest' was almost the only path to promotion and only the very best broke through this barrier, while incompetents with influence rose without effort. During the nineteenth century and the first decade of the twentieth the Navy needed shaking out of its lethargy, its complacency, its belief that ships were the private yachts of their captains, the playthings of the admirals; that the Service was not a mere club for the gentry, its purpose not to present sparkling cleanliness, but to fight wars, and the object of the Admiralty to provide the means by which wars could be fought. Fisher did all this and more; he re-designed the Navy in its personnel and its material; he re-thought its tactics and strategy to utilize the new technology; he kept the Navy ahead of others; he recognized the future of the new elements of the air and submarines and started the methods of utilizing these new dimensions. He was often tactless; 'ruthless, relentless, remorseless' in his pursuit of perfection for the Navy; he *forced* through the reforms he knew to be necessary. He had to battle against privilege, prejudice, vested interest and resistance to change; if his methods were brutal, he would never have succeeded without brutality. But for Beresford's antagonism, the Service would reluctantly have accepted the essential changes. Fisher would have met with resistance, but Beresford was far more guilty of destroying any remnant of the Band of Brothers spirit. Both were brought up in an age when admirals were accorded huge grandeur, which increased as the years of peace passed; Beresford admired and envied such splendour; he looked forward all his life to enjoying it and when his turn came, it was Fisher who spoilt all that. Tributes came from countless sides. Stead wrote:

'I don't know how you feel about it,' said a friend the other day after Fisher's retirement, but I feel pretty bad. It's almost as if Nelson had stepped down from his monument in Trafalgar Square.' That is not exaggeration. We all feel more or less like that, from the King upon his throne down to the scurviest of the curs that snapped at the great man's heels. For Fisher was a great man – one of our greatest men. His greatness was attested alike by the devotion he commanded from all the greatest, and the fierce rancour which he aroused in the worst of his contemporaries.

'"Oh, Jacky! – well Jacky is splendid – simply splendid!"

'There you have it. That is the way in which he impressed everybody who was anybody who had to do with him.[29]

To Fisher McKenna wrote:

I will let you know at once when I hear from Wilson. I wrote to him with a heavy heart, and I have been unhappy these two days at the thought of your leaving. You have been so good to me, so understanding of my difficulties, so skillful in teaching me, so brave in your support of my political anxieties, so affectionate in your personal relations, that I have neither heart nor wish to go on without you.[30]

In the House of Commons he made his formal tribute

In January 1910 the Board of Admiralty was deprived, to their deep regret of the invaluable assistance of Admiral of the Fleet Lord Fisher of Kilverstone, GCB, OM, GCVO, who had asked to be relieved of his post on reaching the age of sixty-nine. Lord Fisher, in addition to most distinguished service as a sea-officer, has had a career of unexampled success in high administrative office at the Admiralty, first as Director of Naval Ordnance, afterwards as Third Sea Lord and Controller, then as Second Sea Lord, and finally as First Sea Lord. The measures which are associated with his name and have been adopted by several successive Governments will prove of far-reaching and lasting benefit to the naval service and the country.[31]

What pleased Fisher most was the flood of letters he received from within the Service. He wrote to Arnold White: 'I forgot to say to you in my letter this morning that I had thought myself very much alone but my eyes have been opened by such a mass of telegrams and letters from all ranks and classes in the Navy, and of course, one thinks of Elijah when he once felt lonely and saw all those chariots of fire around him when his eyes were opened.'[32]

In January he heard from Lionel Yexley, 'I have been asked by Warrant Officers, Chief and First Class Petty Officers, if I would convey to you their very grateful thanks for all you have done for the lower deck.'[33] He continued that he had been asked by a Beresford supporter to help in his election for Portsmouth. Fisher replied: 'I hope you'll fight the good fight at Portsmouth and get annanias carried out dead, as the result of the election. What a show-up your letter contains! I've no doubt you know best what to do.'[34]

But even as he packed his belongings in the Admiralty, his prime consideration was for the Navy he loved so much. He wrote to Mrs. Gerard Meynell (the author, E. Hallam Moorhouse):

> I've had a sad day. I've parted from my moorings this morning and the Admiralty knows me no more! Lord Esher last night and Arnold White this morning (he has a great spirit!) both girding at me to speak and blast my enemies. *I will not.* It might be a great personal triumph, but the Navy would be shown to be so strong as to give good cause for Lloyd George & Co. to build fewer ships. So I welcome hate and odium like the early Christians did the lions – they knew the end was good! I can't say it's pleasant! I overheard myself being called sweet names in my club today, but I fixed my face like a flint!.[35] . . . .

By 1910 Fisher's work had been done. A tornado of energy, enthusiasm and persuasive power, a man of originality, vision and courage, a sworn foe of all outworn traditions and customs, the greatest of naval administrators since St Vincent, 'Jacky' Fisher was what the lethargic Navy had been in dire need of. His five-year tenure of the post of First Sea Lord was the most memorable and the most profitable in the modern history of the Royal Navy. He fell on the old regime with a devastating fury. During those strenuous years there was no rest for anyone connected with the Service. 'It was as though a thousand brooms were at work clearing away the cobwebs'. In the teeth of ultra-conservative traditions, he revolutionized the Navy, cramming in a few years the reforms of generations and laying foundations that could never be destroyed. He gave his countrymen a new Navy, stronger and better organized than he found it, impregnated with the spirit of progress and efficiency, and purged as if by fire of 'those obese and unchallenged old things that stifled and overlay' it in the past.[36]

And Churchill wrote: 'There is no doubt whatever that Fisher was right in nine-tenths of what he fought for. . . . After a long period of unchallenged complacency, the mutter of distant thunder could be heard. It was Fisher who hoisted the storm signals and beat all hands to quarters. . . . But the Navy was not a pleasant place while this was going on.'[37]

But Fisher's work was not done yet. He was to return again to the Navy in war, when the country's need was greatest – and had he been heeded. perhaps the war would have been shortened, perhaps many lives would have been saved. But this is another story.

NOTES AND SOURCES

Chapter 1. Lonely youth and Wild Irishman.
1. Lennoxlove MSS 5100.
2. Admiral Sir Reginald Bacon, *The Life of Lord Fisher of Kilverstone,*(Hodder & Stoughton, 1929), p.9.
3. *Ibid*, p.52–3.
4. ADM. 167/1. NMM.
5. Fisher, *Memories*, (Hodder & Stoughton, 1919), p.130.
6. Marder, Arthur J., *Fear God and Dread Nought*, (Jonathan Cape, 1952), Vol.1, p.69.
7. *Ibid*, p.73.
8. *Ibid*, p.72–74.
9. *Ibid*, p.340.
10. *Ibid*, p.339.
11. *Ibid*.
12. Fisher to Balfour 1910, Balfour MSS.
13. Bennett, Geoffrey, *Charlie B*, (Peter Dawnay, 1968), p.45.
14. Royal Archives, Z459/35.
15. Briggs, Sir John H., Reader to the Board of Admiralty 1827–1892, *Naval Administrations*, (Sampson Low, 1897), p.201.
16. Royal Archives, 51/44.

Chapter 2. Well Done *Condor*.
1. Tarleton, Admiral Sir John Walter, *Diary*, 3 October 1873.
2. ADM. 116/158. NMM.
3. Lennoxlove manuscripts, 1.
4. *Ibid*.
5. Bacon, *Fisher*, Vol. I, p.54.
6. Cited in Marder, *Fear God*, Vol.1, p.87.
7. Bacon, *Fisher*, Vol. I, p.54.
8. *Ibid*, p.55–56.

9. *Ibid*, p.56.
10. *Ibid*, p.58.
11. *Ibid*, p.59.
12. *Ibid*, p.65.
13. *Ibid*, p.68.
14. *Ibid*, p.70.
15. Fisher, *Records*, (Hodder & Stoughton, 1919), p.2.
16. Beresford, Lord Charles, *Memoirs*, (Methuen, 1914), p.191.
17. Bacon, *Fisher*, Vol. I, p.92.
18. *Ibid*, p.91–92.
19. Beresford, *Memoirs*, p.199.
20. Cited in Marder, *Fear God*, Vol.1, p.112–13.
21. Fisher MSS.

Chapter 3. The Truth about the Navy.

1. Bacon, *Fisher*, Vol. I, p.94.
2. *The Times*, 8 January 1883.
3. Prince of Wales to Beresford, 23 August 1884; Beresford MSS.
4. *Ibid*. 30 August 1884.
5. Beresford to his wife, September 1884, Beresford MSS.
6. *Ibid*, October 1884.
7. Beresford *Memoirs*, p.286.
8. Bennett, *Charlie B*, p.115.
9. Prince of Wales to Beresford 27 February 1885.
10. Chilston, Lord, *W.H.Smith*, p.176.
11. Briggs, *Naval Administrations*, p.212.
12. Esher, Reginald, Viscount, *The Tragedy of Lord Kitchener*, pp.5–6.
13. Beresford, *Memoirs*, p.338.
14. An Undistinguished Naval Officer, *The British Navy in the Present year of Grace*,Vol.III, (Hamilton Adams, 1886).
15. *The Saturday Review*.
16. Fisher, *Records*, p.54.
17. Bacon, *Fisher*, Vol. I, p.98.

Chapter 4. The Naval Defence Act.

1. Hamilton, Lord George, *Parliamentary Reminiscences and Reflections, 1886–1906*, (John Murray 1922), p.88–89.
2 *Ibid*. p.88.
3. *Ibid*.
4. Briggs, *Naval Administrations*, p.241.
5. Beresford, *Memoirs*, p.355.
6. *Ibid*, p.355–6.
7. *Ibid*, p.357.
8. Briggs, *Naval Administrations, 1827–1892*, p.225–7.
9. *Ibid*, p.242.
10. *Hansard*, 3rd Series Vol. CCCXXXII,Col. 24–225.

11. *Ibid*, Vol. CCCXXIII, Col. 931–2.
12. *The Times* 4th February, 1888.
13. Beresford, *Memoirs* p.355.
14. Bennett, *Charlie B*, p.145.
15. Salisbury to Queen Victoria, R. Archives, A66/73.
16. Hamilton to Ponsonby, R. Archives, E56/4.
17. Prince of Wales to Prince George, R. Archives, Geo V AA 17/9.
18. *Hansard*, 3rd Series, Vol. CCCXXII, Col. 945.
19. *Ibid*.
20. *Ibid*.
21. Beresford, *Memoirs*, p.358.
22. *Ibid*, p.360.
23. I*bid*.
24. Hamilton, *Parliamentary Reminiscences*, p.112.
25. Dowell Committee Report.
26. *Ibid*.
27. Cited in Marder, *Fear God*, Vol.1, p.170–71.
28. Bacon, *Fisher*, Vol. I, p.104.
29. *Ibid*, p.107.
30. Hamilton, *Parliamentary Reminiscences* .
31. Jameson, Rear Admiral Sir William, *The Fleet that Jack Built*, p.49.
32. King-Hall, L. (Ed.), *Sea Saga*, p.317.
33. Cited in Marder, *Fear God*, Vol.1, p.119.
34. *Ibid*, p.122.

Chapter 5 Sailor or Politician?

1. Ponsonby to Queen Victoria, R. Archives, E56/57.
2. Beresford, *Memoirs*, p.380.
3. Ponsonby to Queen Victoria, R. Archives, E56/52.
4. Lady Brooke to Salisbury, 22 July 1891, Salisbury MSS.
5. Bennett, *Charlie B*, p.166 Note.
6. Salisbury to Beresford, 10 August 1891, Salisbury MSS.
7. Prince of Wales to Waterford, 6 April 1892, Salisbury MSS.
8. Beresford, *Memoirs*, p.386.
9. *Ibid*, p.387.
10. *Ibid*, p.393.
11. *Ibid*, p.394.
12. *Ibid*.
13. Order in Council 19 March 1872, see page 41 ante.
14. Admiral Sir Heathcote Grant, cited in Bacon, *Fisher*, Vol. I, p.115.
15. Bacon, *Fisher*, Vol. I, p.120.
16. Bucknill, Lt-Col. J T, *The Destruction of the United States Battleship 'Maine',* *ENGINEERING*, 1898.
17. W.T. Stead, *Review of Reviews*, February, 1910.
18. Admiral Sir Cyprian Bridge, *Naval Warfare*, p.161.
19. Stead, *Review of Reviews*, February, 1910.

20. Cited in Marder, *Fear God*, Vol.1, p.141.
21. Stead, *Review of Reviews*, February 1910.
22. Beresford, *Memoirs*, p.363.
23. Lee, Sir Sydney, *King Edward VII*, Vol. I, p 722.
24. Lutz, Hermann, *Lord Grey and the World War*, p.34.
25. Marriott, J.A.R., *Europe and Beyond*, p.195.
26. Steinberg, *Yesterday's Deterrent*, p.129.
27. Tirpitz *Memorandum, June 1897, Allgemeine Gesichtspunkte bei der Festellung unseres Flotte nach Schiffsklassen und Schiffstypen.*
28. Bennett, *Charlie B*, p.215.
29. *Ibid*, p.219.
30. Scott, Admiral Sir Percy, *Fifty Years in the Royal Navy*, p.202, note.

Chapter 6. Unruly Member.

1. Cited in Marder, *Fear God*, Vol.1, p.154–55.
2. Marder, *The Anatomy of British Sea Power*, p.352.
3. Bacon, *Fisher*, Vol. I, p.128.
4. Bacon, *Fisher*, Vol. I, p.165–66.
5. Brett, Maurice, Journals and Letters of Viscount Esher, Vol. I, p.31.
6. Beresford, *Memoirs*, p.465.
7. Jameson, *The Fleet that Jack Built*, p.85.
8. Chatfield, Admiral of the Fleet Lord, *The Navy and Defence*, p.41.
9. Roskill, Stephen, *Hankey, Man of Secrets*, Vol. I , p.55, Note.
10. Bennett, *Charlie B*, p.235.
11. Beresford, *Memoirs*, p.469.
12. Cited in Marder, *Fear God*, Vol.1, p.161.
13. Roskill *Hankey, Man of Secrets*, Vol. I , p.54.
14. *Ibid*, p.52.
15. *Ibid*, p.53.
16. *Ibid*.
17. Edward VII to Duke of York, R. Archives, (Geo. V, AA22/61).
18. Marder, *Anatomy*, p.463.
19. Beresford to Salisbury, 21 June 1900, Salisbury MSS.
20. Bacon, *Fisher*, Vol. I, p.138.
21. *Ibid*, p.139–40.
22. *Daily Mail*, 21 June 1901.
23. *Hansard*, 4th Series, Vol. XCV, Col. 1200.
24. *Ibid*, 4th Series, Vol. CVIII, Col. 203-16.
25. *Ibid*, Vol. XCVI, Col. 1349.
26. Bacon, *Fisher*, Vol. I, p.152.
27. Cited in Marder, *Fear God*, Vol.1, p.197.
28. Beresford, *Memoirs*, p.467.
29. Bennett, *Charlie B*, p.240.
30. King-Hall, *Sea Saga*, p.322.
31. Kemp, Peter, *From Tryon to Fisher; Naval Warfare in the Twentieth Century.*
32. Bennett, *Charlie B*, p.238.

33. Bacon, *Fisher*, Vol. I, p.153.
34. *Ibid*, p.152.
35. *Ibid*, p.153.
36. *Ibid*, p.155.
37. Cited in Marder, *Fear God*, Vol.1, p.231–2.
38. *Ibid*, p.218.
39. *Ibid*, p.194.
40. *Ibid*, p.186.
41. *Ibid*, p.210.
43. *Ibid*, p.155.
44. Cited in Marder, *Fear God*, Vol.1, p.143.
45. Bacon, *Fisher*, Vol. I, p.153.
46. Roskill *Admiral of the Fleet Earl Beatty*, (Atheneum, New York, 1881), p.43.
47. Admiralty Circular, December 1901.
48. NMM BRI/15.
49. *Ibid*.
50. *Cited in Marder, Fear God*, Vol.1, p.223.
51. *Ibid*, p.223–4.
52. Lennoxlove Papers, 4203.
53. *Ibid*, 90.
54. Cited in Marder, *Fear God*, Vol.1, p.222.
55. NMM, BRI/15.
56. Bacon, *Fisher*, Vol. I, p.156.
57. Cited in Marder, *Fear God*, Vol.1, p.234.
58. *Ibid*, p.237.
59. *The Times*, 25 April 1902.
60. *Ibid*.
61. *The Times*, 29 April 1902.
62. *Hansard*, 4th Series, Vol. CVII, Col. 613–5.
63. *Daily Mail*, 6 May 1902.
64. *Hansard*, 4th Series, Vol. CVIII, Col. 203–16.
65. *Ibid*.
66. *Ibid*.
67. *Ibid*.
68. *Hansard*, 4th Series, Vol. CIX, Col. 1257–1314.
69. *Ibid*.

Chapter 7. The Iconoclast.

1. Cited in Marder, *Fear God*, Vol.1, p.272.
2. For greater detail of the transition to steam, see *Up Funnel, Down Screw!* by Geoffrey Penn, (Hollis and Carter, 1955).
3. Penn, Geoffrey, *HMS Thunderer*, p.27.
4. Lowys, Commander Geoffrey, *Fabulous Admirals*, p.33.
5. Gardiner, Leslie, *The Royal Oak Courts Martial*, p.18.
6. Lennoxlove Papers, 5415.
7. Cited in Marder, *Fear God*, Vol.1, p.259.

8. *Ibid*, p.263.
9. *Parliamentary Paper*, Cmd. 1385.
10. *Ibid.*
11. Cited in Marder, *Fear God*, Vol.1, p.266 [Leon Gambetta – a French republican lawyer who openly preached the overthrow of Napoleon III].
12. Cited in Marder, *Fear God*, Vol.1, p.243.
13. King-Hall, *Sea Saga*, p.327.
14. Fisher, *Memories*, p.1–2.
15. Cited in Marder, *Fear God*, Vol.1, p.266.
16. Moore, Marjorie, *Adventures in the Royal Navy, 1847–1934*, p.170.
17. Marder, *Portrait of an Admiral*, p.353.
18. *Ibid*, p.255.
19. Penn, Geoffrey, *Up Funnel, Down Screw!*, p.141.
20. Marder, *Dreadnought*, Vol. I, p.30.
21. Cited in Marder, *Fear God*, Vol. I, p. 272.
22. Fisher, *Records*, p.160.
23. For greater detail of the Navigating Branch, see *Snotty*, by Geoffrey Penn, and *Navigation and Direction; the Story of HMS Dryad*, by Vice Admiral B. B. Schofield.
24. Schofield, *The Story of HMS Dryad*, p.21.
25. Cited in Marder, *Fear God*, Vol.1, p.266.
26. *Ibid*, p.273.
27. *Ibid*, p.278.
28. *Ibid*, p.290.
29. *The Times*, 22nd October 1903.
30. Bacon, *From 1900 Onward*, p.54.
31. *Ibid*, p.69.
32. Beresford, *Memoirs*, p.464.
33. Fisher, *Memories*, p.171.
34. Fisher, *Records*, p.176–9.
35. *Ibid*, p.173.
36. *Ibid*, p.176.
37. Cited in Marder, *Fear God*, Vol.1, p.308–9.
38. *Ibid*, p.310.
39. *Ibid.*
40. Lord Roberts to Salisbury, 12 November 1900.
41. Magnus, Philip, *King Edward the Seventh*, p.401.
42. Cited in Marder, *Fear God*, Vol.1, p.241.
43. Hankey, Maurice, *Supreme Command*, p.148.
44. Cited in Marder, *Fear God*, Vol.1, p.287.
45. Ellison, General Sir Gerald, *The Perils of Amateur Strategy*, Prefatory Note, p.xi–xii.
46. Kilverstone MSS packet 41.
47. Lennoxlove Papers, 4928.
48. Cited in Marder, *Fear God*, Vol.1, p.288.
49. Fisher, *Memories*, p.165.

50. Cited in Marder, *Fear God*, Vol.1, p.289.
51. Bacon, *Fisher*, Vol. I, p.206; Fisher, *Memories*, p.167.
52. *Ibid*, p.206-07; *Ibid*, p.172.
53. Cited in Marder, *Fear God*, Vol.1, p.301.
54. Bonham Carter, Violet, *Winston Churchill as I Knew Him*, p.44.
55. Cited in Marder, *Fear God*, Vol.1, p.322.
56. Brett, *Journals and Letters of Viscount Esher*, Vol. II, p.129.
57. *Ibid*, p.166.
58. *Ibid*, p.183.
59. Royal Commission on War Office Reform, *Report*, 11 January 1904.
60. *Ibid*.
61. Cited in Marder, *Fear God*, Vol.1, p.297–98.
62. *Ibid*, p.298.
63. Addl. MSS 50336 British Library.
64. King-Hall, *Sea Saga*, p.324.
65. NMM, NOE/32.
66. Cited in Marder, *Fear God*, Vol.1, p.181.
67. *Ibid*, p.314.
68. *Ibid*, p.366, Note 61.
69. *Ibid*, p.XXII.
70. Cited in Marder, *Fear God*, Vol.1, p.320.
71. Brett, *Journals and Letters of Viscount Esher*, Vol. II, p.59–60.
72. Bacon, *Fisher*, Vol. I, p.221.
73. King-Hall, *Sea Saga*, p.324.

Chapter 8. First Sea Lord.

1. Cited in Marder, *Fear God*, Vol.1, p.325.
2. Magnus, Philip, *King Edward VII*, (Penguin Books, 1967), p.343.
3. Cited in Marder, *Fear God*, Vol.1, p.324.
4. *Ibid*, p.261.
5. 'In 1839, the midst of a time of peace, the rock-nest of Aden, the key to the Red Sea, the Gibraltar of the East, was stolen'. – Treitschke *Deutsche Geschichte*, Vol. V, p.63.
6. Marriott, *Europe and Beyond 1870–1920*, p.189.
7. Figures from Steinberg, Jonathan, *Yesterdays Deterrent* .
8. Callender, Geoffrey, *The Naval Side of British History*, p.250.
9. Steinberg, p.194–5.
10. Marder, *Fear God*, Vol. I, p.259–60.
11. Hurd, Archibald, *Naval Efficiency: The War Readiness of the Fleet.* (1902), p.74–5.
12. Lee, *King Edward VII*; and Cowles, Virginia, *Edward VII and his Circle*, p.318.
13. Von Bülow, *Imperial Germany*, (1914) p.33–4.
14. Richmond, *Statesmen and Sea Power*, p.277.
15. Grey, Sir Edward, *Twenty-Five Years*, p.117.
16. Marder, Anatomy, p.440–41.
17. Beresford *Memoirs*, p.495.
18. *Ibid*.

19. Marder, *Anatomy*, p.441.
20. *Ibid.*
21. *Ibid.*
22. Cited in Marder, *Fear God*, Vol.II, p.18.
23. Cowles, Virginia, *King Edward VII*, p.318.
24. Kemp, Lieut-Comdr P.K., (Ed.) *Fisher Papers*, Vol. II (NRS), p.51.
25. Cited in Marder, *Fear God*, Vol.II, p.17.
26. Bacon, *Fisher*, Vol. II, p.65.
27. Kemp, (Ed.) *Fisher Papers*, Vol. I (NRS), p.6–7.
28. Wemyss, Lady, *The Life of Lord Wester Wemyss*, p.207–08.
29. Aston, Major General George, RMA, *Memories of a Marine*, p.223.
30. Battenberg to 2nd Lord Fisher, *Kilverstone MSS*, 1921.
31. *Ibid.*
32. *Hansard*, 4th Series, Vol. CXXXIII, Col. 220.
33. Kemp, (Ed.) *Fisher Papers*, Vol. II (NRS), p.18.
34. King-Hall, Stephen, *My Naval Life*, p.60.
35. Kerr, Mark, *Prince Louis of Battenberg*, p.218.
36. Richmond, *The Invasion of Britain*, p.80.
37. Kemp, (Ed.) *Fisher Papers*, Vol. II (NRS), p.290.37.
38. *Ibid*, Vol. I (NRS), p.20.
39. *Ibid*, p.101.
40. *Ibid*, Vol. II (NRS), p.83.
41. Cited in Marder, *Fear God*, Vol.II, p.101–02.
42. Kemp, (Ed.) *Fisher Papers*, Vol. I, (NRS), p.19.
43. Brett, *Journals and Letters of Viscount Esher*, Vol. II, p.147–48.
44. Kemp, (Ed.) *Fisher Papers*, Vol. II, (NRS), p.149.
45. Cited in Marder, *Fear God*, Vol.I, p.353, note 40.
46. Kemp, (Ed.) *Fisher Papers*, Vol. I, (NRS), p.20.
47. *The Bluejacket*, September 1900.
48. Carew, Anthony, *The Lower Deck of the Royal Navy, 1900–1939*, p.25.
49. *Ibid*, p.26.
50. *Ibid*, p.29.
51. Cited in Marder, *Fear God*, Vol.II, p.258.

Chapter 9. The Dreadnought Revolution.

1. Report of the Committee on Design.
2. Pollen, Anthony, *The Great Gunnery Scandal; the Mystery of Jutland*, Preface, p.9.
3. $\text{Tan} = \dfrac{\text{Perpendicular}}{\text{Base}}$
4. Sumida, Jon Tetsuro, (Ed) *The Pollen Papers*, (NRS), p.8.
5. *Ibid*, p.72.
6. Pollen, *The Great Gunnery Scandal*, p.37.
7. Cited in Marder, *Fear God*, Vol. II p.87.
8. Pollen, *The Great Gunnery Scandal*, p.56.
9. *Ibid.*

10. Sumida, *The Pollen Papers*, (NRS), p.132.
11. *Ibid.*
12. Pollen, *The Great Gunnery Scandal*, Preface, p.116.
13. Sumida, (Ed) *The Pollen Papers*, (NRS), Preface p.XII.
14. Scott, *Fifty Years in the Royal Navy*, p.262.
15. Fairbanks, Charles H. Jr., *The Origins of the DREADNOUGHT Revolution*, *The International History Review*, XIII 2 May 1991, p.247.
16. KE=$^{1}/_{2}$ (Mass × Velocity^2).
17. The weight of a contemporary 12-inch projectile was 850 lbs compared with 380 lbs for a 9.2-inch shell. The residual velocity at 7,000 yards was 1,783 feet per second, compared with 1,629 for a 9.2-inch shell. The kinetic energy (penetrating power) of a 12-inch shell was about 2.7 times that of a 9.2-inch shell. Moreover, the bursting charge in armour-piercing 12-inch shells was more than double that of 9.2-inch shells.
18. Kemp, (Ed) *Fisher Papers*, (NRS), Vol. II, p.326–7.
19. Cited in Marder, *Fear God*, Vol. I, p.321.
20. *Ibid*, p.326.
21. NL/15432, December 22, 1904.
22. Ordnance Committee Report No 1041, 12 July 1895.
23. Obituary notice of Fisher, *Transactions of the Institution of Naval Architects*, 1920.
24. Kemp, (Ed.) *Fisher Papers*, (NRS), Vol. I, p.212.
25. 'Barfleur', *Blackwood's Magazine*, April 1905.
26. *Ibid*, May 1905.
27. *Ibid*, February 1906.
28. *Ibid.*
29. Kemp, (Ed) *Fisher Papers*, (NRS), Vol. II, p.261.
30. *Ibid*, p.69–70.
31. Dreyer, Admiral Sir Frederic C., *The Sea Heritage*, p.57.
32. Dawson, Captain Lionel, *Flotillas*, p.125.
33. Kemp, (Ed) *Fisher Papers*, (NRS), I, p.212.
34. *Ibid*, p.226.
35. *Scientific American*, January 1910.
36. Ellison, Lieutenant-General Sir Gerald, *The Perils of Amateur Strategy*, 1926, p.4.
37. Kemp, (Ed) *Fisher Papers*, (NRS), Vol. II, p.279.
38. Sydenham, Lord, *My Life's Work*, p.205.
39. Bacon, *Fisher*, Vol. II, p.96.
40. *Ibid.*
41. *Ibid*, p.98.

Chapter 10. Gold Lace and Glitter.
1. James, Admiral Sir William, *A Great Seaman*, p.100.
2. Beresford, *Memoirs*, p.488.
3. Frewen, Oswald, *A Sailor's Soliloquy*, p.60.
4. James, *A Great Seaman*, p.100-01.
5. *Ibid*, p.105.

6. Jameson, *The Fleet that Jack Built*, p.89.
7. Bennett, *Charlie B*, p.259–60.
8. *Ibid*, p.258.
9. Beresford, *Memoirs*, p.495.
10. Kerr, *Battenberg*, p.178–9.
11. King-Hall, *Sea Saga*, p.326.
12. Sturdee MSS.
13. Kemp, (Ed.) *Fisher Papers*, (NRS), Vol. II, p.312.
14. Frewen, *Sailor's Soliloquy*, p.87–88.
15. Bacon, *From 1900 Onward*, p.124.
16. *Ibid*, p.126.
17. *Navy and Statement of Admiralty Policy*, Comd. 2791.
18. *Admiralty Memorandum*, Comd. 271.
19. Chatfield, *The Navy and Defence*, p.14.
20. Cited in Marder, *Fear God*, Vol. II, p.48.
21. *Lennoxlove Papers*, 4762.
22. Bacon, *From 1900 Onward*, p.130.
23. *Lennoxlove Papers*, 4763.
24. *Ibid* 4764.
25. Bacon, *From 1900 Onward*, p.127.
26. *Ibid*, p.146.
27. *Ibid*, p.147.
28. Beresford, Lord Charles, *The Betrayal*, p.7.
29. Cited in Marder, *Fear God*, Vol. II, p.79.
30. *Ibid*, p.80.

Chapter 11. Not in Single Spies.

1. Hankey, *Supreme Command*, Vol. I p.46.
2. Cited in Marder, *Fear God*, Vol. II, p.55.
3. Bacon, *Fisher*, Vol. II, p.87.
4. Churchill, Randolph S, *Winston S Churchill*, Vol.II, p.529.
5. Cited in Marder, *Fear God*, Vol. I, p.367, Note 69.
6. *Ibid*.
7. *Ibid*. p.320–21.
8. Fisher, *Memories*, p.183.
9. Richmond, Admiral Sir Herbert, *The Invasion of Britain*, p.45.
10. Hamilton, General Sir Ian, *Compulsory Service*, Preface, p.21.
11. Esher, *Journals*, II, p.114–15.
12. *Ibid*, p.117.
13. Hart, Liddell, *A History of the World War, 1914–1918*, (first published as *The Real War*), p.57.
14. Beaverbrook, *Politicians and the War*, p.33–4.
15. Grey, *Twenty-Five Years*, Vol. I, p.74.
16. Hankey, *Supreme Command*, Vol. I, p.62.
17. Esher, *Journals*, Vol. II, p.198–99.
18. *Ibid*, p.224.

19. *Ibid*, p.219–20.
20. *Ibid*, p.220.
21. *Ibid*, p.246–7.
22. *Ibid*, p.247.
23. *Ibid*, p.247–8.
24. *Ibid*, p.248.
25. Cited in Marder, *Fear God*, Vol. II, p.131–2.
26. *Ibid*, p.132–3.
27. *Ibid*, p.152.
28. Hankey, *Supreme Command*, Vol. I, p.151.
29. Esher, *Journals*, II, p.257.
30. *Ibid*, p.262.
31. *Ibid*, p.263.
32. *Ibid*.
33. Hankey, *Supreme Command*, Vol. I, p.68.
34. *Report on the Naval Manoeuvres, 1888.*
35. James, David, *Lord Roberts*, p.434.
36. *Ibid*, p.456.
37. *Ibid*, p.455.
38. Repington, Lt-Col. C.A' Court, *The First World War*, Vol. I, p.61.
39. Hankey, *Supreme Command*, Vol. I, p.304–5.

Chapter 12. Blast and Counterblast.

1. *Daily Express*, 28 December 1906.
2. Beresford to McKenna, Beresford inquiry.
3. Marder, *Dreadnought to Scapa Flow*, Vol. I, p.72.
4. Cited in Marder, *Fear God*, Vol. II, p.103.
5. Beresford, *Memoirs*, p.552.
6. Beresford Inquiry.
7. *Ibid*.
8. Cited in Marder, *Fear God*, Vol. II, p.115.
9. Beresford Inquiry.
10. Cited in Marder, *Fear God*, Vol. II, p.114.
11. *Ibid*, p.117.
12. *Ibid*.
13. Hatch, *The Mountbattens*, p.88.
14. Cab. 1/7ff.133–5.
15. Fisher to White, February, 1907, Cited in Marder, *Fear God*, Vol. II p.117, footnote.
16. *Ibid*, p.118, Note.
17. *Ibid*.
18. *Ibid*. p.118.
19. Mackay, *Balfour*, p.62–4.
20. Beresford, *Memoirs*, p.550.
21. Bennett, *Charlie B*, p.283.
22. Cork and Orrery, *My Naval Life*, p.66.

23. Hankey, *Supreme Command*, p.22.
24. Chatfield, *The Navy and Defence*, p.58–9.
25. Bennett, *Charlie B*, p.283.
26. Dawson, *Flotillas*, p.56.
27. Dawson, *Gone for a Sailor*, p.130.
28. Cork and Orrery, *My Naval Life*, p.68.
29. Dawson, *Gone for a Sailor*, p.284.
30. Ponsonby, Sir Frederick, (Lord Sysonby), *Recollections of Three Reigns*, p.132.
31. Cited in Marder, *Fear God*, Vol. II, p.121.
32. *Ibid.*
33. *Daily Express*, 20 July 1907.
34. *Ibid*, 7 August 1907.
35. Report of the Beresford Enquiry.
36. Royal Archives, Windsor 58/80.
37. *Ibid*, 58/81.
38. Kemp, (Ed.) *Fisher Papers*, (NRS), Vol. II, p.464–66.
39. Cited in Marder, *Fear God*, Vol. II, p.125.
40. *Ibid.*
41. Admiralty Memorandum, *Remarks on interview with Commander-in-Chief, Channel Fleet, Friday, July 5, 1907*, Admy. MSS.
42. Royal Archives, Windsor, 58/90.
43. Beresford Inquiry.
44. Cited in Marder, *Fear God*, Vol. II p.139.
45. *Ibid*, p.141–2.
46. Marder, *Dreadnought*, Vol. I p.71.
47. Wester Wemyss, Lady, *The Life and Letters of Lord Wester Wemyss*, p.78.
48. Fisher, *Records*, p.83–86.
49. *The Standard*, 12 November 1907.
50. *Ibid*, 14 November 1907.
51. Williams, Rhodi, *Balfour, Fisher and Naval Reform, Historical Research*, February 1987, p.93.
52. *Morning Post*, 16 November 1907.
53. Cited in Marder, *Fear God*, Vol. II, p.151.

Chapter 13. Paintwork and Pomp.

1. Scott, *Fifty Years in the Royal Navy*, p.202–03.
2. Scott, *A Reply to Lord Charles Beresford*, (*The British Review*, April 1913).
3. Dawson, Lionel, *Flotillas*, p.70.
4. *Ibid*, p.71-2.
5. Padfield, Peter, *Aim Straight: A Biography of Admiral Sir Percy Scott*, p.166.
6. *Ibid*, p.167.
7. *The Morning Post*, 17 December 1907.
8. Padfield, *Aim Straight*, p.169.
9. *Ibid*, p.170.
10. Scott, *A Reply to Lord Charles Beresford*, (*The British Review*, April 1913).
11. Padfield, Peter, *Aim Straight*, p.170.

12. *Ibid.*
13. Cited in Marder, *Fear God, Vol. II*, p.152.
14. Cited in Padfield, *Aim Straight* p.176.
15. *Ibid*, p.177.
16. Marder, *Dreadnought*, Vol. I, p.100.
17. Esher, *Journals*, II, p.280.
18. *Ibid*, p.281.
19. Ibid.
20. *Ibid*, p.282.
21. *Daily Mail*, 24 December 1907.
22. *Morning Post*, 31 December 1907.
23. Manning, *The Life of Sir William White*, p.470.
24. Padfield, *Aim Straight* p.182.
25. *The Times*, 7 July 1908.
26. *Morning Post*, 9 July 1908.
27. *Ibid.*
28. Padfield, *Aim Straight*, p.185.
29. Fisher to Esher, 12 July 1908, Cited in Marder, *Fear God, Vol. II*, p.183.
30. Cited in Marder, *Fear God*, Vol. II, p.184–5.
31. Padfield, *Aim Straight*, p.188.
32. *Hansard*, 4th Series, Vol. CXCIII, Col.1741.
33. *The Globe*, 31 July 1908.
34. Cited in Marder, *Fear God*, Vol. II, p.176–7.
35. *Ibid*, p.201.
36. *Morning Post*, 1 December 1908.
37. Marder, *Dreadnought*, Vol. I, p.104.
38. *Ibid*, p.188.

Chapter 14. The Mutter of Distant Thunder.

1. Roskill, *The Naval Air Service*, p.10.
2. *Fisher Papers; Naval Necessities*, p.97.
3. *Ibid.*
4. *Ibid*, p.106.
5. *Ibid*, p.101.
6. *Ibid*, p.84.
7. *Ibid*, p.91–92.
8. *Ibid*, p.96–7.
9. Marder, *Dreadnought*, Vol. V, p.308.
10. Esher, *Journals*, Vol. II, p.358.
11. *Ibid*, p.375–6.
12. Hankey, *Supreme Command*, Vol. I, p.70.
13. Esher, *Journals III*, p.61.
14. Fisher to King Edward VII, 14 March 1908, *Memories*, p.4.
15. Bacon, *Fisher*, Vol. II, p.72.
16. Fisher to Esher, 21 February 1908.
17. Seymour, *Diplomatic Background to the War*, p.142.

18. Fisher, *Memories*, p.18–19.
19. *Ibid*, p.190.
20. Churchill, Randolph, *Winston S. Churchill*, Vol. II, p.512.
21. *Hansard*, July 1901.
22. *War Memoirs of David Lloyd George*, Vol. I, p.13–14.
23. Marder, *Dreadnought*, Vol. I, p.148.
24. Cited in Marder, *Fear God*, Vol. II, p.203–04.
25. *Ibid*, p.225.
26. *Ibid*, p.226.
27. *Esher Papers*, cited in *Dreadnought to Scapa Flow*, Vol. I, p.160.
28. *The Jellicoe Papers*, Vol. I, (NRS), p.17.
29. *Ibid*.
30. *Ibid*, p.16.
31. Chamberlain, Austen, *Politics from Inside*, p.153.
32. Bacon, *Fisher*, Vol. II, p.91.
33. Marder, *Dreadnought*, Vol. I, p.163.
34. *Ibid*, p.164.
35. Esher, *Journals*, Vol. II, p.375.
36. *Ibid*, p.377.
37. *Ibid*, p.378.
38. *Daily Telegraph*, 24 March 1909.
39. Marder, *Dreadnought*, Vol. I, p.173.
40. *Ibid*, p.173.
41. Churchill, *World Crisis*, p.24.
42. *Comparative strengths in Battleships, and Armoured cruisers of Great Britain, France, United States and Germany, June 1907*, Lennoxlove Manuscripts.

Chapter 15. The Beresford Inquiry.

1. Cited in Marder, *Fear God*, Vol. II, p.199, Fisher to McKenna, 28 October 1908,
2. *Ibid*, p.200, Fisher to Arnold White, 2 November 1908.
3. *Ibid*.
4. Lambton had changed his name to Meux.
5. Esher, *Journals*, Vol. II, p.322.
6. *Ibid*, p.357.
7. *Ibid*, p.189.
8. I*bid*, p.190.
9. *Ibid*. p.191.
10. Bacon, *From 1900 Onward*, p.132.
11. *Hansard*, 5th Series, Vol.III, Col. 1132, 6 April 1909.
12. *Ibid*.
13. *Ibid*.
14. Marder, *Dreadnought*, Vol. I, p.191.
15. *Ibid*.
16. *Daily Express*, 20 March 1909.
17. Naval Library, Ministry of Defence, M3, attached to proof of minutes of Beresford Inquiry.

18. Cited in Marder, *Fear God*, Vol. II, p.254, Note.
19. Cab. 16/9. *Report and proceedings of a sub-Committee of the CID to inquire into questions of naval policy raised by Lord Charles Beresford.*
20. Marder, *Dreadnought*, Vol. I, p.200.
21. *The Times*, 25 October 1909.
22. Naval Library, Ministry of Defence, M3, typed copy, (incorrectly dated 22 August, 1907) attached to proof of minutes of Beresford Inquiry.
23. Marder, *Dreadnought*, Vol. I, p.201.
24. *Ibid*, p.204.
25. Cited in Marder, *Fear God*, Vol. II, p.272.
26. *Ibid*, (Note).
27. Bacon, *Fisher*, Vol. II, p.103.
28. Cited in Marder, *Fear God* Vol. II, p.202.
29. Bacon, *Fisher*, Vol. II, p.105–06.
30. *Ibid*, p.106.
31. *Ibid*.
32. *Ibid*, p.105.
33. Cited in Marder, *Fear God*, Vol. II, p.289, Note.
34. *Ibid*, p.290.
35. *Ibid*, p.291.
36. *Ibid*, p.218-19.
37. Churchill, *World Crisis*, p.54–5.

BIBLIOGRAPHY

Admiralty Circulars, 1834–1914.
Admiralty Orders in Council, 1663–1856, (Admiralty, MDCCCLVI).
Admiralty Orders in Council, February 1903 to December 1907, (Admiralty, 1908).
Altham, Captain E., *Jellicoe*, (Blackie, 1938).
Ashley, Maurice, *Churchill as Historian*, (Secker and Warburg, 1968).
Aspinall-Oglander, *Roger Keyes; A Biography*, (Hogarth Press, 1951).
Asquith, Earl of Oxford and, *Memories and Reflections, 1852–1927*, (Cassell, 1928).
Aston Major General George, *Memories of a Marine*, (Murray, 1919).

Bacon, Admiral Sir Reginald, *The Life of Lord Fisher of Kilverstone, Admiral of the Fleet*, 2 Vols, (Hodder and Stoughton, 1929).
    The Life of John Rushworth, Earl Jellicoe, (Cassell, 1936).
    A Naval Scrapbook, 1877–1900, (Hutchinson, nd).
    From 1900 Onward, (Hutchinson, 1940).
    The Jutland Scandal, (Hutchinson, 1925).
'Barfleur',
    Naval Administration, (*Blackwood's Magazine*, May 1905).
    The Battle of Tsu Sima, (*Blackwood's Magazine*, February 1906).
    Naval Policy: A Plea for the Study of War, (Blackwood, 1907).
Barthorp, Michael, *War on the Nile*, (Blandford Press, 1984).
Bayly, Admiral Sir Lewis, *Pull Together!*, (Harrap, 1939).
Beaverbrook, Lord, *Politicians and the War, 1914–1916*, (Doubleday, Doran & Co, NY., 1928).
Beckett, Ian and Gooch, John,
    Politicians and Defence: Studies in the Formulation of British Defence Policy, 1845–1970, (Manchester University Press, 1981).
Bennett, Geoffrey,
    Charlie B: The Life of Admiral Lord Charles Beresford, (Peter Dawnay, 1968).
    Naval Battles of the First World War, (Pan Books, 1974).

Beresford, Admiral Lord Charles,
    Memoirs, (Methuen, 1914).
    The Betrayal, (King, 1912).
Beresford Committee, *Report of the Sub Committee of the Committee of Imperial Defence appointed to enquire into certain Questions of Naval Policy raised by Lord Charles Beresford*, Comd. 256.
Bonham Carter, Violet, *Winston Churchill as I Knew Him*, (Eyre and Spottiswood, 1965).
Bradford, Admiral Sir Edward, *Admiral of the Fleet Sir Arthur Knyvet Wilson*, (Murray, 1923).
Brett, Maurice, *Journals and Letters of Viscount Esher*, 3 Vols, (Nicholson & Watson, 1934).
Briggs, Sir John, *Naval Administrations 1827 to 1892*, (Sampson Low, 1897).
Broad, Lewis, *Winston Churchill: The Years of Preparation*, (Sidgwick and Jackson, 1963).
Brock, Michael and Eleanor, (Ed.), *H. H. Asquith, Letters to Venetia Stanley*, (OUP, 1982).
Brodie, Bernard, *A Layman's Guide to Naval Strategy*, (Princeton University Press, 1942).
Brown, David K, *A century of Naval Construction: The History of the Royal Corps of Naval Constructors*, (Conway maritime Press, 1983).
Brownrigg, Rear-Admiral Sir Douglas, *Indiscretions of the Naval Censor*, (Cassell, 1920).
Bülow, Von, *Imperial Germany 1914*.

Cable, James, *Britain's Naval Future*, (Macmillan, 1983).
Callender, Geoffrey, *The Naval Side of British History*, (Christophers, London, 1924).
Calvocoressi, Peter, and Wint, Guy, *Total War*, (Penguin Books, 1972).
Carew, Anthony, *The Lower Deck of the Royal Navy,1900–1939*, (Manchester University Press, 1918).
Chalmers, Rear-Admiral W S, *The Life and Letters of David, Earl Beatty*, (Hodder & Stoughton, 1951).
Chamberlain, Austen, *Politics from Inside*, (London, 1936).
Chatfield, Admiral Lord, *The Navy and Defence*, (Heinemann, 1942).
Chatterton, E. Keble,
    Dardanelles Dilemma: The Story of the Naval Operations, (London, 1930).
    The Big Blockade, (Hurst & Blackett, nd).
Churchill, Randolph S, *Winston S Churchill*, (Heinemann 1967), Vol. I & II.
Churchill, Winston S.,
    The World Crisis, 1911–1918, (London 1923), 3 Vols.
    The World Crisis, 1911–1918, Revised Edition, (Odhams, 1938). 2 Vols.
    Great Contemporaries, (Macmillan, 1937 and the Reprint Society, 1941).
    The Second World War, (Cassel, 1951).
Clarke, Lt-Col. Sir George, and Thursfield, James, *The Navy and the Nation* (Murray, 1897).

Clausewitz, Carl Von,
    On War, (Trans. Colonel J J Graham; Kegan, Paul, 1908).
    On War, (Trans. Anatol Rapoport; Penguin, 1968).
Coles, Alan, *Three Before Breakfast*, (Kenneth Mason, 1979).
Colomb, Vice-Admiral P H, *Memoirs of Sir Astley Cooper-Key*, (Methuen, 1898).
Committee on Designs, *Report, 1904*, (MOD Library).
Compton-Hall, Commander P R, *Submariners' World*, (Kenneth Mason, 1983).
Corbett, Sir Julian,
    Naval Operations, (Longmans, Green & Co., 1929).
    Some principles of Maritime Strategy, (Conway Maritime Press, 1927).
Corbett, Sir Julian, and Newbolt, Sir Henry,
    History of the Great War, Naval Operations, (Longmans Green & Co., 1920–31), 5 Vols.
Cork and Orrery, Admiral of the Fleet Lord, *My Naval Life*, (Hutchinson, 1942).
Cowles, Virginia, *King Edward VII and his Circle*, (Hamilton, London, 1956).
Cramb, J A,
    Germany and England (A series of lectures at Queen's College, London), (Murray, June 1914).
Cunningham, Admiral of the Fleet Viscount, *A Sailor's Odyssey*, (Hutchinson, 1951).
Custance, Admiral Sir Reginald, See 'Barfleur'.

Dardanelles Commission, *First Report, Comd 8490; Second Report Comd. 8502.*
Dawson, Captain Lionel,
    Flotillas, (Rich & Cowen, 1933).
    Gone for a Sailor, (Rich & Cowen, 1936).
    Sound of the Guns, (Pen in Hand, 1949).
de Chair, Admiral Sir Dudley, *The Sea is Strong*, (Harrap, 1961).
d'eyncourt, Sir E Tennyson, *A Shipbuilder's Yarn*, (Hutchinson, 1948).
Denham, H M, *Dardanelles: A Midshipman's Diary*, (Murray, 1981).
Doenitz, Admiral Karl, *Memoirs: Ten years and Twenty days*, (Weidenfeld & Nicolson, 1959).
Dewar, Vice Admiral K G B, *The Navy from Within*, (Gollancz, 1939).
Dictionary of National Biography.
Dixon, Norman F, *On the Psychology of Military Incompetence*, (Cape, 1976).
Domville, Admiral Sir Barry, *Look to Your Moat*, (Hutchinson, nd).
Douglas, General Sir Howard,
    Treatise on Naval Gunnery, (Murray, 1856).
    On Naval Warfare with Steam, (Murray, 1858).
Dreyer, Admiral Sir Frederic C, *The Sea Heritage*, (Museum Press Ltd., 1955).
Duff, David, *Alexandra, Princess and Queen*, (Collins, 1980).
Eade, Charles, (Ed.), *Churchill by His Contemporaries*, (Hutchinson, 1953).
Eardley-Wilmot, Rear-Admiral Sir Sydney, *An Admiral's Memories*, (Sampson Low, nd).
Ellison, Lieut-General Sir Gerald, *The Perils of Amateur Strategy*, (Longmans, Green, 1926).

Esher, Viscount, *The Tragedy of Lord Kitchener*, (Murray, 1921).

Farrere et Chack, *Combats et Batailles sur Mer*.

Fisher, Admiral of the Fleet Lord,
    Memories, (Hodder & Stoughton, 1919).
    Records, (Hodder & Stoughton, 1919).

Fisher, Admiral Sir Frederic, *Naval Reminiscences*, (Muller, 1938).

Fisher, H A L, *A History of Europe*, (Edward Arnold, 1936).

Fremantle, Admiral Sir Sydney, *My Naval Life*, (Hutchinson, nd).

Frewen, Oswald, *Sailor's Soliloquy*, (Hutchinson, 1961).

Gardiner, Leslie, *The Royal Oak Courts Martial*, (Blackwood, 1965).

Gerard, James W, *My Four Years in Germany*, (Hodder & Stoughton, 1917).

Gilbert, Martin, *Winston Churchill, 1914–1916*, (Heinemann, 1917), Vol. III and CV III.

Goldrick, James, *The King's Ships Were at Sea*, (Naval Institute Press, Annapolis).

Goodenough, Admiral Sir William, *A Rough Record*, (Hutchinson, nd).

Goodspeed, D J, *Ludendorff*, (Hart-Davis, 1966).

Gretton, Vice-Admiral Sir Peter, *Former Naval Person*, (Cassell, 1968).

Gretton, R H, *A Modern History of the English People*, (Secker, 1929).

Grey, Viscount, of Falloden, *Twenty-Five Years*, (Hodder & Stoughton, 1925).

Haldane, R B, *Autobiography*, (Hodder & Stoughton, 1929).

Halpern, Paul, (Ed.), *The Keyes Papers*, 2 Vols. (NRS 1979–82).
    A Naval History of World War I, (US Naval Institute, 1994; UCL, 1994).

Hamilton, General Sir Ian, *Compulsory Service*, and *Gallipoli Diary*, (London, 1920).

Hankey, Baron, *Supreme Command*, 2 Vols, (Allen & Unwin, 1961).

Hart, Liddell, *A History of the World War, 1914–1918*, (Faber, 1930).

Hatch, Alden, *The Mountbattens*, (1966).

Hazlehurst, Cameron, *Politicians at War, July 1914–May 1915*, (Cape, 1971).

Hickling, Vice-Admiral Harold, *Sailor at Sea*, (William Kimber, 1965).

Hickey, Michael, *Gallipoli* (John Murray, 1995).

Hindenburg, Marshall Von, *Out of My Life*, (Trans. F A Holt, New York, 1921).

Home, William Douglas, and Jennifer Brown, *The Prime Ministers: Stories and Anecdotes from No 10*, (WH Allen, 1987).

Hough, Richard,
    Admirals in Collision, (Hamish Hamilton, 1959)
    Former Naval Person, (Weidenfield & Nicolson, 1985).
    First Sea Lord, (George Allen & Unwin, 1969).

Howard, Michael, *The Causes of War*, (Unwin Paperbacks, 1983).

Hurd, Archibald,
    Naval Efficiency: The War Readiness of the Fleet, (Chapman & Hall, 1902).
    Who Goes There?, (Hutchinson, 1941).

Jackson, G Gibbard, *The Ship Under Steam*, (Fisher, Unwin 1927).

James, Admiral Sir William,
    A Great Seaman: The Life of Admiral of the Fleet Sir Henry Oliver (Witherby, 1956).

The Eyes of the Navy: A Biographical Study of Admiral Sir Reginald Hall, (Methuen 1956).

James, David, *Lord Roberts*, (Hollis & Carter, 1954).

James, Robert Rhodes,

    Churchill: A Study in Failure, 1900–1939, (Weidenfeld & Nicolson, 1970).

    The British Revolution: British Politics, 1880–1939, (Hamish Hamilton, 1977).

    From Asquith to Chamberlain, 1914–1939, (Hamish Hamilton, 1977).

Jameson, Rear-Admiral Sir William, *The Fleet that Jack Built*.

Jellicoe, Admiral Viscount, *The Grand Fleet, 1914–16*, (Cassell, 1919).

Jordan, Gerald (Ed). *Naval Warfare in the Twentieth Century*, (Croom Helm, London, 1977).

Keegan, John,

    The Price of Admiralty, (Hutchinson, 1988).

    A History of Warfare, (Hutchinson, 1993).

Kemp, Lieut-Comdr P K, *The Papers of Admiral Sir John Fisher*, 2 Vols, (NRS, 1960 and 1964).

Kerr, Mark, *Prince Louis of Battenberg*, (Longmans Green & Co 1934).

Keyes, Admiral of the Fleet Sir Roger, *The Naval Memoirs, 1910–15, 1916–18*, (Eyre & Spottiswood, 1934–5).

King-Hall, L, (Ed.), *Sea Saga: The Naval Diaries of Four generations of the King-Hall Family*, (Gollancz, 1935).

King-Hall, Stephen, *My Naval Life*, (Faber, 1951).

Laffin, John, *Damn the Dardanelles: the Agony of Gallipoli*, (Alan Sutton, 1989).

Lean's Royal Navy List, (Witherby, 1902).

Lee, Sir Sydney, *King Edward VII: A Biography*, 2 Vols, (Macmillan, 1925–27).

Leslie, Sir Shane, *The Film of Memory*, (1938).

Lewis, Michael, *The Navy of Britain*, (Allen & Unwin 1948).

Liddle, Peter H, *The Sailor's War, 1914–18*, (Blandford Press, 1985).

Lipson, E, *Europe, 1914–1939*, (Black 1945).

Lowys, Commander Geoffrey, *Fabulous Admirals*, (Putnam, 1957).

Lloyd George, David, *War Memoirs of David Lloyd George*, 2 Vols, (Nicholson & Watson, 1934).

Lumby, E W R, *Policy and Operations in the Mediterranean, 1912–14*, (NRS, 1970).

Lutz, Hermann, *Lord Grey and the World War*, (Trans. E W Dickes: Allen & Unwin, 1928).

Maber, Lt-Comdr John, *The Ironclad Huascar*, (Journal of Naval Engineering, Vol 28, No 3).

Mackay, Ruddock F,

    Balfour, Intellectual Statesman, (Oxford University Press, 1985).

    Fisher of Kilverstone, (Clarendon Press, Oxford, 1973).

Macksey, Piers, *The War in the Mediterranean*, (London, 1957).

Magnus, Philip, *King Edward VII*, (Penguin Books, 1967).

Mahan, Captain A T, USN, *The Influence of Sea Power upon History*, (Sampson Low, 1889).

Manning, Frederic, *The Life of Sir William White*, (Murray, 1923).

Marder, Arthur J,

   The Anatomy of British Sea Power; a History of British Naval Policy in the Pre-Dreadnought Era, 1880–1905, (Alfred A Knopf, New York, 1940). Published in Britain as *British Naval Policy, 1880–1905: The Anatomy of British Sea Power*, (Putnam, 1941).

   Fear God and Dread Nought, The Correspondence of Admiral of the Fleet Lord Fisher of Kilverstone, 3 Vols, (Cape, 1952–59).

   From the Dardanelles to Oran; Studies of the Royal Navy in War and Peace, 1915–1940, (Oxford University Press, 1974).

   From the Dreadnought to Scapa Flow, 5 Vols, (Oxford University Press, 1961–70).

   Portrait of an Admiral: The Life and Papers of Sir Herbert Richmond, (Cape, 1952).

Marriott, J A R, *Europe and Beyond*, (Methuen, 1921).

Martin, Hugh, *Battle: The Life Story of the Rt. Hon. Winston S. Churchill*, (Sampson, Low, Marston, nd).

Mathew, David, *The Naval Heritage*, (Collins, 1944).

Maurice, Major-General Sir Frederick, *Haldane*, (London, 1937).

Mitchell, *Report on the Dardanelles*, MOD, Naval Library.

Moorehead, Alan, *Gallipoli*, (Hamish Hamilton, 1956).

Navy Lists, 1834–1979, (HMSO).

Newbolt, Henry, *A Naval History of the War, 1914–1918*, (Hodder & Stoughton, nd).

Nicolson, Harold, *King George the Fifth: His Life and Reign*, (Constable, 1952).

Orders in Council and Acts of Parliament for the Regulation of the Naval Service, (HMSO 1856 and 1908).

Padfield, Peter,

   Aim Straight: A Biography of Sir Percy Scott, (Hodder & Stoughton, 1966).

   Doenitz, the last Führer (Gollancz, 1984).

Patterson, A Temple, (Ed.),

   The Jellicoe Papers, 2 Vols, (NRS, 1966).

   Jellicoe: A Biography, (Macmillan, 1969).

Penn, Geoffrey,

   Up Funnel, Down Screw!, (Hollis & Carter, 1955).

   Snotty: The Story of the Midshipman, (Hollis & Carter, 1957).

   HMS Thunderer: The Story of the Royal Naval Engineering College, Keyham and Manadon, (Kenneth Mason, 1984).

Pollen, Anthony, *The Great Gunnery Scandal*.

Ponsonby, Sir Frederick, *Recollections of Three Reigns*, (Eyre and Spottiswood, 1951).

Price, William Harold, *With the Fleet in the Dardanelles*, (Andrew Melrose, nd).

Prior, Robin, *Churchill's 'World Crisis' as History*, (Croom Helm, 1983).

Raft, Bryan,

   Beatty Papers, (NRS 1993).

Technical Change and British Naval Policy, 1860–1939, (Hodder & Stoughton, 1977).

Repington, Lt-Col. C A'Court, The First World War, 1914–1918, (Houghton Mifflin Co., New York 1921).

Richmond, Admiral Sir Herbert,
The Invasion of Britain, Methuen, 1941).
Statesmen and Sea Power, (Clarendon Press, 1946).

Robertson, C Grant, Bismarck, (Constable, 1918).

Robinson, Commander Charles N, The British Fleet, (Bell, 1894).

Rodger, N A M,
(Ed)., The Admiralty (Terence Dalton Ltd., 1979).
The Naval Miscellany, Vol. V, (NRS, 1984).

Roskill, Stephen W,
Admiral of the Fleet Earl Beatty, (Atheneum, New York, 1981).
Churchill and the Admirals, (Collins, 1977).
Documents Relating to the Naval Air Service, Vol. I, 1908–18, (NRS, 1969).
Hankey, Man of Secrets, 3 Vols, (Collins, 1970–74).

Schofield, B B, The Story of HMS 'Dryad', (Kenneth Mason, 1977).

Scott, Admiral Sir Percy, Fifty Years in the Royal Navy, (Allen & Unwin, 1919).

Schurman, D M, The Education of a Navy, (Cassell, 1965).

Seymour, Diplomatic Background of the War.

Smith, Engr. Captain Edgar C,
A Short History of Naval and Marine Engineering, (Babcock and Wilcox Ltd., 1937).

Smith, Vice-Admiral Humphrey Hugh, A Yellow Admiral Remembers, (Edward Arnold 1932).

Somervell, D C, The Reign of King George the Fifth, and English Chronicle, (London, 1935).

Spender, J A,
A Short History of Our Times, (Cassell, 1934).
Life, Journalism and Politics, (Cassell, 1927).

Steevens, G W, With Kitchener to Khartoum, (Nelson, nd).

Steinberg, Jonathan,
Yesterday's Deterrent: Tirpitz and the Birth of the German Battle Fleet, (Macdonald, 1965).

Sumida, Jon Tetsuro, The Pollen Papers, (NRS), (Allen & Unwin, 1984).

Sydenham, Baron, of Combe, (See also Clarke), My Life's Work.

Sydenham, and others, The World Crisis, by Winston Churchill, a Criticism, (Hutchinson, nd).

Taylor, A J P, The First World War: an illustrated History, (Hamish Hamilton, 1963).

Taylor, A J P, and others, Churchill, Four Faces and the Man, (Allen Lane, the Penguin Press, 1969).

Tirpitz, Grand Admiral Von, My Memoirs, 2 Vols, (Hurst & Blackett Ltd, nd).

Trevelyan, G M, *Fifty Years: a Composite Picture of the Period 1882–1932*, (Thornton Butterworth, 1932).

'Undistinguished Naval Officer', *The British Navy in the Present Year of Grace*, 3 Vols, (Hamilton Adams, 1885–1886).

Van de Vat, Dan, *The Ship that Changed the World*, (Hodder & Stoughton, 1985).

Wemyss, Lady Wester, *The Life and Letters of Lord Wester Wemyss*, (Eyre & Spottiswood, 1935).
Wemyss, Admiral of the Fleet Lord Wester, *The Navy in the Dardanelles Campaign*, (Hodder & Stoughton, nd).
Williams, Hamilton, *Britain's Naval Power*, 2 Vols, (Macmillan, 1896).
Winton, John, *Convoy*, (Michael Joseph, 1983).
Wyatt, H F and Horton-Smith, L G, *The Passing of the Great Fleet*, (Sampson Low, 1909).

INDEX

254

259